A Wobbly Life

Ed and Chiky, 1915

A WOBBLY LIFE

IWW *Organizer E. F. Doree*

ELLEN DOREE ROSEN

Introduction by
MELVYN DUBOFSKY

Wayne State University Press Detroit

08 07 06 05 04   5 4 3 2 1

Library of Congress Cataloging-in-Publication Data

Rosen, Ellen Doree, 1924–
A Wobbly life : IWW organizer E. F. Doree / Ellen Doree Rosen ; introduction by
Melvyn Dubofsky.
        p. cm.
Includes bibliographical references and index.
ISBN 0-8143-3203-X
1. Doree, E. F. (Edward Frederick) 1889–1927. 2. Industrial Workers of the
World—History. 3. Labor unions—United States—Officials and employees—
Biography. 4. Labor leaders—United States—Biography. I. Title.
HD6509.D67R67 2004
331.88'6'092—dc22

                              2004000533

FOR
Ed and Chiky

Contents

꧁

PREFACE

꧁꧂

IN A TIME WHEN divorce was rare and "everybody" had a father, the death of the family's protector left a child feeling "different" and vulnerable. I did not feel so, consciously, at the time, but in retrospect and through the dreams that accompanied my writing of this narrative I know that it was so. Because my mother was older, in fragile health, heartbroken, and preoccupied with the struggle to provide a living, my absent father became my lodestar. I idealized him. But every child knows that if someone is sent to jail, he must have done something bad. And somehow my mother's reluctance to broach beyond our doors the subject of my father's imprisonment made me suspect something vaguely shameful. I didn't want to know. I could not afford to find out that he had feet of clay.

And so, although I knew that the black satchel in our closet held my father's papers and his letters from prison, I did not read them. I was afraid of what I might find. Had my father been misguided, as his conviction by the United States government would have me believe? Or had he been right, and punished unfairly, as I had been taught at home? Either answer promised pain, so I kept my ignorance intact. As I grew older, the distractions of life took over—forty-eight-hour workweeks during the Second World War, college classes at night, marriage, motherhood, pursuit of the master's degree and then the doctorate in political science, professorship at John Jay College of Criminal Justice. Finally, as a secure adult, I read my father's letters. I discovered a principled, brave, competent, caring, fun-loving, honorable man.

Encouraged by my colleagues, I began to research the Industrial Workers of the World and my father's role in it. I found that he was much more important than I had known. I found that my mother's claims that he had been unjustly convicted were true. I had to write this book.

It is made up of many materials: my own writing, my father's affidavits, excerpts from the trial transcript and congressional hearing records, but mainly my father's letters. In reading these letters, I ask you, the reader, to take your mind back to a time when America was only recently industrialized. Formerly independent farmers and miners, and waves of immigrants flooded the labor supply. Society provided no safety net. Unemployment meant starvation. The newly emerged corporate giants of mining, lumber, and agriculture were at their full power, unrestrained by government regulation, free to use workers—especially unskilled, immigrant, and black workers—as they saw fit. That is the setting for this story.

In writing this narrative, I became indebted to so many people. John Jay colleagues, most notably Professor Blanche Wiesen Cook, encouraged me to begin the book and, along the way, provided advice and leads. Distinguished Professor Melvyn Dubofsky of the State University of New York at Binghamton has been more than generous with his time, his valuable advice, and the introduction with which he has enriched this book. My friend Elinor Gabriel reviewed the manuscript and other good friends, too numerous to cite here by name, have read portions of the manuscript and provided advice and encouragement. My daughter, Leslie Rosen Levy, traveled with me to Detroit to assist in my research and later proved to be a meticulous and creative critic; she will recognize some words as her own. The person to whom I am most indebted and, to coin a phrase, without whom this work would not have been possible, is my husband, Professor (of Chemistry) Milton J. Rosen. The most purposeful man I have ever met, he prodded me on and picked me up when the going got rough. He is an honest, sophisticated, invaluable critic. He is also my best friend.

Edward Weber and Julie Herrada of the Labadie Collection at the University of Michigan have been of great help in many ways. Archivist William LeFevre of Wayne State University's Walter P. Reuther Library has been generous in making materials, most importantly the trial transcript, available to me. I am grateful also to the Tamiment Institute Library, the Great Neck Public Library, the Lloyd Sealy Library at John Jay College of Criminal Justice, and reference librarians at the Kansas City Public Library in Kansas City, Missouri. Alice Nigoghosian of the Wayne State University Press first saw the potential in my father's story and has shepherded it with skill and consideration. Editors Adela Garcia and Sandra Williamson have, with warmth and wit, brought their impressive skills to bear upon the manuscript.

A Note to the Reader: I have retained my father's misspellings and grammatical errors, in the belief that they will remind the reader of how little formal education he had, and trusting they will not pose an impediment to the reading.

At the suggestion of the publisher, a glossary has been added to help the reader identify (insofar as I have been able to ascertain) people and events alluded to in the letters.

My father is referred to variously as Edwin and Edward. The name on his birth certificate is Edward, but he was always called Edwin. When I met my grandmother for the first (and last) time, the year she turned ninety, she looked at me and said, in her Swedish singsong, "Ven I look at yew, I see Ed-vin."

I can think of no greater compliment.

Great Neck, New York

INTRODUCTION
Melvyn Dubofsky

✥

ELLEN DOREE ROSEN's *A Wobbly Life*, a book which perhaps merits the title used by Theodore Dreiser, *An American Tragedy*, does not fit into any easily identifiable scholarly or literary genre. It is not a conventional scholarly study; neither is it traditional biography or autobiography; although it consists in large part of a collection of prison letters, it is not really a set of edited letters. Rather, it represents a daughter's search for a father whom she never really knew, other than through passing remembrances by her mother and the prison letters that Ellen read long after her father and mother had died. As a personal story of human interest, the sort of story beloved by our "up close and personal" newspapers, news magazines, and television news shows, it should pique the interest and touch the emotions of readers. But Ellen's father also happened to be a quite extraordinary ordinary man.

E. F. Doree was a leading member of the most famous band of labor radicals in United States history, the Wobblies, members of the IWW (Industrial Workers of the World). If not of a stature or renown comparable to William D. "Big Bill" Haywood, Elizabeth Gurley Flynn (the "Rebel Girl"), Vincent St. John ("the Saint"), or Joe Hill, the Wobbly bard, Doree may have actually been more important to the everyday work and success of the IWW. It was Doree and other men and women like him who went out into the field to organize the workers who joined the IWW between 1910 and 1917. Whether among timber workers in Louisiana, their brothers in the woods of the Pacific Northwest, iron ore miners on the Mesabi Range, rubber workers in Akron, dock wallopers on the Philadelphia waterfront, or itinerant harvesters on the Great Plains from

Texas to Canada, Doree moved among them, struggled with them, understood them, and sought to organize them. And for his services to the IWW, like nearly all his brother prewar and wartime Wobbly leaders, federal authorities arrested him in 1917 for sedition and espionage, tried him on those charges in the infamous Chicago IWW trial of 1918, and sentenced him to a term in the Leavenworth federal penitentiary where he wrote the bulk of the letters featured in this book.

Let me stress that *A Wobbly Life* does not add substantially to the history of the IWW. It will not alter our understanding of why in the year 1905 a group of diverse radicals disaffected from the American Federation of Labor (AFL) and its style of craft unionism met in Chicago to create an alternative labor movement, one its founders believed would usher in a cooperative commonwealth built by hand and brain workers. This book will not tell readers anything about the internecine battles and schisms that crippled the fledgling IWW between 1905 and its resurrection in 1909–1910. It also will not help us understand the struggles among anarchists, syndicalists, anarcho-syndicalists, industrial unionists, and other radical factions to define the character, ideology, and ultimate goals of the IWW. Only between the lines does it tell us anything about the successes and failures of the IWW during its glory years between 1910 and 1917, the years when Doree was most active as a Wobbly and participated in some of the organization's most famous struggles and its two greatest successes, the organization of migratory harvest workers between 1915 and 1917, and the creation of union power on the Philadelphia waterfront among black and white longshoremen. It does, however, portray graphically how the wartime federal persecution, prosecution, and imprisonment of the IWW leaders, Doree among them, crippled the organization far more effectively than the Wobblies' own persistent internal disagreements. And in describing Doree's personal disaffection from the postwar leadership of the IWW, it partly explains why the post-1920 IWW ultimately disappeared into what the journalist Dan Wakefield described in 1955 as "haunted halls."

Doree's prison letters make this book unique and enable historians, scholars, and readers to do one of the hardest things imaginable, actually enter the mind and heart of an ordinary working person. Most of what passes for knowledge about working people comes from reports and observations of social investigators and journalists, official government commissions and public documents, public testimonies at trials and hearings, or carefully plotted biographies and autobiographies. All these sources are either "socially constructed" or personally designed after the fact. Indeed, not long ago I glanced at a review in a recent issue of *Labor History* concerning a book about the Agricultural Workers' Organization of the IWW, an organization with which E. F. Doree had an intimate and crucial association. The reviewer noted that "exploring the minds of workers, even activists, is often next to impossible. Still, I cannot help but wonder if [the author] could have explored more deeply the young, white men at the AWO's core."[1] And that, of course, is precisely what Ellen Rosen's *A Wobbly Life* does.

Ellen offers us something totally different from what is generally found in the literature about working people and radicals. Her book consists in large part of a series of letters her father wrote while serving time as a federal political prisoner in Leavenworth penitentiary between 1918 and 1922. Unlike the kind of sources I mention above or even the biographies and autobiographies of IWW leaders like Big Bill Haywood, Elizabeth Gurley Flynn, Ralph Chaplin, Ben Hayes Williams, and Covington Hall (and many others),[2] these letters are personal and private. They offer unrivaled insight and glimpses into the deepest feelings and longings of an ordinary working man. To repeat myself, E. F. Doree was one of the most important members, organizers, and officials of the pre–World War I and wartime IWW. His letters tell us more about the values, beliefs, and yearnings of the committed Wobbly than anything I have ever read. The man who comes alive in these pages seems in part to resemble the prototypical Wobbly as described in the opening pages of James Jones's *From Here To Eternity*, when an army veteran tells a young recruit: "You don't remember the Wobblies. You were too young. Or else not even born yet. There has never been anything like them before or since. They called themselves materialists-economists but what they really were was a religion. They were work-stiffs and bindlebums like you and me, but they were welded together by a vision we don't possess." He bears scant resemblance to the poverty-impaired, homeless, family-less, culturally deprived casual laborer described so memorably by the economist cum sociologist Carleton Parker. Wobblies who shared lives of brutality, degradation, and violence "starting with the long hours and dreary winters of the farms they ran away from, or the sour-smelling bunkhouse in a coal village, through their character-debasing experience with the drifting 'hire and fire' life in the industries, on to the vicious social and economic life of the winter unemployed."[3]

More than three decades ago, when I first began research for the book that became my history of the IWW, *We Shall Be All,* I met the human counterparts of the conventional stereotype of the Wobbly rebel and his alter ego. At the time I resided a little more than an hour west of Chicago, where a famous surviving Wobbly and the organization's then most recent historian, Fred Thompson, lived and worked. Eager to interview Thompson and discuss with him his memories of fellow Wobblies and his perspective on the IWW's place in history, I contacted him. At first, however, we could not find a convenient time to meet because our personal work and family schedules conflicted. Then one day Thompson phoned to say that he had time to see me. Good, I replied, how come? To which he answered, "I just had an argument with my foreman and I punched him on the jaw. So, I am out of a job and with time to spare." Ah, said I, the prototypical rebel Wobbly as portrayed by Jones and also John Dos Passos, one who says to an abusive boss, "take this job and shove it," or perhaps utters what a World War I–era Wobbly, much to the dismay of a federal agent, scribbled as a salutation, "Here's to mud on the stick of the boss." Around the same time I located and interviewed the last surviving member of the prewar IWW executive board, Richard Brazier. Like Doree, Brazier organized almost everywhere for the IWW, participated in free speech fights, served time in local jails, and was one of the political prisoners along with Doree at Leavenworth. When I met Brazier, then retired and living on Social Security with his wife, they occupied an apartment in municipal housing just north of the Columbia University campus on the westernmost fringe of Harlem. Before I could begin to discuss with Brazier his memories of the IWW, he asked me to share a glass of wine and a toast. What, I asked, was the occasion for the celebration? Brazier and his wife had just learned that day that they would be able to vacate their current apartment and move to another city housing complex farther downtown, near Lincoln Center. Why, I asked, was that worth a celebration? Without missing a beat, Brazier responded that it meant liberation from the Black Muslims, nationalists, and adolescent toughs who made his daily life a living hell. What, I then wondered, was the reality of the tough-as-nails, super-manly IWW rebel? The elderly Fred Thompson still eager to punch out an abusive boss even at the loss of a job, or the even more elderly Richard Brazier, who feared mid-1960's black nationalists and militants?

Doree's prison letters offer us an opportunity to answer that question by glimpsing the interior life and feelings of an ordinary working person who became a dedicated labor radical. Bill Haywood and Gurley Flynn published autobiographies (in the former's case almost certainly ghost-written), but their purpose was to justify their subjects' ultimate loyalty to Soviet-style Communism, not to explore and reveal their most intimate feelings and personal desires. Ben Hayes Williams and Covington Hall, two other prominent prewar Wobblies, wrote autobiographies, but they, too, focused on the public arena, not the more private sphere of family, sentiment, and affection. Doree's letters, by contrast, expose his most personal and private feelings. Mostly written to his wife, they express his deepest longings, his ardent love, his faith in family, and his devotion to a son whose presence he was denied by imprisonment and who died a tragic death not long after Doree gained his liberty. The person who emerges from these letters bears scant resemblance to the sort of Wobblies and labor radicals known best to us through their polemical writings, the biographical portraits fashioned by creative writers, or the work of most scholars.

Doree scarcely resembles Haywood, who deserted his wife and two daughters early on and who outraged his Pinkerton abductors in 1905: not because they seized him as a suspect for multiple murders, but because they found him, a married man, in a Denver brothel. Nor does Doree resemble Flynn, who married as a teenager, escaped that unhappy, loveless marriage, developed a relationship with the Italian radical Carlo Tresca and thereafter led an unconventional personal and family life. Nor does he seem at all comparable to other itinerant workers, men typically described as leading footloose, women- and family-free, hand-to-mouth lives; men who gambled, boozed, and screwed away what little money they earned; who apparently had little respect for serious literature, the play of ideas, and deep thought. The man who emerges from Ellen's reconstruction of her father's life and his own letters remains committed to a monogamous relationship with the woman he loves, seeks to be a presence in the lives of the children he so desperately desires, and, above all, strives to build a stable home life for his family. Indeed, so important were home and family to Doree that after his release from prison he labored to create a more normal life for his wife and children, a life in which he would not be away from home repeatedly, a life away from the labor radicalism to which he had once committed himself, a life reconstructed as a stable, salaried, white-collar employee. The Doree who emerges in the following pages could build such a new life because he self-educated himself in the best sense of that process. He read widely and deeply in literature, both fiction and theory; he could discuss complex subject matter with perception and precision; and, despite spending so much of his life as either an itinerant worker or a prison inmate, he displayed a wealth rather than a paucity of culture. In many ways, then, this book is more a bildungsroman than a biography or an edited collection of letters.

Anyone who reads this book must conclude that Aileen Kraditor's portrait of the labor radicals of Doree's generation as partly neurotic, partly psychotic, and totally out of touch with the quotidian life of her "John Q. Worker" is quite wrong.[4] In ways too numerous to count, Doree's letters portray a man as loyal to family, as devoted to a stable home life, as commonplace and mundane as Kraditor's "John Q. Worker." No unbridgeable gap, then, separated the world of radicals from the universe of "John Q. Worker." Ordinary workers and radicals could speak the same language, share the same visions, join together as brothers and sisters in solidarity, and move, depending on time and circumstances, back and forth between a world of revolutionary dreams and a commonplace existence.

Salvatore Salerno has tried to recreate what he characterizes as the complex and syncretic culture of typical Wobblies, an amalgam of concepts brought to Western shores by European immigrants and acquired by U.S.-born workers immersed in an indigenous culture of opposition. Salerno has also tried to save those labor radicals from the condescension of such scholars as me, Louis Levine, and Paul Brissenden.[5] Yet he is forced to conclude that little has survived to provide a sense of the lived activity and culture of the Wobbly.[6] Doree's life and letters provide readers an opportunity to judge the validity of Salerno's portrait of Wobbly culture.

Doree's letters also put into question Donald Winter's assertion that "the lesson of the IWW . . . is about how religious sensibility and imagery

helped mobilize the radical element of the labor movement" by endow-
ing it with "the soul of solidarity."[7] Doree's correspondence and his com-
ments about fellow prisoners hint at the fundamentally secular essence
of Wobbly culture. In print and speech, song and poem, IWW polemi-
cists and bards used biblical rhetoric and imagery, turned Jesus into a
working-class rebel, his disciples (apostles) into organizers of revolt,
Judas into a scab or labor fink. Yet as the absence of words about faith,
religion, and God in Doree's letters attest, theology, the church (or for
that matter the synagogue or temple), and the Lord carried little weight
for the committed Wobbly and the working-class milieu from which he/
she emerged.

The letters also raise questions about themes emphasized in the most
recent scholarly literature about workingmen in the past: their hyper-
masculinity, the place of "whiteness" in working-class culture, and the
status of newer immigrants as "in-between peoples."[8] Nothing in these
letters suggests that the relationship between Doree and his partner was
built on patriarchical beliefs and expectations or that the woman
remained responsible for the domestic sphere while the man acted in the
public one. Doree's words and language convey convictions as nurturing
and affective as those associated with the most feminine personality. The
man of the house, he felt totally bereft because he was denied the presence of his young son, whose nurture and training he desired to share in
every way. As his son ultimately proved unable to fight off the illness that
took his life, the father donned no mask of stoic, hyper-masculinity but
shed freely the tears of sadness. To be sure, we can never be certain how
typical or atypical Doree's sentiments were among other men who led
transient lives of casual labor and eventually settled down with families,
but we can question whether such men, as a rule, simply dismissed the
mutual obligations of partnership, parenthood, and compatibility, and
whether they typically treated women with scorn and derision. (In a letter of September 8, 1921, Doree reports the results of his own study of fellow political prisoners, in which he finds that, after three years'
imprisonment, of the sixty-four married "Reds" in Leavenworth, only four
had been deserted by their wives.)

Doree and his close IWW friend, fellow organizer of agricultural
workers and Philadelphia longshoremen, and Leavenworth inmate, Walter Nef ("the big stiff")—both children of the older Northern European

immigration—had no aversion to linking themselves to "in-between people." In fact, they chose to tie themselves through marriage to women of Eastern European Jewish extraction. Doree was certainly aware of the racial distinctions that marked U.S. society and culture, but one of his best friends and a fellow Wobbly, Ben Fletcher, was coal black, and Doree's letters never hint at any sense of "whiteness." Moreover, his wife and son were literally adopted and subsidized by Philadelphians of the best sort, and his own Scandinavian (Nordic) family accepted without reservation his Jewish spouse and children. Anyone who reads this text and the letters in it will be hard-pressed to associate Doree with a sense of "white privilege" or "whiteness" or to conclude that Doree, Nef, and the Eastern and Southern European workers they mingled with in the IWW and in prison ever considered themselves to be "in-between people" who had to negotiate a perilous passage before "becoming white." In an ironical footnote to the story, when Doree died suddenly and unexpectedly in West Texas, his wife moved herself and two young children back East, to Brooklyn, New York, where they settled in a Bedford-Stuyvesant rooming house she ran in order to support the family. They were often visited by Ben Fletcher, and they remained there as the neighborhood turned black; they persisted as the last white family in an all-black block and an all-black community.

The role played by wealthy and socially prestigious reformers in sustaining the morale of such political prisoners as Doree, and also quite literally supporting his wife and child in Philadelphia, casts another doubt on themes of "whiteness" and "in-betweenness." Insofar as one can discern from Doree's correspondence with these reformers or his discussions about them with his wife, these Philadelphia "Mainliners"—most of whom were Quakers with a long tradition of good works, including W. I. Biddle, the warden of Leavenworth, who proved so solicitous of Doree, and who was descended from one of the more famous old Philadelphia families—and their old-stock, upper-class Protestant counterparts in Boston and New York, among other places, never doubted his or his spouse's standing as full "American" citizens who had no need to establish their credentials as "white." Certainly, racism in its many forms pervaded U.S. culture and society during World War I and the ensuing decade. It remained commonplace to refer to the Hebrew race, or the Irish (Celtic) race, or the Nordic, Anglo-Saxon, Teutonic, Negro, and

Mongol races—among the multifarious races different observers and even social scientists identified. Some of the analysts of "race" even built a complex hierarchy of race that descended from superior to inferior types. But for Doree, the circles in which he moved and the reformers with whom he became close were all part of a common human race in which similarities bulked larger than differences.

Doree's letters describe the vast gulf that separated the prewar Wobblies from the people who took over the organization after the imprisonment of nearly all its leaders during the war. They tell us how estranged Doree and most of his cohort felt from the post-1919 leadership of the IWW. For example, in a letter written on August 20, 1922, he observes of the postwar IWW, "Any movement that becomes dead to human emotions, is as dead as it can ever become." Some letters he wrote in prison deal more openly and fully with politics at home and abroad. In them, one sees how Doree rethought many of the principles and revolutionary aspirations that initially drew him to the IWW, and how and why the consequences of the Bolshevik revolution made him question the uses of violence. They also hint at why he ultimately consented to the terms of the pardon offered by the Harding administration. Doree denounced what he felt to be the reorganized IWW's desertion of the Leavenworth political prisoners. He found inexplicable the IWW national office's alacrity in suspending from membership the successful local of Philadelphia longshoremen and other units that bargained with employers and achieved real material gains for members. Upon his release from prison, Doree disassociated himself from the IWW not only because he wanted to build a more stable and commonplace life for himself and his family but also because he now felt totally estranged from the organization's leaders. He resented their disdain for those who had suffered so greatly to build the IWW as a practical alternative to the AFL and craft unionism.

There is so much to learn from this book and its letters that I hardly know where to begin or end. They tell us a great deal about prison life among convicts who are not common criminals but political prisoners. They tell us how painful and destructive prison life is not only for those behind bars but even more for their families and loved ones outside. And they offer a cautionary lesson concerning how easily fears of subversion and terrorism (the diseases associated with the IWW in 1917–1918) can lead to unjust and tragic consequences. Think of the tragic results that due process and constitutional jurisprudence brought to Doree and his family. Then consider what might be the reality for those, U.S. citizens, who in the future are charged with links to terrorism and denied the basic rights enjoyed by Doree and his cohort.

Ellen, as I said at the beginning, might well have titled her search for a missing father, *An American Tragedy*. Think of the blows that rained down on the Doree family between 1917 and 1927: imprisonment and marital separation; the premature death of the firstborn son; the premature death of E. F. Doree, leaving behind a daughter and an infant son who never knew their father, and a mother who for the remainder of her life inhabited an empty, affectless universe. This is a story told mostly in the private and innermost words and thoughts of its protagonist, the lost father that Ellen sought to rediscover. This, then, is a story that should attract and hold the attention of readers.

PROLOGUE

❦

ON SEPTEMBER 7, 1918, one hundred men were on their way together to prison. They rode a train specially prepared to carry them from Chicago, directly into the walls of the federal penitentiary at Leavenworth, Kansas. They were big men, rough, scarred, and weatherbeaten, who called one another "Fellow Worker." The newspapers called them "The Chicago Hundred."

These were the leaders of the IWW, the Industrial Workers of the World, the "Wobblies." They were its officers, union heads, editors and writers, its best organizers. One of these men was my father. On the rocking train, bound for ten years in prison, he wrote my mother a short note in pencil on a folded piece of paper.

Enroute to Fort Leavenworth
Aboard Train.
Sept. 7, 1918.

My dearest little Chiky:

Hope that this line will reach you before you leave. We are having a fine trip. Everybody happy. The whole hundred on three cars.

Write me from time to time on the road home, wont you?

[Forrest] Edwards and I are hand-cuffed together. We were the last two aboard the train, but we got the best seats.

Well, love and kisses to you and Bucky. My next letter will be addressed to home. Bye, bye, baby. Hope you are as happy as I am.

Your loving Ed

I never got to know my father. My earliest specific memory is his funeral. I am in a room with many people. I see the room and people from a low, small child's perspective. The people are talking quietly. My mother is not in the room, but everyone is being very nice to me, so I am happy.

That was in Amarillo, Texas, two months before my third birthday. I retain an impression of the train that carried us— my mother, my infant brother, and me—to New York. I recall clearly my delight as I ran from floor to floor, discovering room after room in our new house in Brooklyn. Only later would I understand that my father's life insurance had paid for the brownstone, once an elegant town house, now subdivided into furnished units whose rent could support a widow and her children.

Children know. I think I always knew that my mother lived in two worlds. Her hands were in the mundane world of renting out the rooms, cleaning, stoking the coal furnace, putting meals on the table, sewing my dresses, cutting paper bags into schoolbook covers for my younger brother Eddy. But her heart, I knew, dwelt in the past, the lost world of my father and their first child, Bucky. It was a world I could not approach or comprehend. She would not—could not—talk about it.

The house, however, hinted everywhere at the past. In the basement sat a trunk, and inside it was an urn with Bucky's ashes. My father's charcoal drawings looked down from our walls: a woman's face, a Santa Claus, a muscular workman entitled "The Slave of the Mill." My father's brown suit hung in the bedroom closet. In the hall closet, resting on a shelf, was a black leather satchel with a leather-bound tag in his fine lettering: E. F. DOREE.

Inside the satchel was my father's life, reduced to a few possessions. A white envelope with clippings of his dark red hair. His right-hand glove, the pinky and ring fingers cut away and neatly resewn at the base. His gold Hamilton pocket watch, along with a device for sharpening razor blades. Also a set of baby-carriage clips, a lace baby cap, and a miniature book that belonged to my brother Bucky. Then the newspaper articles about our family, the photographs, various official documents, and the family treasure, my father's letters from Leavenworth penitentiary.

At first, all I knew from my mother was that my father had been in prison and I should be proud of him. He had been in prison because he was a member of the IWW. The IWW organized workers because in union there is strength. That was about the extent of my childish understanding.

When I was small, my mother would take us to the annual Wobbly Ball in New York, where I would inevitably be pulled to the front of the room to lead the singing of songs from the "Little Red Songbook." I sang Ralph Chaplin's "Solidarity Forever," Joe Hill's "The Tramp" and "Casey Jones." I didn't understand most of the songs. Never having heard the word "fort," I sang, "Hold the fork, for we are coming, Union men be strong." But my favorite song was T-Bone Slim's "The Popular Wobbly," with its refrain: "They go wild, simply wild over me."[1]

The annual ball was the only IWW reality in my young life. I knew two Wobblies as I grew up, but they almost never talked about the past, and I saw them simply as people I knew, not as Wobblies, ex-convicts, or even men who had known my father. One was Walter Nef, my uncle, married to my mother's sister Feige. He was a big man with clear blue eyes, jug-handle ears, and a strong cleft chin in a poker face. He was a well-born but inarticulate, humorless Swiss whom my father had dubbed "the big stiff." A straight arrow, Walter was helpless in the face of his small wife's strength of character, ready tongue, and exquisite manipulative skills. When she finally showed him the door, he came to stay with us for a while. Like so many during the Great Depression, he was unemployed. He did odd jobs and spent his evenings in the basement, doggedly turning out "One Big Union" flyers on his mimeograph machine, alone and ineffectual. In time, and to my surprise, I would learn just who he had been and what he had accomplished.

The other Wobbly lived nearby. Ben Fletcher was the blackest man I have ever met; his cherubic face gleamed like polished ebony. Unlike Walter, Ben smiled and found the humor in every situation: it was he who said Judge Landis used poor English because his sentences were too long. I adored Ben's wife, Clara, with her no-nonsense warmth and practical energy. My mother explained that I was to bear two things in mind about Clara. Firstly, although we knew that she was Ben's wife, for some reason they passed as brother and sister. Secondly, although I could call her "Clara" at home, I was to call her "Miss Fletcher" in the street. Clara was sensitive that people might think, because she was colored, that I was summoning a servant.

The truth is that my childish interest lay not at all in the Wobblies but in my father. I hungered to know more about him, and I often fantasized that he would one day appear at our door, alive. In the self-centeredness of childhood, I wanted him as my champion. It was said that I took after him. I was certainly different from my mother and brother Eddy, both of whom were sensitive, poetic, and depressed by nature. I was coming to see my optimism as a defect, evidence that I lacked soul. If I really took after my father, I wanted him on hand to validate my character. He never appeared.

1

E. F. DOREE

They accuse me of ras-cal-i-ty,
But I can't see why they always pick on me;
I'm as gentle as a lamb, but they take me for a ram,
They go wild, simply wild over me.

WHEN I WAS a child, my father's family lived in towns scattered along the West Coast, from Watsonville, California, to Sitka, Alaska. In those days of thin pocketbooks and slow travel, that was a world away from Brooklyn. Although my mother kept up a sporadic correspondence with my grandmother, I knew little about them.

As a teenager, I began to speculate about the family name. Knowing that my father's parents were born in Sweden, I wondered why we had a French name. In high school I learned that Napoleon's Marshall Bernadotte became King of Sweden, and I made the romantic assumption that we descended from some lesser French officer who came to Sweden and, of course, achieved nobility there. Years later, my father's sister Florence provided what turned out to be a partial explanation: my grandfather ran away from home, saw "Doree" on a box, liked the word, and adopted it as his own: he would be Frederick Doree. No one knew his real name. Florence's tale shattered my illusion: I was descended not from aristocrats but from a crate. Eventually, Florence divulged the whole truth. She wrote, "Of Dad's parents I know very little. His father was a red headed school teacher who got a girl . . . pregnant and refused to marry her so having no way of taking care of the baby she took it to his home and left it on the porch. A tailor and his wife took Dad and raised him. I think their name was 'Walstead.' Any way my Father was a very fine man. Honest as the day was long."[1]

The unwanted baby grew up to be a handsome young man skilled in the craft of cabinetmaking. At the age of eighteen he left Sweden for America and found work in Elizabeth, New Jersey, preparing the wooden interiors of railroad cars. As soon as he was established he sent for his sweetheart, Maria Brandt, and they were married on April 14, 1888. He was tall and red-headed, with calm blue eyes and a ferocious moustache; she was diminutive, brown-eyed, and feisty.

They soon moved to Philadelphia, where my father, Edwin Frederick, their first child, was born on February 6, 1889. Hilma, Frank, and Alford followed in short order. My grandmother was lonely and unhappy in the city, so the Dorees moved to eastern Washington, near Coeur d'Alene, Idaho, where my grandmother's siblings had settled. My aunt Florence was born in Cannondale, Washington.

In 1900 an opportunity presented itself to my grandfather. Gold had been discovered in the Klondike. A new railroad line was being built to provide access between White Horse, in the Yukon, and the port of Skagway, in Alaska. The rail line was a marvel of trestles and tunnels, climbing steeply up from the coast through narrow mountain defiles. Frederick went alone to Alaska, to work at building cars for the new railroad. Finding Skagway quite livable, he sent for his wife and children. The windows of their house looked out upon mountains, rising like sheer walls from the small valley floor that is Skagway. There the youngest child, Edna, was born, and there the family would remain until 1911, when they settled permanently in Oregon.

Edwin was eleven years old when the family moved to Skagway. At the age of thirteen, he left the Skagway school and went to work on a truck farm. He attended night school for the next two years—and with that his formal education ended.

At age fifteen he began to work, like his father, for the railroad. He was hired as an apprentice in coach and car building. One day in 1905, when he was sixteen, Edwin lost two fingers from his right hand in a sawmill accident on the job. As his sister Florence told it, the railroad company's reaction was to fire him—no medical care, no compensation—with the warning that any fuss would cost my grandfather's job as well. The young man had to leave Skagway. Before he left, the family had its portrait taken. The picture shows all six children, from Edna, still a baby, to Edwin, a handsome, even dapper young man, his deformed right hand resting on the back of his mother's chair.

This object lesson in corporate ruthlessness and labor powerlessness must have marked the beginning of a radical. Edwin moved to Coeur d'Alene, to live and work with his bachelor uncle Axel.

THE NORTHWEST

Of my father's years in the Idaho-Washington area I know almost nothing. At some point he began identifying himself as E. F. Doree. He was a member of the Western Federation of Miners when he joined the newly formed IWW in Spokane in January 1906.[2] He dropped out of the IWW after a few months.[3] He worked for a time as a logger, but his passion was baseball. He played as "Skag" Doree, managed the Hayden Lake team of the Northwestern League, and dreamed of a professional baseball career. That dream was shattered one day in 1908, when his horse stepped into a posthole. My father was thrown to the ground, his horse on top of him. The horse had to be shot. My father's leg was badly injured, and he spent almost a year in the hospital, probably in nearby Spokane. According to my mother, the leg would not heal, and the doctors talked of amputation, so my father "crawled out of the hospital one night and had the leg till the day he died."

Spokane was an important city for the IWW. Lumberjacks, fruit pickers, and roustabouts from near and far wintered over there, waiting for work to begin when the weather allowed. In the town, two forces vied for their souls. Soldiers of the Salvation Army preached redemption while, across the street, Wobbly speakers on soapboxes preached the union gospel. The IWW was a grassroots movement in the best American tradition—the little guys, fed up with abuse, joining hands to confront tyranny. Their abusers were the turn-of-the-century "robber barons" of industry, who worked their loggers seven days a week, their harvesters from sunup to sundown in the prairie heat, and the children in their textile mills for ten hours a day—and charged them for their drinking water. The weapon of the "little guys" was unionization. While existing unions had never taken up the cause of the unskilled, the migratory, the immigrant, or the black worker, the Wobblies strove to bring them and all the other workers of an industry into one big union, skilled and unskilled together. (Decades later, with the help of Wobbly John Pancner, the automobile workers would do just that by forming the CIO Auto Workers Union.)[4]

The corporations were powerful. They "owned" legislators, town officials, and police forces. Fighting was dirty, and often bloody. In 1908, while my father was bedridden, a free speech fight erupted in Spokane. To silence the Wobblies, the municipality had outlawed public speaking on the streets. The Wobblies countered by civil disobedience, inviting, or at least not resisting, arrest. Wallace Stegner has captured the scene as the conflict spread along the West Coast: "The Wobblies crammed half the jails from Everett to San Diego with belligerent workers fighting ordinances against free speech and street meetings, piling in till they jammed a town's whole system of law and order, pouring down from the woods and the camps, beating their way from skid roads and winter boarding houses, streaming in from the harvest country. . . . They organized and kept their jails spotless, and they sang till townspeople gathered laughing outside to listen."[5]

My uncle Walter took part in that fight. The only time he ever spoke to me about his past was to describe how he was treated in the Spokane jail: watered down with a hose and forced to march around outdoors, wet, in the cold of winter.

The Spokane fight raged for two years. My father must have emerged from the hospital into that Wobbly campaign. It is clear he rejoined the IWW in 1910. But when did he become an organizer? Undated pictures from the black satchel show him, looking very young, addressing crowds in the streets and parks. A nearby sign reads, "Lumberjacks and Roustabouts, Organize." His career had begun.

DEAREST LITTLE CHIKY

It was as an organizer that he met my mother. In September 1914 my father was speaking in Rochester, New York, attempting to organize clothing workers. My mother, working in a clothing factory, went to a rally to hear the IWW organizer. It was every cliché in the book: love at first sight across a crowded room. Three days later they were married, which is to say they made pledges to each other. No need of a state or religious authority to tell them they were one! And they loved each other from the day they met to the day he died. In twenty-seven years of widowhood my mother never thought of another man.

I always thought of my parents' love for each other as a physical entity, a palpable presence, an extraordinary, transcendent "thing." It dwelt with us even after his death. It was a lodestone for gauging daily life. Nothing real compared with it in importance. Beside it, all emotions were superficial. It was immortal. The love shared by father, mother, and Bucky occupied a place and defined a world that not even I and my younger brother could enter. We were in a different time warp.

My father called my mother "little baby" or "girlie" but mostly "Chiky," from her Yiddish name that he never could pronounce properly. It was "Chai-ky," little Chaya, but, unable to master the gutteral "ch" sound, he spoke her name as if she were a baby chicken. Early in their marriage she adopted the "American" name Ida, and he referred to her as Ida when he spoke or wrote to others. But for him she was always Chiky.

Chiky, with her ivory complexion, chestnut hair, and hazel eyes, was an immigrant from Lithuania. As was typical of Jews in Eastern Europe, her family lived in poverty in the Pale of Settlement, prohibited from owning land and periodically attacked in pogroms. Her intelligent, literate, witty mother had given difficult birth to fourteen children in sixteen years. Six died in childhood and seven emigrated, two to England and five to America. My grandparents, Lebel and Sarah Salinger, would never learn the unspeakable news that in America daughters Belle, Chiky, and Feige all married gentiles. But the three intermarriages did not escape the active disapproval of Orthodox brother Yudel in Rochester and revered elder sister Ruchel Weber in Galeton, Pennsylvania.

Ed and Chiky shared a passion for justice, a rejection of formal religion, and faith in the possibility of making the world better. In every other respect, they were, by most standards, oddly matched. Chiky was five years older than Ed; when they met he was twenty-five and she was thirty. He was a torch—six feet tall, thin, straight, aflame with red hair. She was a dumpling—a full foot shorter than he, full-breasted, overweight. He was born Christian, she was born Jewish. He came from a world of action, she from a world of reflection. Ed was an American at home, a product of open spaces, mountain, ranch, and farmland, of Washington, Alaska, and Idaho. Chiky was a "greenhorn," a transplant from the shtetl, a product of the inhibiting Old World of strict religious orthodoxy in a hostile environment.

They had very different personalities. Ed, I came to learn, was always hopeful, finding the best in a situation. He was at home with others, ready to give and ready to accept. He was playful, outgoing, and liked to observe people. Chiky was quintessentially domestic and irredeemably sad. Her sadness carried a Russian aura of futility, reinforced by a Jewish certainty of the inevitability of suffering. She recited to me a poem she wrote, in Yiddish, when she was young. It was about the wind:

> Where is the wind running,
>   As if poisoned?
> Why driven, why hastened,
>   Unsure where it steps?
> Does it mean to drive the clouds away?
> Does it mean to drive the clouds together?
> Or does it run without purpose,
>   Like all of us.[6]

She was introverted, aesthetic. She loved music, especially Mozart, and sang in a pure, sweet, high voice. She had a natural flair for mathematics, a sure, elegant sense of design, and an extraordinary, subtle gift for color. But she was not social. She was ill at ease with others, unskilled in small talk, humorless, lacking tact, prone to misjudgments. I will never know by what miracle they produced such a glowing and enduring unity.

Everything was against the new couple. Poverty kept them apart for the first year. As an unpaid organizer, Ed could not provide a home for his wife. While he rode the rails to Kansas and worked to organize grain harvesters, she remained in Rochester. When she fell seriously ill and had no choice but to live with her disapproving brother and his wife, Ed wrote from Kansas City:

> Jan. 27, 1915
> If anybody wants to kill me, the quickest way to do it is to hand me a job or a ten dollar bill. . . . There is one thing that I insist on, and

that is, at least one good meal a day, and believe me I get it, even if I don't get any more.

Feb. 22, 1915
Yes, girlie, I wish I knew what your trouble is. It worries me, some what. You always say that you will tell me when we meet. . . . I hate to think of you as being sick or unhappy. To tell the truth, I some-times curse myself for ever having dared to love in such a world as this. It makes me feel worthless. A world full of plenty and yet I cant get together enough so that we might live together and love as nature intended we should.

May 13, 1915
I am going to stick with you until one of us dies. . . . Girlie, I will not forget you or even try to forget you. You haven't broken my heart at all because if you don't come to me I shall come to you, even into your brother's house. Chiky, I love you. Sick or well, you have won a place in my life.

July 24, 1915
I am not so sorry because you cannot become a mother as I am that you must take the operation. . . . Girlie, you are the one bright spot in this world to me, you are my everything in life. . . . Do anything to get well.

Whatever the medical problem was, it was cured. In December 1916, when they moved from Baltimore to Philadelphia, Chiky was seven months pregnant with their first child. Frederick Lee (Bucky) Doree was born on February 18, 1917.

But we are getting ahead of our story.

2

$1,000 Reward, Dead or Alive

Oh the "bull" he went wild over me,
And he held his gun where everyone could see;
He was breathing rather hard when he saw my union card,
He went wild, simply wild over me.

MOST OF MY father's young life was spent in organizing American workers: lumberjacks in the far West, softwood loggers in the Deep South, rubber workers and ore handlers in the Midwest, harvest workers on the Great
Plains, textile workers and longshoremen on the East Coast. Yet all I know
about that life rests upon clues from the occasional letter, article, photograph, testimony, reference. Like glimpses between the boards of a high
fence as one moves past it, the view is discontinuous and tantalizing.

THE DEEP SOUTH

If the West Coast years are lost in the fog, the year 1912 is sunlit. Here
the view through the fence is clear.

The defense strategy at the 1918 trial of the Chicago Hundred cen-
tered on having selected defendants describe, from their own experience,
what the IWW was fighting for—and against. (Such was their faith that
a reasonable jury would see the righteousness of their cause!) My father
was one of those who testified about his experiences as an organizer,
guided by defense attorney George Vanderveer.

9

Q *Did you have occasion to go down into Louisiana, in behalf of the IWW?*
A Yes, in 1912.

Q *What did you go down there for?*
A Well, there was a strike down there of the Brotherhood of the Timber Workers, an independent organization, and on the 7th of July, 1912, a riot occurred. . . . Practically all of the Union officials were arrested. . . . The Brotherhood of Timber Workers, I understand, called upon the IWW for some one to assist them in the strike, and I was one of the men sent down there.

Q *How long were you in Louisiana on that occasion?*
A In Louisiana and Texas nine months.

Q *Traveling around a good deal?*
A Traveling around through all the mill towns and camps.

Q *Now describe to the jury, please, what a mill town is and the conditions existing within it?*
A A mill town is a town that is built by the milling companies themselves. . . . Around the whole thing, the mill and saw mill and piles and houses and business houses and everything else, is erected a fence . . . most of them with barb wire on top, and some of them with an electric wire stretched around the top and charged with electricity, so that no one can either get in or out over the wire or through the fences. . . . Practically all the mill towns have what they call their own money. . . . It is absolutely a little empire; a little domain all of its own. In most mill towns, the ordinary officials of the law are not permitted to enter. . . . If a constable, for instance, of DeRidder [a free town] wants to get a man in a [mill] town three miles from there, he goes down to the gate and tells the guard who he wants, and if the guard wants to bring him out, all right. If the guard don't want to, it is all right again. . . . Often the gunmen go out of the mill town and start to police the free town. . . . If there is anything like a Union meeting or anything like that, the gunmen go up there into the free towns en masse and what is known as law existing normally, ceases to exist entirely in face of increased power.

Q *What are the domestic arrangements of the people who live in these mill towns? The colored people particularly?*

A Well, I don't know just. . . .

Q *When a colored man moves from one shack to another?*

A Well, if he moves from one shack to another there is not very much takes place, but if he moves from one mill to another, there is likely to be a whole lot take place.

Q *What is that?*

A There is a policy in the South to keep the negro in debt. Say a negro would go to work at a wage of 85 cents a day loading lumber, piling lumber or something. He works his month out. He has bought stuff in the commissary. . . . He does not try down there to argue with the time keeper or the commissary clerk over how much he drew out of the commissary or how much his wages ought to be. If he argues too much, well they have got a funeral, that's all, and he knows it. It costs $7 to kill a negro in Louisiana. . . . They just tell him he is in debt, and that settles the argument. They don't show him any figures. . . . So if he wants to go to another camp, he cannot leave Bon Ami, for instance, to go to Carson . . . where he could get $1.25. . . . If he goes over there himself, he is brought back. . . . If this company don't want a negro, they peddle their debt and send the negro along with it. That is very prevalent.[1]

Q *At the time you went [to DeRidder] you said there was a strike on? . . . How long did this strike last, Mr. Doree?*

A Now [the strike at Merryville] went on for approximately two months. The mill joined the Southern Lumber Operators Association. . . . Gunmen were brought in . . . by the hundreds . . . it was estimated there were about two thousand gunmen in Kalkasoo Parish. . . . They organized a drive on the . . . strikers. . . . The gunmen . . . tore down everything that belonged to the union. . . . They stole the clapper out of the church bell. That is what we used to use to call the union meetings with. . . . They took [some of the leaders] away from the crowd and throwed them into automobiles and took them to Singer, nine miles away; they gave two of them a good beating. . . . I received a wire to go to Maryville [Merryville]. I did not know what had happened at that time, so I took the train to go around to Maryville. . . . I got off at the depot . . . one of the gunmen who happened to be a Burns detective . . . one whom I had previous experience with, he told me . . . "Back on, old Man, back on, this is an unhealthy climate for you fellows"; so I jumped off the other side . . . and somebody caught me across the face. . . . When I woke up I was on the platform of the car and we were just ready to start again. So, I left Maryville, and Fellow Worker Fallino left about as rapidly, coming from the other direction. . . . Then, the bosses put out little posters . . . $1,000 reward for the body, dead or alive of J. Smith, Covington Hall, C. H. Fallino and E. F. Doree.

[At Quandray] I tried to go out to the camp and was met by a man whom I did not know . . . and asked him where the camp was located. . . . He says, "What do you want with the camp?" I said, "I want to go over there to see some of my friends there." . . . He says, "You are from the north, ain't you?" I says, "Yes." "Well, I reckon you ain't got no business around that camp at all. . . . I is a Deputy Sheriff, I is." "Oh, that's different." He says, "You can't go to that camp at all." I says, "All right." Now, he says, "You all start right down that way." (Indicating), and I started in that way (Indicating). I got about 50 feet and he took a shot at me. Well, I was 50 feet further before he got the next shot. Well, we ran a hide and tag race for nine miles out of Quandray back into Quandray. . . . Then I went back to Alexandria and went down to New Orleans.

Q *You referred to meeting a Burns man on some former occasion. I want you to tell that by way of illustrating what the Burns people do.*
A Well, . . . it was an open fact that the Burns Detective Agency was operating down there. I wanted to go down to see [the strike leaders] in jail. . . . I went to Mr. Reed, Mr. Kenny Reed, the sheriff, and I asked him if I could go in and see Emerson and the rest of them. He said, "You come back tomorrow; I will tell you tomorrow." . . . So the next day I came back. Well, at the door there was a deputy there, and he said, "Sit down," and I sat down in the sheriff's office. Well, while I was sitting there a man came through and walked into the back room. A little later Mr. Reed came in . . . and went in there also, into this same room. I waited about half an hour and they came back out together. I stepped over as I says, "Can I go in and see Mr. Emerson?" "No." He said, "No, I don't think I will let you in any more. I have had too damn much trouble with you anyway." "All right." . . . So I started to walk out of the buildings, and this other fellow

came up alongside of me and he says, "Your name is Doree, ain't it?" I says, "Yes"; he says "My name is So-and-so" . . . I don't recall the name. He says, "I am just here to tell you to lay off of the Burns detectives." I says, "All right. That is Jake with me." "Now, you lay off of them." I says, "All right," and we kept on walking until we got to the top of the stairs. . . . He says to me: "Now, you all, cut out everything about the Burns detectives." I says, "All right," and started to step down the step, and he stepped by me and stepped around in front of me, and he said, "I am going to tell you to cut out all talk about the Burns detectives." I says, "You have told me that about a half dozen times. Now, that is all, that is enough." . . . Now, he said, "You be damn sure it is all right." I says, "All right." And I went to step down again and he stepped in front of me and I slammed him. He went down the steps and I hit for town. I went up to see a lawyer and ask him if there was anything that could be done about it. He said there was not. I said, "I don't know what he is likely to do." He says, "I don't know. After he does it, we have got plenty of law to handle it." I says, "That don't sound good to me," so I started out of there, and he [the Burns man] met me down stairs. . . . He says, "I want to see you back over to the court house." I says, "I am not going back over to the court house." He says, "Kenny Reed wants to see you." I says, "If Kenny Reed wants to see me, let him send somebody to get me." He says, "He wants to see you." I says, "I am not going over there." So he took his gun out of his pocket and he put it up under my coat here against my back, and he says, "Now I reckon we will go." . . . So of course, I went up to the court house with him. When he got up there, he says "Now, I want to talk to you." I said, "Don't Reed want to see me?" He says, "I don't give a damn whether Reed wants to see you or not." Now, he says, "You lay off the Burns detectives." I says, "That is about the fourteenth time I have heard that. I am willing to do anything now that you say. You have got a gun and that settles the argument." He says, "You be damn sure of it." I says, "If I have said anything or done anything that you don't like, here we are right in the court house. Here is the sheriff. Get me pinched." He says, "I wouldn't pinch you for a thousand dollars." I says, "Why?" He says, "Too damn much fun shooting people like you." So, with that admonition I left and went up to the lawyers. . . . He said, "If he shoots you, then we have got our come back." I said, "That wasn't worth the exercise," and I asked the lawyer what advice he could give me. He said, "My advice to you is to get a 44 and hang on to it. If he comes around the corner first, let us have the law suit over him and not over you." So that was his advice to me.

Q *What was the condition of the law down there while you were there?*
A There wasn't any law. I didn't see any law the whole time I was there.

Q *Who was administering what law there was?*
A The sheriff and the deputy sheriffs.

Q *Well, I mean in the mill towns.*
A The sheriffs and deputy sheriffs; they belong to the mill company.[2]

It was not in the testimony, but my aunt Florence wrote me, many years later, "In Louisiana [Ed] was clubbed over the head one night and spent a long time unconscious in a hospital which we did not know about until after he was well. When I was with them after you were born I could put my hand on his head and move the scalp around. It was loose from the skull."[3]

The jury acquitted the Louisiana union leaders. The authorities reacted by arresting my father on charges of jury tampering. This was, after all, the Deep South, the year was 1912, and he was trying to organize black and white workers into a single union!

Writing to the *Industrial Worker* from his jail cell, he quoted Shelley's lines from "The Masque of Anarchy":

Arise like lions after slumber
In unvanquishable number.
Shake your chains to earth like dew
Which in sleep have falled on you.
Ye are many, they are few.[4]

I do not know under what conditions he was released; I do not know when. Was it in this jail that he was hit on the head, as his sister describes? Glimpses through a fence.

E. F. Doree's parents, Frederick and Maria Brandt Doree, probably taken soon after their marriage in Philadelphia in 1885. *Photograph courtesy of Walter P. Reuther Library.*

The Doree family, Skagway, Alaska, 1905. Back row: Hilma, Frank, Florence, Alford, Edwin. Front row: Frederick, Edna, Maria. Edwin had just lost two fingers from his right hand in a sawmill accident on the job. He was 16 years old. *Photograph courtesy of Walter P. Reuther Library.*

E. F. ("Skag") Doree as professional baseball player and manager, Hayden Lake (Idaho) team, Northwestern League, 1907. *Photograph courtesy of Walter P. Reuther Library.*

Doree speaking to workers on the street, probably 1911 in Washington state. Soapbox speeches spread the IWW union gospel; often, across the street, Salvation Army members spread their word. Many IWW songs were parodies of their hymns. *Photograph courtesy of Walter P. Reuther Library.*

Doree speaking, probably 1911 in Washington state. The workers thronged to listen to the IWW speakers. *Photograph courtesy of Walter P. Reuther Library.*

IWW organizers sent to Louisiana in 1912 to help striking soft-wood loggers. Left to right: J. Smith (?), E. F. Doree, Covington Hall, C. H. Fallino (?). The lumber companies posted a reward of $1,000 for the body of each, dead or alive. *Photograph courtesy of Walter P. Reuther Library.*

Louisiana loggers, 1912. Note the racially mixed audience: Doree and the other IWW organizers (squatting, right front) were striving to bring black and white loggers into the same union. *Photograph courtesy of Walter P. Reuther Library.*

Doree in Akron, Ohio, 1913, helping rubber workers to organize. His haggard look evinces the nine months in Louisiana, where he was beaten, jailed, and shot at. *Photograph courtesy of Walter P. Reuther Library.*

E. F. Doree and Frank Little, 1913, probably before leaving for the Mesabi Range to organize ore handlers. Little was kidnapped by local businessmen, freed by reporters. Four years later he was lynched by vigilantes in Butte, Montana. *Photograph courtesy of Labadie Collection.*

Chicky (Ida) and Edwin Doree, early in their marriage, 1914 or 1915. *Photograph courtesy of Walter P. Reuther Library.*

IWW head "Big Bill" Haywood, speaking at the 1915 Chicago funeral of the Wobbly bard Joe Hill. The man to Haywood's left holds a photograph of Hill. Doree is in the back, to the right of the big tree. *Photograph courtesy of Walter P. Reuther Library.*

One of the IWW ethnic branches represented at the Joe Hill funeral, when thirty thousand people marched through the streets of Chicago. Doree is to the right of the flag in the back. *Photograph courtesy of Walter P. Reuther Library.*

Group of mourners at Joe Hill's funeral. Doree is second from right in the second row. His wife is third from right in the first row. *Photograph courtesy of Walter P. Reuther Library.*

Business card of National Organizer, E. F. Doree, 1916. *Photograph courtesy of Labadie Collection.*

Clothing Workers Industrial Union 192

Polish Branch No. 1, Lithuanian Branch No. 2, Italian Branch No. 3, Jewish Branch No. 4, English Branch No. 5

Baltimore, Maryland.

AN INJURY TO ONE AN INJURY TO ALL

INDUSTRIAL WORKERS OF THE WORLD

Baltimore, Md. April 18th, 1916, 191

1819 Mc Culloh St.,

Dear Folks at Home:-

Have not written you for a while, so here goes. Every thing
is O. K. at this end of the line. I am feeling fine but Chiky has her spells.
She has been getting along fine lately until today she feels a little off but
I guess it isnt much. If she feels good tomorrow she will go to Washington, D. C.
to see Mrs. Margaret Sanger, a well known rebel nurse who is to lecture there.
Perhaps Mrs. Sanger can tell her what is the matter.

I am pretty busy but Joe Ettor will be here for a day or two
this week and that will help a little.

Have not been able to go to Philadelphia but I wrote to
Abel Holmstrand and Otto Osterlund. I got word from Holmstrand but not from
Osterlund. Holmstrand seemed very glad to hear from me and asked me to send his
very best to you. He is still secretary of the Swedish Benefit Society and
lives at 860 Bucknell St., Philadelphia. Osterlund I found in the directory as
Otto Osterlund, Drug Store, 4600 Baltimore St., I wrote there but no answer to
date.

How is every one at home? Let us hear from you often if only
a short letter. There is no real news of interest to you so will close for the
present,

With very best wishes from both of us, we are

YOUR KIDS.

Ed & Chiky.

E. F. Doree letter to his parents, April 18, 1916. Note the reference to Margaret
Sanger, leader of the birth control movement. *Photograph courtesy of Labadie
Collection.*

Edwin and Chiky with Frederick Lee ("Bucky") Doree, age six months, 1917. This was taken on the eve of Doree's surrender to jail to await trial. Note the IWW ribbon at Chiky's waist. *Photograph courtesy of Walter P. Reuther Library.*

The Midwest

The next year, my father accompanied Frank Little on an expedition to "carry the Wobbly gospel north," in the words of historian Melvyn Dubofsky.[5] They went to Duluth, Minnesota, with plans to move on to the Mesabi Range. The enterprise was cut short when Frank Little was kidnapped by local businessmen. Luckily, he was rescued by reporters. The next time he was not so fortunate.

It is a common literary device to have the hero's friend killed off to illustrate just how close to disaster our hero has been. My father's vulnerability was brought home to me by the fate of Frank Little, a colorful, contentious man, blind in one eye, "part American Indian, part hard-rock miner, part hobo, he was all Wobbly."[6] One picture from my father's satchel shows him and Little together. They signed the photograph and captioned it "Pals."

Dashiell Hammett, later a famous detective story writer, was a Pinkerton detective in 1917 when, to his horror, the Anaconda Copper Company offered him five thousand dollars to kill Frank Little.[7] He refused, but a mob did the deed. When Frank Little was in Butte, Montana, his broken leg in a cast, "six masked men, heavily armed, broke into Little's hotel room, beat him up, dragged him down in his pajamas to their car, tied him by a rope to the rear fender and dragged him along the dirt track to the Milwaukee Railroad trestle several miles out of town. There, in the harsh light of their car's headlamps, they hanged him, and pinned a note to his lifeless body saying, 'First and last warning.'"[8]

The killers were never pursued.

To RETURN TO the trial transcript, by the end of 1913 my father was in Ohio:

Q Just take a moment and tell the jury what occurred in Akron, what was it?

A Why, it was in . . . the winter of 1913 . . . there was some trouble in Akron in the Rubber Workers Union, and I had been asked to go there and see if I could not help the local fellows, to find out what was the matter, why the union did not seem, with a fine sentiment, to grow, to become anything. . . .

. . . Working together with some local members . . . we finally got one man who was the recording secretary of the union, went out to his house, had a long talk with him . . . tripped him up in two or three of his statements . . . and then one of our boys got right alongside of him and told him he might just as well cough up now as any time, be just as healthy for him.

Q *. . . What was the condition that you ultimately discovered . . . ?*
A Well, the Union, they could not make a union; just as soon as a man joined he got fired; that was the condition.

Q *Yes.*
A Anyway, we got this fellow—he at last confessed . . . that he was a corporation auxiliary detective, as they were known. . . . We worked around for a while longer and got, by watching the Cleveland office of the company . . . every officer of the Union was a detective in the employ of the company, and every member of the strike committee in the strike just preceding that time had been a detective in the employ of the company.[9]

It turned out that, on company orders, the detectives had fomented a strike with the objective of provoking government action against the union. They were successful: the Akron rubber workers' local was "never heard from again" within the IWW.[10]

THE GREAT PLAINS

As 1915 began, Ed left his bride Chiky behind in Rochester. In bitter January cold, he rode unheated boxcars to Kansas City to look for work and take part in what has been described as "one of the most dramatic union efforts to ever appear on the American scene."[11] The hero of this action would be none other than my uncle, the inarticulate Walter T. Nef.

In those days, America's golden waves of grain were harvested not by machines but by hand. Migratory harvesters worked their way north as the grain ripened, moving from job to job by hopping onto freight cars, what they called "riding the rails." On the trains all sorts of predators lay in wait to part a worker from his hard-earned pay. My father described the situation in an article that appeared in the *International Socialist Review* of June 1915.

Gathering the Grain

About the middle of June the real harvest commences in Northern Oklahoma and Southern Kansas. . . . The exceedingly long work day is the worst feature of the harvesting so far as the worker is concerned. The men are expected to be in the fields at half past five or six o'clock in the morning until seven or half past seven at night, with from an hour to an hour and a half for dinner. It is a common slang expression of the workers that they have an "eight-hour work day"— eight in the morning and eight in the afternoon. . . . Twenty-five men died from the heat in one day last year in a single county in Kansas.

About the time that the headed grain is reaped the bundle grain in Central and Northern Kansas and Southern Nebraska is ready for the floating army of harvesters. . . . Small wages are paid and accepted because thousands of workers are then drifting up from the headed wheat country and because of the general influx of men from all over the United States, who come to make their "winter's stake."

In North and South Dakota no worker is sure of drawing his wages, even after earning them. Some farmers do not figure on paying their "help" at all and work the same game year after year.

The best paying occupation in the harvest country is "the harvesting of the harvester," which is heavily indulged in by train crews, railroad "bulls," gamblers and hold-up men. Hundreds of workers lose their "stake" annually at the point of a gun. As is the rule with a migratory army, the harvesters move almost entirely by "freight," and here is where the train crew gets theirs.[12]

In Kansas City, a group of Wobbly organizers came together to establish a union, the Agricultural Workers Organization. Walter Nef was put at its head. He was, it turned out, an organizational genius. The IWW took control of the hobo camps and the railroad boxcars. They threw out the gamblers and intimidated the train crews. The union card became a safe-passage guarantee. Nonunion workers were ejected, so that the workers who arrived at the work site were already organized and capable of negotiating effectively.

The IWW began to charge a membership fee and real dues, which enabled it to establish union halls and pay its organizers for the first time. Seven paid traveling organizers, each assigned an allotted district, directed the activities of "job delegates" who were on-the-job volunteers, their "office" (IWW literature, union cards, and songbooks) in the pockets of their overalls. [13]

The campaign was superb. "In 1914—before the AWO campaign—migrants earned $2 or $2.50 for a twelve- to sixteen-hour day. By the fall of 1916 the Wobblies had won a pay scale of $4 for a ten-hour day, with comparable improvements in room and board."[14] Beyond such bread-and-butter benefits, the IWW provided the itinerant harvesters with something equally important—a community. "A migrant Wobbly bumming his way across a strange and hostile land could now count on one safe haven—the IWW hall."[15] (By 1917 the AWO would grow to a membership of 70,000,[16] only to fall "completely disorganized" following the indictment of the Chicago Hundred in September of that year.)[17]

Regular pay meant that Ed could send for Chiky, and they were finally united. Photographs from November 1915 show them together.

The occasion was the funeral of the Wobbly bard, Joe Hill. Perhaps the Wobbly most remembered today, Joe Hill was executed for murder by a Utah firing squad. Reportedly his final words were "Don't mourn. Organize." His funeral was in Chicago (Hill had said that he did not want to be caught dead in Utah!). Thirty thousand mourners marched through the streets to the cemetery.

The East Coast

After one year in the grainfields, my father was called to Baltimore, national headquarters of the IWW's textile union, which had been mismanaged and was badly in debt. He assumed its leadership in February of 1916. In December the union's national headquarters were moved to Philadelphia. There, in the city of Ed's birth, his first child, Bucky, was born.

In November of 1916 Walter Nef resigned his AWO post over differences with the IWW head, "Big Bill" Haywood, who wanted to exert central control over all IWW activities. Walter now also came to Philadelphia, to organize longshoremen on the city's waterfront. Two months later, Walter married my mother's sister Feige. As 1917 began, the sisters were together, and so were their husbands: Walter T. Nef, secretary-treasurer of the Marine Transport Workers Industrial Union, No. 100, shared an office with E. F. Doree, secretary-treasurer of the Textile Workers Industrial Union, No. 1000.

On September 5, 1917, this office—along with every other IWW office across the nation—was raided by federal officers. During the simultaneous raids, federal officers seized everything they could put their hands on: documents, files, and office equipment.

TEXTILE WORKERS INDUSTRIAL UNION
Main Office Address
509 Parkway Building
Philadelphia, Pa.
Phone Bell, Spruce 5466

Sept. 21st, 1917
Wm. D. Haywood
1001 W. Madison St.
Chicago, Ill.

Fellow Worker:

Regarding the raid. I was not here at the time of the raid but Nef and Pazos were in the office. They were given a receipt for the contents of the office. Nothing was specified in the receipt except the typewriters and adding machine and mimeograph. Went over the whole thing with Pazos this morning. Find list enclosed.

E. F. Doree
Secy-Treas., # 1000

SUPPLIES, ETC., TAKEN
Day Books
Ledgers
Book containing names and addresses of all delegates of # 1000
3 Typewriters, 1 Adding Machine, 1 Duplicator, 1 Check-writer, . . .
All check books, bank books, receipt stubs, canceled checks, etc. . . .
All unopened mail.

> All communications and copies of replies to same. All membership
>   records.
> All seals and rubber stamps. . . .
> All IWW papers. All Literature, such as IWW pamphlets, leaflets and
>   Stickers. Only one song book left after raid.
> All buttons. . . .
> All constitutions and IWW pennants
> All drawers from filing cases and half the drawers from the desks. . . .
> Contents of waste paper baskets.

THE UNITED STATES entered World War I on April 6, 1917. On September 28th federal indictments were handed down against Walter Nef, my father, and 111 other IWW leaders, accusing them of conspiring to hinder the execution of certain wartime laws of the United States, conspiring to injure United States citizens in the enjoyment of certain rights and privileges, conspiring to induce IWW members either to fail to register for the draft or to desert the service, and conspiring to cause insubordination in the wartime military. Rather than fight extradition, they obediently made their way to Chicago. For rebels, they held remarkable trust in the system!

Twelve cases were dismissed at the outset of the trial. The trial of the remaining "Chicago Hundred" began on April 1, 1918, and lasted longer than any previous trial in American history. After four and a half months of testimony, it took the jury less than an hour on August 17 to find each of the defendants guilty on all counts. On August 31 the judge, Kenesaw Mountain Landis, imposed sentences of one, five, ten, and twenty years (the legal maximum) in the federal penitentiary in Leavenworth, Kansas.

Ed was sentenced to ten years, Walter to twenty. Before leaving for prison, Ed sent his wife and child "home" to Oregon, commending them to the care of his parents.

440 N. Dearborn St.
Cell 454, Chicago
September 5, 1918

Dear Folks at Home:

I received your welcome letter and photos. They were fine. Gee, you both look well and that is a whole lot.

Some fool or crank placed a bomb in the Federal Building here, killing four persons and wounding several more. It was a miserable affair, a thing which makes the heart revolt at the thought, but, the police have, at least through the newspapers, laid the blame at the door of the IWW.

Aside from the terribleness of the whole thing, which every member hates, nothing could have happened to have hurt us more. . . .

I will make no attempt to get bail now and am writing to Chiky, today, to take little Bucky and go to you. In this tense atmosphere, she will not be likely to remain well and, of all things, she must not get sick while I am in prison. Take good care of Chiky. She is a good, kind little girl. You will be proud of her.

Well, mamma dear, I am in a peculiar position. Guilty of no crime, in prison, I, who thought of love, think the thoughts peculiar to criminals. I, who have all my life fought against violence am now told that my life theme was violence. Well, never mind, some day will the truth be known and in that day will we be freed from the terrible stigma of today. It is not being in prison that bothers me, it's being told that I am a believer in such outrages as happened yesterday in the Federal Building. . . .

Should it prove that the real criminal is caught before long, then I will try again for bail. If Chiky is with you, I will try to come out there should I get out.

Well, bye, bye, for now. From your loving son.

Ed

Chiky dutifully took the year-and-a-half-old Bucky and went to live on an Oregon farm with the family she had never met.

3

LEAVENWORTH I

Oh the jailer, he went wild over me,
And he locked me up and threw away the key;
It seems to be the rage, so they keep me in a cage,
They go wild, simply wild over me.

Leavenworth, Kansas
Sept. 15, 1918

My dearest little Chiky:

Well, girlie, how are you? And how is little Bucky boy? I guess he has forgotten his papa altogether. Well, so much the better for him for the time being.

How are the old folks at home? Dear old mamma! You and mamma will get on finely, I am sure. This will have to serve as a family letter, to wife, baby, mother, father, sisters and brothers, so when you get it, call the whole family together and read these lines. It must be a solemn moment, for it is not the good fortune of the Doree family to have representation in a first class penitentiary. I said "first class," I mean it. It's a home. Everybody likes it so well that they settle down here for long periods. Enough of this foolishness.

I am feeling fine. Got to be a regular fiend for food. Frankly, I eat at least three times as much here as I ate "outside." The food here is wholesome and there is more than plenty. It's one's own fault if he goes hungry here. The cells are clean and airy. Plenty of sunlight.

Now let me give a brief description of the place as we found it on entering. We arrived here, hungry and sleepy, on Saturday, Sept. 7th at about 4 o'clock in the afternoon. The train was run right into the penitentiary yards. Our handcuffs, which we wore the whole way down, were taken off, and we were marched to the "auditorium"—a real theater, stage and all. The warden gave us a short talk and a real human one. He met us on the "man to man" ground, an attitude admired by everybody. We then emptied our pockets, then came supper—and did we eat? We did. After supper we went to our cells. The cells—what a contrast to the filthy cells at Cook Co. Jail. Next morning we had our pictures taken, were numbered, etc. Then a bath and shave—good-night moustache—and then we got our prison clothes. (Our hair is not touched) Monday, we were photographed again, weighed and passed physical examination and were vaccinated. Then we were assigned to our work. I am in the kitchen. Haven't got a regular job yet except to wait on table. The seating capacity of the dining room, I think is about 1500 persons. The band plays during dinner and supper—from the time the men start to march in till they are gone.

Every afternoon we go out to the ball park for about an hour. Yesterday afternoon, we all went to the ball game between the white and colored teams. Some fine game. I'm going to try to get on the team next year.

On Oct. 7th, school starts. I am going to take a course in stenography. When I have completed that, I'll take up something else. I'm determined to come out of here better physically and mentally than when I came in.

Now, Chiky, take good care of yourself. I know you'll do everything in the world for Bucky. But, above all, take good care of yourself. Don't worry. I'm all right. I'll come thru here with colors flying. My thoughts are of you and Bucky and the old folks. You all be well and happy till I get out of here. I'll be out in May, 1925, if not sooner. We'll only be kids, yet, Chiky, just kids. Say, Chiky, send me one of the last pictures we had taken of Bucky.

Now, what do I want? First about $5.00 cash. It is useless to send me tobacco, I can buy it so cheaply here. Before cold weather sets in, if you can, send me 2 suits of underwear and a plain black collarless sweater, and the fountain pens.

Nef is in the tin-shop. Haywood in the clothing department. Our boys are scattered all over the place. They all look fine and are in fine spirits.

I can write out of here once a week and oftener by special permit. I shall write you regularly every Sunday. Should I have to write other letters, I will use my special privilege. But to you, baby, every week. Write me as often or oftener. I am sure you will.

Got two letters from you so far, one written just after you left Chicago and the other mailed at Cheyenne, Wyo. I received none mailed in Chicago. The first letter I got on Thursday and you can't imagine how glad I was to get it.

Now, tell me, Chiky, how are you? How is everything at home? Write me a long letter about everything. Have the girls write, and mamma—everybody.

Well, I must close for this time. Love to mamma and papa and all. And to you, Chiky, all the love and kisses we have so long enjoyed— and will enjoy. Kiss Bucky from his papa. Be good and above all, be healthy. Take life as easy as I do and all's well. Love to you my little baby

From your hubby
Ed

Sept. 22, 1918

Got your special delivery letter last Tuesday and have heard nothing from you since. I think that the mail must be straying some where. For a while I would suggest that you send your letters registered. I am sure that they are not held up here at the prison but are being held in the mails.

The boys are looking fine. Chaplin and Corder have jobs in the office now. Believe me, girlie, this is some place for a prison. Didn't think they could be so human. If it were not for being away from you and Bucky, I wouldn't care if Landis had said three times ten years. To tell the truth, this place affords me the first real rest in years.

. . . Girlie dear, after ten weeks you are entitled to aid from the [IWW] General Defense Committee. If you need anything let me know. There is a move on now at Washington, to allow prisoners to work for wages. I hope such resolution passes. Then I could make enough to care for you and Bucky. I'd really sooner work at something worth while than be fooling around a kitchen. A KITCHEN. I laugh at the thought. And "BIG BILL" handing uniforms to convicts—and THOMPSON laying bricks. Some melting pot!! Some leveler!!! Many of the boys are building a new jail here—to get locked into some day!! Some turn for the Wobblies. The ignorant say we wanted to tear down society, tear down, the deuce, we're building, building jails.

There is a good library here. Have had Shelley's Poems and am now reading Zangwill's "Children of the Ghetto"

. . . Be healthy above all things. Be good when there's nothing better to do. Love to all. Love and kisses to baby, and Chiky, girlie, love, love and many sweet kisses.

The mail *was* "straying somewhere." Every letter that my father wrote or received was diverted to a prison typist, who prepared a copy for the Department of Justice.[1] Washington received typewritten copies of the correspondence of all the Wobblies in Leavenworth. In the eyes of the Wilson administration, the Wobblies, even behind bars, bore watching.

Sept. 29, 1918
Your letters . . . arrived last week and I was surely happy to hear from you so often and to know that you find it so fine at home. . . . I was sure that you would find real rest there. At home? Surely you would be at home with mamma. Who wouldn't? You think that they all like you. Surely they do. Who would not like you, girlie?

So Bucky talks? You always tell me that he talks. What does he talk about? Why certainly Edna and Florence take up with Bucky and why in the world should he not take up with them, they are his daddy's sisters.

Now, baby, regards money to me. I won't need much. We cannot transfer money here to another prisoner, and can buy only so much tobacco and some merchandise. This rule makes it quite impossible to spend much and impossible to give any away. I must have some work done on my teeth right away. Most of it will be done without cost but some I will have to pay for. It won't be much, tho.

Got "Official notice" of my "time" here. Our "time" started September 7th. I am subject to parole on Jan. 6, 1922, and my "good time" term expires on May 25, 1925. . . . I am sure, however, that I will never do the full time. Secy of War Baker in a letter to Upton Sinclair says that he is sure that there will be a general amnesty of "political prisoners" at the close of the war.

However, I am not going to "hitch my wagon to a star." I'm settling down for six years, eight months and nineteen days. And in that time I intend to be better mentally and physically than I am now or have been for years. I feel much better now than I did when I came here. I weigh 6 pounds more.

You wish I could take it "easier"! Say, baby, I'm the clown of the ranch. Takes more than this place to make me "long in the face." Did you ever know your hubby to growl about anything. "Everything" is all right with me. Here's my daily schedule. We "crawl out" at 6:30. Think of me getting up at 6:30 with no strike on. But it is true. Dress (naturally) and make the bed (most unnatural for me) at 7:15 we leave our cells for the kitchen, dress up in white jackets and aprons till we look like a Thompson Restaurant "hasher." Then we feed mush and muffins to the "big mess" (1230 men) then we wait on the "small mess" (about 250 to 300 men). Those working on the farm eat before we come down. After that the "waiters" (?) eat. Then we clean off the tables. I take the dishes off of 17 tables (six plates to a table) and wash twelve tables. Then we mostly loaf till 10:30 when we set the tables, then we "waiters" eat. Then the small mess, then the big mess, then we clean tables again. At 2 o'clock, we go to the base-ball park till 3 o'clock. Then "set up" again, we all eat and at 5 o'clock we do as we please till 9:30 o'clock when the lights go out—and we go to our dreams. This is our day—rain or shine. And, it's a merry day for a jail. On Saturday we either go to a ball game or to the yard for one hour and 30 minutes and see all the boys.

They are all looking fine. Those who were sick are being fixed up in the hospital. They have a fine hospital here. Nef has got over his spell and is getting real friendly to me.

About bail. Baby, I will do nothing at all. I will not try to get it. If Miss Inglis or Wm Bross Lloyd wants to go my bail, all right. You will do as you please about trying to get bail. I feel that it is a settled policy to keep us in jail till the war is over and I am satisfied with the arrangement. You can surely stand it, and will stand it. It is worse on you than on me, for that reason I don't want to close all doors, but, personally, I should much prefer to stay here. I need a rest and am getting it. With schooling and physical attention, I'll be all the better when my time is done here. This jail is not a spirit breaking institution. Men can improve here. I propose to do so.

. . . Now, Chiky, baby, remember there is nothing so sweet as a letter from you. It's a great feeling to have the mailman stop and hand in a letter to me, especially if it's from you. I know it's a lot to ask, but it is the greatest pleasure here, a letter.

Have finished reading "The Children of the Ghetto" and am now reading Mark Twain's "The Connecticut Yankee in King Arthur's Court." It's great!!!

Oh, yes, I almost forgot. I've been indicted again. This time in Wichita, Kansas. Embree has been indicted at Seattle. Don't know whether I'm indicted there or not. Don't matter. Met Haywood the other day. He says, "Been indicted yet this morning." A standing joke! Let er ride.

. . . Kiss little Bucky from his papa. Tell him papa wants him to be a good boy.

It is unclear just when and how Miss Agnes Inglis of Ann Arbor, Michigan, came to know my father. Like the "Millionaire Socialist" William Bross Lloyd, Agnes Inglis was an upper-class maverick, ready to act on her radical beliefs despite the disapproval of her social set and the wartime public. Within a week of his arrival in prison, she visited my father and offered to provide bond for his release.

October 6, 1918
I understand that our case will be appealed directly to the U.S. Supreme Court . . . [but] . . . I am sure that we have little to hope for till the war is over and people regain their power of normal thinking. After the war no court will sustain the rulings of Judge Landis which make our conviction at all possible. You know my case. Not one word—not one syllable of evidence against me. Not one witness not a written or spoken word. Nine witnesses for me. You know them all, from Navy Yard longshoreman to U.S. Army lieutenant—but what's the use—wasn't my name in the indictment? That's enough.

Look at the cases of Manuel Rey and Clyde Hough, given 20 and 5 years respectively for violating the Espionage Act. This act was passed by Congress and went into effect on June 18th, 1917. Both Rey and Hough were arrested on June 5th, 1917. Rey for strike activities in Buffalo and Hough for refusing to register under the Selective draft act. The law was not passed, that is, the Espionage Act, until 13 days after they were arrested. They have not been out of jail a single minute since. How they were able to violate a law while in jail is a mystery to me.

Some of the boys figure that they would be able to secure a pardon as soon as the war is over. As for me, I prefer to stay here to taking a pardon from anyone. I have done nothing I must be pardoned for. If released today I would go on just as I did when arrested. I have every legal and moral right to do so and because a few corporation tools have gotten temporary hold of what should be free institutions in this nation is no reason why I should bow to anyone for pardon or forgiveness for crimes which I did not commit nor ever contemplated committing.

We have but one possible and honorable path to follow, that being to wait for a calmer day when people reason and then place our case before the people.

. . . When affairs get in such shape with you financially so you can stand it, try to send me $15.00 to get my teeth fixed with. Much of the work is done free but to save two teeth I will have to get them crowned. I would hate to lose the only molar that I have left on the upper right hand side of my mouth.

. . . By the way, I have always before forgotten to mention my number here is 13125.

Gee, its good to hear of the good time you are having. We enjoy ourselves here a whole lot, too, playing base-ball and foot-ball. Went to the movie show today. . . . Every night we have music (?) you see, musical instruments are allowed in the cells and the inmates surely enjoy to punish them.

Well, I guess that I have said my say, except that I surely enjoy your little stories about Bucky. . . . It would be great to play with him for a while but he is happy as it is. . . . Take my greatest love and fondest kisses.

Your loving hubby,
Ed

October 10, 1918

Now, I had better answer mamma's letter. I am so glad to have the pleasure to read happy words like mamma writes.

. . . Poor old aunt Sophia. I can imagine how she did cry. Well, that does no one any good at all, at all. The one thing that I admired about the rebel girls at Chicago was that they did not cry. They bore up like real rebels. Gee, mamma, I never hope to see a finer picture of real rebel spirit in action than I saw the day we were sentenced. No faltering, no whimpering, no begging for mercy, neither was there the slightest show of braggadocia on the part of anyone, man or woman. All seemed reconciled to the fact that the class war required victims and that sooner or later we must pay the penalty for our agitation for human freedom. A real class conscious rebel becomes hardened to persecution. He looks upon it as a part of life, a part preferable to that of an abject, submissive slave, and fortunately or unfortunately you must be one or the other unless, of course, if you are a clever thief.

See that [brother] Al has been called to the army. Well, he won't stay away long. . . . The war is over even tho at this time the armistice is not signed. Whether or not they ever sign it is of small importance as it will never be lived up to by either side. The revolution is on. . . .

Just to show what an awful psychological condition the Germans had to over come. We have several "Vons" in here, chief among them Von Bopp, the dynamiter. . . . When one of the "Vons" condescends to speak to a common stiff who happened to be born on the other side of the Rhine, this poor boob stands like a Prussian Guard all the while the "Von" sprinkles words of wisdom into his dome. Imagine a servile race like that telling the "Vons" to go to hell!!! Well, my dear little girlie, it is true!!! The red flag flies over German cities and ships today. The longsuffering, round faced German is master of the "Fatherland." When such a condition is possible there, then J. P. [Morgan] and J. D. [Rockefeller] had better watch their step, that's all. The war is over, the revolution is on. Gee, how I wish I could stand beside Leibknecht today. Liebknecht—a prisoner a year ago, today— words fail. ——Trotsky, a year before the Czars downfall, an exile, today—the most hated and loved man in the world. Today, I sat and looked at Big Bill with numbers on each knee and on his back—in jail. Tomorrow he may be the Leibknecht or Trotsky of America, who can tell: Bill has that quality in him. . . . We live in the days of revolt! Gee, I'm glad I'm alive today, yes, even in jail. This is the decade when labor is coming into its own—the world.

. . . I feel as tho I should take a rest for a while when I get out. Do nothing, find a job for a while and forget the great struggle for a while. I wonder if I can. I almost wish that they would make it a condition of the bond. A real rest would do me good.

October 13, 1918

[Attorney] Fred Moore was here to see us last Friday. . . . We discussed the appeal, etc. . . . I asked Moore about the Wichita indictment. He said I was named but would never be arrested on it, that I did not need to worry about it at all. The same was true of the Spokane indictment. . . . The main thing is to get out of here, for, if I once leave here after peace is declared, I will never have to come back. The appeals will drag a couple of years or more and before that time amnesty will be declared for all political prisoners such as we. Clarence Darrow told Pres. Wilson more than two weeks ago that the war would be over in six weeks and that as soon as it was over, he would have to turn all IWW and Socialists out of prison.

. . . Well we got in a week already at school. We are progressing very finely. I have 100 mark on my first lessons. I think that shorthand comes very easy to me. I have no trouble to remember the characters nor to connect them. Of course, I may hit a snag later but hardly think so. Taken, all in all, the school is great. It is the one redeeming feature of this place.

You spoke in a letter of fear that this place might make a criminal of me. Chiky, baby, you have it all wrong. I mix only with the prisoners, and as long as I am here I won't run into any politicians, so you see I have no way in which to come into contact with criminals. The criminals are all on the outside. Only their victims are in here. I think that there is only one way to make congress and legislatures honest, that being, to insist that all candidates must have served a prison sentence. There are more men that you can trust in here than I ever met on the outside . . . Fred Moore is the only lawyer that I know whom I would vouch for as honest. There is no such thing as an honest politician except some Socialists and they are illusioned. So there we are. Criminal? No danger of ever becoming one here. No. No. None at all. In fact, it wouldn't hurt me to develop some of the traits of a crook as it would aid materially in keeping me out of jail. But somehow, I think I'd sooner play square and be in jail every now and then, than be crooked and remain on the outside. Don't you feel that way about it?

Oh, yes, I had my Bertillion measurements taken. I am told that the main reason for taking them is to secure future convictions when they have no other evidence.

. . . Am in fine humor today because we did not have to go to church. Believe me, I hate to go. It is like so much twaddle and tommy-rot to me. Don't believe in the junk and hate to waste time on it but this is prison. Of course, they cannot stop me from thinking my own thoughts.

October 17, 1918

If the powers-that-be had the sense that God gave geese, they would open these prison doors in a minute, with "Pardon us, gentlemen, we made a mistake, which we now repair as best we can." But, no, they haven't that much good horse sense, no, no, they will go on jailing and holding men in prison, till they have Bolshevism at their door, crying for the high offices that these political and financial parasites now think they hold securely.

Can't these Kaiserites of America learn from the original Kaiser? Answer that question in the light of history and the reply is, "No, absolutely NO!" Those in power never see the real danger, the mass.

. . . When the mass really learn "how" and "for what" and "upon what evidence" we were sent to prison for many years, they will protest, and vigorously. And usually, so history says, when the mass asks, they ask for, or rather, take, a thousand times more than they set out for.

. . . By all means, I say, let the workers fight for our release. I hope Pres. Wilson does not act too quickly. Nor do I think he will. I'd sooner be in jail than see a good fight go to waste. All I say is, "Hold these boys in jail and you've planted the seeds of Revolution in America."

Say, please send some candy. Any kind of junk. Peanut candy prefered. Lots of it. Never wanted it so bad in my life before.

October 20, 1918
It is so good to get such sweet letters from you. You speak of being proud of me. Me? I have no choice. I have to stay here. I must pay the penalty of having my own mind. It was I who was to be punished and, I suppose, according to the letter of the law, I alone, and I wish it were so, but, I fear that it is really you who suffer, you it is who are paying the penalty. Once here, I have a definite course to persue, I can take no other, I need not bother my mind as there are no two roads. But, you, baby dear, you are serving your penalty as a true rebel and dear loving wife, by choice. You are not bound to me except by strands of love, nor to the movement we hold dear except by your honor and courage.

. . . You say that the world is not altogether dead. You are right. We have received news this week thru foreign exchanges that means much to us. The leading socialist and syndicalist paper of Italy, and incidently, the paper with the largest circulation of any paper in that country, is giving great publicity to our conviction. . . . Hundreds of protest meetings are being held thru out Italy. . . . The Italian and Spanish syndicalists have called upon the French and English unionists to meet. . . . One of their principal demands will be, the release of all political prisoners of all countries.

. . . Am glad that you got your glasses. Will make your head feel better. You feel lonesome. I do sometimes, especially when I look over the pictures. Really, I miss Bucky very much. . . . To be continually away from children . . . for me, it's sometimes a torture, I do love children, all of them, I guess.

Am feeling very fine. I've gained 12 pounds now since coming here. I can't see where it's at, but its on my bones anyway.

October 27, 1918
I got a letter from [sister] Hilma this week. It was really amusing, anyway, I got a good laugh. She said it was dreadful for an innocent man to be kept in jail. "Innocent." I'm not "innocent." I am not guilty of

the crime that I was sent to prison for but I am very guilty of opposing the repressive methods of Rockefeller, et al., and that is a crime.
The courts will go thru hell and high water to do Mr. Morgan or John
D. a small favor like putting a few IWW in jail while they (Morgan,
et al) rob both the worker and the government, as instanced by the
Hog Island expose and the . . . investigation of the wholesale rob-
bery . . . of the Beef Trust. We, I, all the bunch are opposed to "industrial tyranny" in America. Can a greater "crime" be committed? No!
No! not if courts are to decide.

   . . . I am coming on finely with my studies. . . . On Wednesday
the school "children" are treated to an illustrated lecture. Last
Wednesday we had a series of stereopticon views and the Chaplain
gave a lecture on "Holland." For his fine review of that little country's
peculiar characteristics, I could almost forgive him for his sermons
on Sunday.

November 3, 1918
I got the $15.00. Fine, girlie. The tooth I was going to save is gone.
Started to ulcerate last week and had to get it pulled.

   . . . Baby dear, hang on to the relief money. You are entitled to it.
You and I have given our best to the cause of our fellow workers, now
let them aid in our hour of need. . . . You can't work. I wish you
wouldn't try. Keep well above all things. Remember, health is the
greatest of all human assets.

   . . . I was glad when I read your last letter and again heard your
words of love. Baby, dear, I don't know how I could express myself,
there is something peculiar in our love, I think. Even from the day
we met. We have had a poor field for real love, what with me in strikes
and you continually sick. Most of the time we were broke financially.
Even Bucky was born in an ice box!! Really, I think that the only
warmth we have had in four years has been our profound love for
each other—and Bucky. Four years without a real cross word and
nothing approaching a quarrel, I think is something of a record. I
think most of it is due to your wonderful patience and silence. Often,
I remember, when I was worried or tired or worked half to death, I
would feel impatient and cross. It is peculiar that I never felt cross at
you yet, sometimes Bucky made me half mad, think of it, dear little

Bucky. But this is true. In all of four whole years I do not recall an incident that wasn't really pleasant in spite of the struggle.

It is these thoughts and memories that cheer one along so well. I can not even think of the day when we shall ever be other than we are today—except that I expect to be out of jail part of the time.

November 24, 1918
There is another angle in our case that must be considered. I wish I could write of it but I can't. It has to do with some of the crooked works we suspected the Dept. of Justice of using in the Chicago Case. I feel that some of their underhanded work is leaking out. I know a whole lot but this is no time to speak of it.

. . . The world revolution is on. I only wish that we were able to get all the facts. There must be a whole lot more than we have learned. From a spare glimpse in the day-lie press, we can learn that the left wing in Germany is rapidly gaining control.

. . . Haywood, Debs, et al, get 10 to 20 years in prison in the freest (?) of all countries. For treason? No! For opposing war profiteers. Democracy, thy name is mud! Long live the Bolsheviki.

. . . Here I am in jail. I am not charged with having injured one living thing, hurt nothing, no one charged that I tried to get anyone else to injure anyone. Yet, in jail. Democracy, hell. The more I think of this grand fake the more I hope to live until the world gets some sense.

. . . What do I do? Read one of my first letters over again. Same thing.

December 1, 1918
My greatest hope is that we shall not be forced to follow the steps of the Russian rebels. I look forward with dread and revulsion to a possible "red terror" here before we shall win our fight. I do not believe in revenge. Because others injure me and mine, offers to me no reason why I should ask their misery and blood when I and mine see power.

. . . My hope is that the brutality of man to man shall cease when the workers assume control, but, it is an idle hope. Those in power do not vacate easily, nor, when vacated do they remain idle in their efforts to again assume control. In this lies the danger. . . . It is hard enough to build up a smooth running co-operative common-wealth . . . but . . . when this crowd who has been in power is continually throwing monkey-wrenches into the machinery, it is an almost unbearable job, and, if they show enough persistence and power, then, it may be necessary to resort to extreme terrorism—such as the capitalists now use against us. I hope, however, that we shall never have to resort to such methods. The Russian rebels have told the bourgeoisie that unless they behave their lives are not worth anything. It sounds brutal—it is brutal—but perhaps, it is necessary.

. . . All a world revolution needs is one thing to momentarily hang upon. It may be . . . the case in which I am a part.

December 8, 1918

It is not a month since the armistice was signed, yet a great deal has been done toward securing our release. The Seattle Labor Council and the Chicago Federation of Labor have made demands for the release of all political prisoners. . . . Old Mother Jones . . . said that she will fight to a finish for our release. There is no mistaking the fact that she will do us a lot of good. She still carries a lot of weight in the A.F. of L. . . . Amnesty leagues are being formed all over the east, some of them with some mighty powerful people back of them. For tactical reasons they are not making their names public at this time. You already know of the demand made by the Mexican delegates to the Pan-American Labor Congress. Well, now get this,—in January a conference will be held at Selina Cruz, Mexico, the purpose of this conference being to place a boycott on all American manufactured goods, and, for the Marine Transport Workers to refuse to load or unload American ships in Mexican ports so long as IWW prisoners are held in jail because of their union activities. What do you think of that?

. . . I am still in the kitchen but expect to be transferred into the Clothing Department in a day or two. There I will have a pretty good office job. My work will consist of taking care of civilian clothes and such stuff which is being held in storage. I think that will be a far better job.

Today, we were in the yard and I put in a full hour and a half at handball. When I came here I couldn't play for 15 minutes without being completely played out, now I think I could play for ten hours without getting the least bit sore. Playing hand-ball every day has brought my weight down a little but I am all the harder for it. I weighed 158 pounds in my shirt sleeves today. When I came here I weighed 137 pounds with my coat on. Believe me, I sure lost weight in Chicago.

Say, baby, what's the matter with the rest of the bunch at home. All got arms broken—or something. I never hear from them any more. Stick a pin in some of them and see if they are alive. A fellow surely likes letters in a place like this.

December 15, 1918

Your dear letters . . . came to me during this last week, and mighty happy I was to get all of them. Mamma's letter, so full of cheer, was a real treat. Come often, mamma. . . . Belle sent me a pound of candy which I am now chewing. [Attorney] Otto [Christensen] writes that he has had word from Miss Inglis that bail is certain for Pancner and me, so, that seems settled all right.

. . . It sounds so very pathetic to me to read of Bucky's calling "Where is Afford." I am trying to make a drawing of Alford from his picture. Don't know yet how I will succeed but will try and try again. Maybe some day, I'll succeed.

. . . Say, baby, there are stories appearing in the capitalist press about the wobblies here. All that I can say for those stories is that they are all lies, pure and simple. We are getting along here first rate, that is, for a prison. I have every privilege that a prisoner can have and perhaps more than some. I, like the other boys, do what we have to do, and get along well. The press, of course, has to have something to yell about. These stories have about as much foundation as the old "German Gold" stories, so, if they hit the west just give them the same consideration.

I am getting to be quite a handball expert. Am playing on the "Kitchen team" now. We are cleaning up the opposition fast. There was a football game today. "Mixed Vegetables" the white team, beat

"Pork-chops" the colored team. It was some game. The IWW boys provide quite a few of the best athletes here. Prashner, Scarlett, McEvoy and Clyde Hough all play on the football team. Several of the boys are playing baseball altho the season is well over. Chaplin, Miller, Gordon, Harrison George and I are the handball enthusiasts.

. . . When I look about me and see only bars-bars-bars and a great high wall, I wonder what is the difference between us and wild beasts. I have watched, day by day, the great mass of prisoners file past me in the big dining hall, and, I wonder why they are there. Sure, a jury found them guilty of some "crime" and a judge sent them away for years. I talk with them, we recount our struggles and our triumphs and losses and all those things. . . . I have a cell-mate who is all the time wondering when he will get out. He has ten years, too. Just a kid, a deserter from the army. I don't think he really realizes yet what it all means. Sometimes he says to me, "Do you think it is right for them to send me to prison for ten years for what I did." Ten years! No one outside of prison realizes what a long time ten years is.

. . . Taking all in all, the prison population, they are of little use to themselves or anyone else. They are mostly men of little or no moral stamina. I do not mean by this that they are an immoral body of men, but rather, men who lack moral courage, they are men who float with the stream; as a rule weak men such as is generally found at the meanest labor. There are practically no dangerous men. . . . There are some men in here that have really done something and you can recognize them clear across the yard—these men have brains—whether they be train robber or revolutionist. This latter type have possibilities and prison life makes them the more determined to follow their old paths with greater thought and cunning. As for the rest, the great mass, prison life does nothing, except perhaps to make them carry around a greater hate from which neither they nor society reap any benefit. Prisons are failures in their purpose, yet, I am happy to have the experience of this one.

December 29, 1918
Every time that I think of [brother] Frank up in White Horse, I feel that about the only difference between us is that I know that I'm in prison and he doesn't.

. . . As for staying away from the movement. I may for a while but surely not long. I am not my own property, I am in a sense "public" property, property of the rebel movement.

. . . Men really come to their true value in a crisis and those who stood the test best are the best. I don't ever want to give anyone the oppertunity to call me a quitter or a coward. If permitted I would gladly take a back seat for a while and enjoy the world, <u>You</u> and me and <u>Bucky</u> and the folks. But, I say, Chiky, shall I walk the streets and let my fellow workers lay here in jail and not enter a cry of protest? Would that be right? But, I shall make no plans till we get together and rest a week or two. We both have a right to a rest and shall have it. The affairs are taking such a turn in the world that one can not guess what the tomorrow holds. . . . The soldiers have been called out to do strike duty in the street car strike in Kansas City. Thus do they fight for "democracy" at home. Well, let us remember, that those whose heels press heaviest today may be the ones to strike the hardest blow tomorrow.

The best fighters for the Bolsheviki in Russia are the old Cossacks and the champion scrappers of the Spartacus movement in Germany are the sailors from the same fleet that murdered the Finnish Reds a year ago. So it goes. Those who today crush labor with rifles and clubs are very likely to be one who, with rifle and club, will strike the first real blow for the benefit of labor.

January 5, 1919

Do you know, it is funny, but a fact. I've got used to it here. I'm willing to bet that you feel more ill at ease than I do. I never thought that I could become accustomed to prison life. This same is true to many others. Big Nef never looked better in his life. . . . You recall how he worried after the conviction. None of that any more. He is smiling every time I see him.

. . . Perhaps you wonder what takes up most of my moments of thought. Well, I can hardly say myself. As a rule, I think very little of life outside these walls. Such things as theaters, etc., never come into one's mind. . . . I never think of our old homes, of street scenes, nor much of people. In a way, they seem too far away. My thoughts are mostly you, and then not in a very personal sense. . . . I have no

overwhelming desire to be with you, my chief worry—it is a worry—
is about your health. Frankly, I would rather do every minute of these
ten years than to be free with you, if you had to go thru the tortures
which you went thru after we were married. I am continually afraid
that you would take sick again. . . . I do not think that I could bear
to be here with you ill outside. Somehow, I have no fear for Bucky's
health. Bet he doesn't have a sick day in his whole life.

My father was a poor prognosticator. My mother would find the strength
to do what she had to do. It was Bucky who would prove fragile.

January 12, 1919
Some interesting things are happening around the country. The
Omaha cases are to be dropped according to the district attorney. The
Spokane cases are as good as dropped and the Butte cases are wiped
from the slate. We may expect the Wichita Cases dropped before
long.

In the Chicago "Tribune" of the 10th the following appears. "Basil
M. Mauley, co-chairman with Wm. Howard Taft of the War Labor
Board, told the reconstruction congress today, that in many cases of
alleged disorderly conduct and sabotage [by] the IWWs which were
reported to the Board it was found that the employers had deliberately hired operatives from big detective and strike breaking agencies
to go among the men and instigate them to acts of violence." At the
same meeting, Louis F. Post, asst. secy of labor, said "that he had long
known about the conditions which Mauley described." Further, he
said, "that the American flag had been used to 'cover the dirt on the
log' by many of the capitalist employers during the war."

But, we who have been "framed" on are in jail and those who used
the "flag to cover the dirt on the log" are still at large, yea, more, they
are very respectable citizens of these United States.

But why should I sit here and rave this way? I'm coming home
pretty blame soon and then we can get comfortably into a corner and
philosophize over all these things, because, you know, we have
promised ourselves a little rest from all this turmoil.

. . . Say, tell Bucky to be waiting for his papa and not to be bash-
ful when he comes.

The Chicago Hundred trial was only the first of a series. Conviction of the IWW leadership was followed quickly by other mass trials of Wobblies. In Sacramento, almost fifty prisoners were convicted together on January 19, 1919. Half these men were held for over a year before trial; some died in jail. At about the same time, prison sentences were imposed on twenty-six Wobblies in Wichita. In Omaha, sixty-four IWW members, non-leaders, who were arrested in November of 1917 still lingered in jail, awaiting a trial that would never materialize. They were freed in April of 1919.

January 19, 1919

I got a letter from Moore which was dated Chicago, Jan. 16th. . . . He said things looked fine there for us. . . . He also wrote that there would be some delay in presenting the application for bond because he and Van [Vanderveer] wanted to have the bill of assignments complete 100% before presenting it to the court. He says he does not want to give the court the slightest loophole to crawl thru.

. . . It is far better that all matters relating to the appeal should be correct in every detail than that we should get out on bond a week or two earlier. Don't you think so? I am perfectly frank, baby, I want to leave here not to return, when I do leave. I would far prefer to remain here, if necessary a couple years and then be free, than to get out for a few months and have to come back. I don't want to come back that way.

. . . I'm done with shorthand and go to school no more. I spend evenings writing and reading, especially writing. I've always wanted to be able to express myself in writing and here is my chance so I'm making good use of it. The dear bosses are at least going to make me a bit more proficient in the struggle. I also rehearse speeches so as to keep in trim. When they break this chicken's spirits we'll both go skating in hell in July. . . .

Oh! Say! We are going to have some more visitors pretty soon. The Sacramento boys who were convicted are to come here.

Say, baby, you had better get out more. Go to town, see a show once in a while and take in a meeting once in a while. Don't go to prison because I'm in one. Keep dressed up. Keep yourself looking well and you'll feel better. Some things I've learned in here, among them dress as well as you can, look neat. Eat carefully and sleep as long as you can. Never miss fresh air. I'm taking more care of myself here than I did on the outside. Take good care of yourself—mentally and physically. I feel much better, so will you. . . . Kiss Bucky boy from papa. My sweetest kisses and many hugs to my sweetest girlie.

January 26, 1919

The boys came here from Sacramento yesterday. They looked bad, most of them. Well, why shouldn't they. Months in jail and then a hard trip here. We'll fix them up all right. They will look some different after we feed them up.

Talking about looks. Say, I want to tell you a good one. We were out in the yard today "chewing the rag." Well, you know, we stand or walk around in groups and talk, etc. To make a short story long—a group of us were standing together, when a fellow worker butted in and said, "Hurrah for the reds, long may she wave!" We asked him what was eating him and he replied:—"Some 'red's' hair is white and some is black but, by God, soup-strainers are pink this year." Well, we took stock:—There was St. John, Law, McKinnon, Nef, Buckley, Hardy, Thompson and I all standing together—all with red mustaches—and no two had the same colored hair. But, why shouldn't they be red? Weren't they grown in here?

Believe me, baby, we have our happy moments here lots of times. It may sound foolish, but I can say truthfully that I never saw this bunch in better humor at any time. We have lots to keep us interested with. Letters come from all over. The news in them is passed around and every week we hear from all over the country. I think we have a pretty good news system here now. And, it is always interesting to get together and try to solve social puzzles which are daily arizing in the press.

. . . From the best that we can estimate, more than three million workers, either directly or thru their chosen representatives, have demanded our release. . . . The workers of America want us out. Another factor is: The workers of England wants us out. Already the Scotch and Welsh workers and a good part of the English workers have made this demand upon Pres. Wilson. England has already released most of her war prisoners. The Sinn Feiners are to be released shortly according to press reports.

The official organ of the C.G.T.—(the Confederacion Generale du Travail) the largest and practically the only labor organization in France—is using the two center columns, front page, of every issue demanding the release of class war prisoners in America. This practice will continue during the entire period of Pres. Wilson's stay in Europe.

A big feature also is: Pres. Wilson's actions and attitudes abroad, and his perported private statements here. He can not talk democracy forever and fail to deliver some of the goods at home.

Something also worth considering is the statement of Senator Borah of Idaho. He stated that he was going to enter a resolution in the Senate asking the repeal of the Espionage Act and the release of war prisoners.

It is going to be hard for America to hold her war prisoners after every other country on earth has released theirs. . . . I am confident of release and I don't expect to wait very much longer either.

After giving so much of himself to improving the lives of workers, Ed was sure that the workers would fight for his freedom. For a while, labor groups in many countries did. But, in the long run, the vast majority of workers did not bestir themselves. And he became increasingly disillusioned.

February 2, 1919

I smile sometime when you speak about being lonesome. I'll be hanged if it wasn't some job to get you to go out when there was a "out." Well, girlie, maybe pretty soon, we shall know something about what is what with us.

. . . As I hardly expect to be home on Bucky's birthday, I'm sending in this letter a little birthday poem, which I concocted here one evening. As you see, I'm not much of a poet but my heart's in the right place anyway.

All I need now is to be out of here and back with you and Buck and all the rest. Say, the very thought makes me happy, and, to think it may not be long. . . . Say, baby, we will never part again, except, of course, some other jail opens up it's lovely doors and begs me to come!!! It's a hard job to stay out of jail now a days when they can try a fellow on his "frame of mind" and give him ten and twenty years.

Dog-gone it, I wish I had the ability to write a history of this time.
Say, future historians are going to have some job. But, those poor devils who claim that evolution is an ever-forward movement have come
in for an awful jolt. Once upon a time Jesus was crucified. We are
told that the world has advanced since then, well, it has in the art of
making shoes, etc., but in its conduct man to man, well, I'm in doubt.
Some sky-pilots tell us that Jesus is coming back to earth in our time.
Really, I hope not. For haven't we enough trouble keeping ourselves . . . out of jail without having to have a permanent defense
committee to keep Jesus out of jail. If Jesus had been on trial with us
he would have got more than Bill Haywood.

1919

BIRTHDAY GREETING

February TO BUCKY Eighteenth

When to this sun-kissed world you came,

Two years ago,

You knew not what you meant to me,

Nor do you know,

Nor will you know, nor will you ever care

That ev'ry year you pass still leaves me there.

But when I'm old and near the death

I'll think of thee. . . .

Not as the man, full-grown; but as the child,

The new-born babe, the pure, the undefiled.

No. 13125

February 9, 1919
Your two letters which arrived during this last week were a pleasure to
me. . . . I also got the joint letter from Edna and mamma. I shall
answer them first. But before, I got a fine letter from Fellow Worker I.
Gaines, a colored lad, in Maryville, Louisiana. He says he and the boys
are more active than ever. We shall give a cheer yet for the old south.
      . . . Now for mamma's letter. Thanks very much for your fine
birthday greetings. I really appreciate reaching the sober age of 30
years. You see up to that age its hustle and bustle and climb, from
that time on, one sits down and slides down. It's so much easier, you

know. Oh yes. Don't let any more conscientious objector releases interest you so far as I am concerned. I never was and am not now, a conscientious objector. There are some good fellows among them— some, I said, a few—the most of them are either cowards or religious freaks. I hope I am neither of these. Surely, my worst enemy will not say that I am a coward—that I would run in any fight, and, as for religion—I have none. The acrobatic stunts of the sky-pilot brigade from Moses till today is more than I can stand.

When I was called to register for the draft, I registered and had I been called for service, I should have gone, I am sure, not because I was afraid to oppose the draft, etc., but because I wanted to see German Militarism crushed forever, and, if to accomplish that end some one must fight, I'd fight. I've never yet asked any man to go where I will not go myself. I don't say this boastingly, mamma, I say it because it is true. I hate war. Yet, once there is a war, my theoretical hatred for war become drowned in the major issues of war. One issue, the largest to me, was militarism. I had, and will, fight it in this country, then why should I have not been willing to fight it in another country. No! I'm not a conscientious objector.

I fought for the principle that the workers in the United States had the "right" to organize. . . . I hold that labor has the "right" to use its organized power to dispose of every privilege now enjoyed by the exploiters of the laborers of the world. For these views, and for the propagating of them, I was sent to prison, and in prison I'd stay till hell froze over before I'd recant a word or act of mine that tended to gain victory to the slaves. Perhaps, this is enough of this.

. . . Haywood was around today with questionaires to be filled out. The purpose of this questionaire was to find out who if anyone could pay for his appeal.

One of the questions asked was—"What is your present income"—one of the boys answered—"Stew." Another wrote, "One sack of tobacco a week and $5.00 at the end of 20 years, board found."

. . . Have moved to another cell. Am celling with Arthur Boose. We have a great time. It surely is much better to be in with a wobbly than with a scissor [Wobbly term for a worker who is not class-conscious]. He's having an awful time getting thru with his letter. He has one page to write. He started before I did and he has not finished yet.

I'm kidding him about it. I'd like to read it when he gets thru, his dutch accent and style is rich, bet his letter has all kinds of "Shut the gate wide open" and "throw the cow over the fence some hay" stuff in it.

February 16, 1919

Say, baby, have you been following the press lately? It's a rich game they are playing now. The IWW is some bird. According to the press, this sizes up the whole thing. The IWW—a hell of an outfit. In 1916 it had it's headquarters in Berlin. For some reason, . . . the said head-quarters were moved to Moscow or Petrograd (one or tother) and the treasurer changed from Kaiser Bill to Lenin or Trotsky (one or tother). Some weeks ago the headquarters were moved to Dublin, Ireland and a German by the name of Kelly who runs a saloon in Chicago was treasurer. Now, comes the latest. The press is now insisting that its headquarters is in Chinatown of either Chicago or New York (one or tother). Now, what do you know about that! And listen! They have found the way to cure the world of Bolshevism, IWWism and all other terrible diseases. This is good! Deport 'em. We will deport 250 to England and England will deport 250 to this country. That will rid both countries of these pestiferious I.W.W. Great idea so long as they don't wear out the Atlantic Ocean.

There is one thing that worries me. You getting fat! Gee, whiz, girlie, use some sense. Lay off that fat stuff. A picture comes to my mind now of you when we were first married, a round, fat little maedel. You are a whole lot more becoming without the double chin and you get around better. Don't you think so?

I'm continually gaining weight but more slowly now, a half a pound to a pound a week but steadily upward. I can stand it, for I had to stand in one place five minutes to throw a shadow.

Really there is nothing to write about. Everything is just the same as it was this time last week. . . . You see I have no Bucky here whom I might watch grow and make foolish pranks. Here everything is the same—ALL THE TIME.

February 23, 1919

Do you know that your optomism is a great thing. It is most inspiring. It is the greatest tonic one can receive. I often wonder what I should do if it were not for you. You are truly the one shining spot on this earth to me. All the judges and jails this side of hell cannot take you from me. Can they, baby?

What I shall do when I get out, really, I don't know, but I shall ask you a question. If after this affair is cleared up and the iron heel is not lifted . . . what would you say to us going to Russia? I have thought this over long and carefully, and my only answer to the hell erected here, is to leave. I do not think that any man is of value so long as he is in prison, and, if to move, means prison, why not then leave the fight to those less known? I do not intend to run from any fight where I can be of value, but when I am forced finally to conclude that I am valueless except as prison fodder, then I feel my duty is to those whom I love most. I can not humble myself to any oppressor. So long as a man tries to oppress me, I will—must fight back. I would sooner be a rebel spirit in prison than a servile slave on a job, knowing I was driven there. I would sooner die. . . .

Bucky, too. What of him. Shall I not struggle that he may live in a better world. I would sooner see him dead than to have traveled my world so far. I have been happy in a sense, but, you, and the folks and a few friends have been my happiness.

Chiky, baby, I doubt if you have ever known what is in my heart. I've been heart sick most of my latter years, what with the poverty I have seen, strikes I have taken part in, and all the horror and misery of the world have haunted me. I have sat for hours contemplating it with a heavy heart. I have brooded in silence and sometimes I got angry with you, baby, when you asked me if I was sick. The face of some poor kid upset me for weeks. I have never confessed this before because I have always felt that it showed weakness. Perhaps it is. Well, then I am weak.

Yes, Bucky. A whole world to you and me. What of him. Either we must strive on for a better world for him here or we must bring him to a better one. If we cannot be potent factors here toward the creation of a better world, why not go to Russia. In a few years it will blossom into a great free country. There can Bucky become educated and be a little somebody. There the school-book will not read "If a man buys 5 yards of ribbon at 8 cents a yard and sells it at 12 cents a yard, how much profit will he make?" . . . There, too, can we become of real use. There I shall work, not so that some parasite may grow fat, but to help feed, clothe, shelter and give recreation and amusement and knowledge to my fellow workers. Why should I slave to feed the boss when I can work to feed the workers. Think this over, baby. This new land of freedom! Damn! I wish I was a Russian so that I could be deported. It would be like the devil kicking a poor sinner out of hell into heaven!!!

. . . Say, I'm fixing up our cell. Pictures on the wall, carpet on the floor, and all modern improvements. Boose and I have great times here arguing. We agree only on the letters—IWW After that we disagree on everything, yet we get along fine. As soon as we get thru with our letters, I'll start another argument.

Oh, yes. Pres. Wilson [returns from Europe] Monday. . . . The N.Y. Civil Liberties Bureau crowd is going to take our case before him. Wonder what he'll say.

March 2, 1919
I read so much of Bucky that I can not but keep hoping to see him pretty shortly. . . . Gee whiz, he must be growing. I can hardly imagine him being three feet tall and not the round fat chubby kiddie that I left him. You remember, the last time I saw him was in the Cook County Jail. You will recall that he got tired of trying to look thru those screens and sat down by the stairway and began to play. That picture will ever remain vivid in my mind.

I have decorated the cell here with pictures of all kinds, but those of Bucky I often stop and "study." I see his little hand and I often wish I could squeeze it and kiss it. Bucky was surely papa's boy!

. . . The one great thing now is, that there is quite a howl around the country because we are behind the bars. Today's paper tells of some 290 soldiers who have seen service in France and have just been returned to this country, who have sent a letter to Pres. Wilson demanding him, in the name of democracy, to liberate all who have been sent to jail in this country because of alleged anti-war activities.

Say, baby, where and when you want to go anywhere is a matter for you to decide. I am in prison. Should I get out soon I surely want to come west for a while at least. Then we may return east. Maybe so, maybe not, we will see then. Should I have to stay here then—it's up to you entirely. Of one thing I am sure, you wont stay with Belle long. You know and I know that you would not. Much as I like Belle in many ways, I must say honestly that the devil could not live with her long. . . . I am sure that if you would get out and around more, you would feel better. There are lots of people yet, in this world, whom you might get acquainted with. I'll tell you honestly baby, if I were you, I'd stay west even if you had to move into town. Summer is soon here and I think that if you put in one summer on the coast you wouldn't want to put in another one anywhere else.

You must feel as I do here lots of times. Just get kind o' tired of everything. If I came to the Pacific Coast, you would like it all right, wouldn't you? The fact is, you can be no more satisfied than I can while we are forced to be apart. Let us wait a little longer and we will see what happens in this case. Then maybe we can do some better figuring. What do you think?

March 9, 1919

Included in the mail of the week was a letter from Edna, to which I shall reply first.

My dear Edna, why blame God for the weather. If you must blame him for your bad weather, I should have to praise him for the fine atmospheric condition he permits here. I remember once hearing a fellow start a prayer and instead of saying, "praise God from whom all blessings flow" he said "praise God from whom all cyclones blow." No matter what happens, God seems quite indifferent. So let him sleep on undisturbed. I see you all have colds and that the governor died. You speak of both events in the same breath so I am wondering if he died of your cold. Now, little (?) sister, please make Chiky run a few foot races. Anything to keep down the fat. If you let Chiky get fat, I shall consider that you have failed in a great duty to your brother who art in prison.

Now, Chiky baby. . . .

The first thing I strike in going over your letters is where you speak of how you have picked up the language. I must admit, and happily, that you are making great progress. I find paragraph after paragraph where the composition is absolutely correct, where the flow of words are in their proper places. . . . Keep it up. You will find it greatly beneficial to read good literature. If you can get some of Oscar Wilde's works in prose and especially his plays, you can learn, with pleasure, the very finest of conversational English. Wilde used unusually fine and simple English.

. . . Respecting Russia. Well, I'd like to go. I am pretty sure that if we were to go that the best time would be as soon after I get clear of this case as possible, for, as you know, when I once throw my heart into anything the very devil can't change my course. I would like to study at first hand, what is actually going on there.

. . . In your second letter on Russia, I fear that you are somewhat illusioned. . . . Of this, I am sure, Russia is neither a heaven or a co-operative commonwealth. Revolution must yet follow this revolution. Russia's later revolutions were not economic, but political. Russia merely changed, in turn, from monarchial autocracy to bourgeois autocracy to proletarian autocracy. You may wonder why I object to proletarian autocracy. Listen, I'm opposed to any autocracy. . . . The present trouble with Russia seems to be that it is ruled by the Bolsheviki, a political party, having control of the Soviets, a political system or machine, instead of having an economic union of industrial and agricultural workers in charge of the industries and lands. Russia today has Government Ownership instead of "Workers" ownership. Get the point?

. . . Well, baby dear, I'd surely like to see you and pick you up and half squeeze you to death. Baby, I surely do miss you, but it's great to know that I've got a little Chiky waiting for me, and a Bucky boy, too. And all the folks. Some day will be a day of great joy.

March 16, 1919
Do you know, when I miss your letters for a couple of days, I start laying for the mailman with a club. He always delivers the letter, tho, so as to save himself from abuse.

Yes, the Supreme Court held that Debs was fairly tried and convicted, but, they did not pass upon the constitutionality of the Spinage [Espionage] Act. So there we are.

The most important event of the last week was the Wichita Case. They went to trial on the 12th. Got a jury the first day. Then Vanderveer began a legal argument holding that the letters, etc., were illegally seized . . . and that the indictment was faulty in that it did not say where the conspiracy was supposed to have taken place.

Federal Judge Pollock seemed to agree with Vanderveer and, while he did not make a ruling, he fired the jury and posponed the case till September, an action which I am sure means the end of the case.

. . . Our papers are getting thru the mails in pretty good shape from what I hear and mail is coming thru. The powers-that-be are easing up to quite an extent from a federal point of view at least.

In 1905 Socialist leader Eugene V. Debs joined with Bill Haywood of the United Federation of Miners to found the Industrial Workers of the World. But the IWW's reliance on direct action and its disdain of the ballot soon led Debs to desert its ranks.

Debs ran for president of the United States on the Socialist Party ticket in 1912, receiving six percent of the vote. Then, with the passage of the wartime Espionage Act, he was sentenced to ten years in prison for an antiwar speech he delivered in Canton, Ohio. In 1919, the Wobblies were following his case with interest.

March 30, 1919

Last Thursday night, I got a wire from Vanderveer stating that the bond hearing had been postponed from that date till Wednesday morning, April 2nd. His wire said no more but from the Chicago papers we learned that the delay was allowed so as to give Prosecuting Attorney Clyne time to go to Washington and return.

Say, baby, have you heard? You remember Bill Shatoff of New York. You have met him, I am sure. Well, he is now Chief of Police in Petrograd. Bill Shatoff was one of the levelest headed fellows we had in this country. Funny thing, too, he and Trotsky knew one another pretty well in this country. They were not very good friends here. Several men like Shatoff can do a whole lot toward industrially organizing the workers in Russia.

. . . Lenine seems to have a wonderfully long head on him. I think that among keen observers of international affairs, Lenine is considered the world's greatest statesman. Of course, this view would hardly be held among those who rely upon the daily press for their information regarding turbulent Russia.

I see in the Christian Science Monitor that the O.B.U. [One Big Union] in Australia is sweeping the country. Think of it, girlie, in a country where it means 6 months imprisonment to be a member, 6 months to contribute to the defense of an arrested member and, mark you, a lawyer who attempts to represent a wobbly in court is liable to 6 months imprisonment for so doing. Yes, the O.B.U. is the biggest thing in Australia today. Less than two years ago 12 of its leading officers were sent to prison for 15 years each. They are back in their offices now.

Oh, yes, girlie, I got a better job as I expected. I'm in the bakery now. I have a little more work to do—but, do we eat? I should say so!! I'll give you an idea of what my bill-of-fare consists of now. I'll just give what we had today (it's about the same every day) Breakfast—2 fried eggs, 3 hot-cakes, syrup, hot biscuits, butter, coffee, and, oh yes, fried spuds. Dinner—Roast pork—boiled potatoes, fried parsnips, sage dressing, gravy, bread and coffee. Supper—Fried pork tenderloin, fried potatoes, corn fritters (fried as one would doughnuts) bread, butter, coffee and cake. It is made of good fresh food materials and well and tastily cooked. I believe we eat better than any other prisoners in the institution. I have gotten along finely here, taking all in all. Have never been reported for the violation of any rule, have done what I had to do, and, also, have taken advantage of every privilege granted and asked for more. If I have to live here I want to make it a decent place to live in. . . . I have observed many things here, and from what I can gather, "isolation" or "prison life" that is to say, "locking a person away from the world," is the most unjust punishment in the world. It is not by any means an "equal" punishment. To illustrate, we will say that a group of men are sent to jail for the same period of time for the committing of a similar crime . . . one is keen mentally while another is a dullard; one is single while another is married and has a family, perhaps starving, one man's family is well while sickness overtakes the others, one has lived well and learned to enjoy luxury while the other never had a better board or bed; one sees his whole life ruined because of his prison term, the other sees his future made. To illustrate this latter case, I understand that there is a bank cashier here who took from the funds entrusted to him, some money used to loan a needy friend. . . . He sold his home, everything, borrowed what he could, and he did make good every cent, but he broke the law and came here for seven years. He is disgraced, yes, his life is broken—that's how he sees it. Then take my case, disgraced when I get out? I should hope not. If I could, I would have my picture, together with my prison number and my prison record placed in big electric signs accross every main street in the world, so everybody could see it. I am now and always will be proud of my prison sentence. By that token I can prove that when the struggle for human freedom was bitter, I was not afraid. I did not compromise my principles for my freedom. Can it be said that prison life means the same to us? He suffers mental agony while I am happy. His children bow their heads in shame at their father's misfortune while Bucky says, "Papa, far, far away in jail." For my "crime" we may and are all proud, you and me and Bucky. It may be a bit hard now, baby, but tomorrow belongs to us.

April 2, 1919

Well, at last, comes the news. Bond has at last been set. I do not know what the bond conditions are. If they will take the bond which Miss Inglis and Mrs. Hendrie has to offer, then I should be out of here in a week or ten days.

. . . So you may know all the news that I have to date, I am sending a copy of the telegram I got a couple hours ago.

TELEGRAM   Chicago, Ill, Apr. 2,

E. F. Doree, Leavenworth, Kansas.

Bail fixed as follows. Ten thousand each for Andreytchine, Ashleigh, Chaplin, Clark, Doree, Edwards, Fletcher, Gordon, Jaakkola, Johannson [Johannsen], Laukki, Lossief, Law, McDonald [MacDonald], Miller, Nef, Pancner, Prashner, Thompson, St. John.

Five thousand each for Avila, Fanning, George, Parenti, Perry, Plahn, Rothfisher, Stenberg, Tanner, Westerlund, Wetter. One thousand each for Nelson, Speed, Nigra, McWhirt. Fifteen thousand for Haywood.

Signed Geo Vanderveer, Otto Christensen

All those named in the telegram have bail in sight.

April 5, 1919
My bail is $10,000. Property to twice that amount must be put up.
Bond will be accepted from anywhere in the United States, which
makes it great for me.

. . . I'll try to explain the proceedure thru which we must go in
order to make bond.

First, our blank bond forms must be sent from Chicago by our
lawyers to our prospective bondsmen (in my case to Miss Inglis at
Ann Arbor) then the bondsmen must take the papers, fill them out
and swear to the truthfulness of their statements contained in the
bond papers, before the local U.S. Commissioner. The papers are
then sent to the clerk of the Appellate Court at Chicago. He will
accept the bond unless the district attorney objects. When he objects,
he notifies the district attorney of the district in which bond is made,
then this attorney looks up the property and informs the attorney at
Chicago of its value. If the Chicago dist attorney is then satisfied the
bond is accepted by the clerk and orders sent here to release us.

Was over to the Clothing department and got my order in to have
my suit and overcoat pressed. Looked all the stuff over and it stood
storage fine. Was over to the tailor shop, too, and got measured for a
new suit.

I expect that the Wichita Cases will be dropped very soon. We see
no more about it in the papers and we have not been charged with
trying to murder anyone lately. The newspapers must have fired a few
of their hop-heads!

Oh yes, baby, I came near forgetting to tell you what our bond conditions are. Merely that we shall not violate the Espionage act. We
may take part in any and all organization activity. [Federal attorney]
Clyne was forced to admit, by Vanderveer, in open court, that no law
was violated by anyone when he confined his activities to organizing
the workers along the IWW line.

Had he admitted this at the time of our trial, we would never have
been here.

April 13, 1919
As you see, I'm still here and don't know how much longer I'll have
to stay here. One thing I do know is, that my bond was all gathered

together in Detroit last Monday and probably has been sent to Chicago before this time.

There is one thing certain. I am not sorry that I came here. I've learned a great deal here. One really should have a little penitentiary experience. While it is not pleasant or anything like that, yet one learns much about men, he could not otherwise learn.

There are no petty disturbing influences, there is nothing which does not permit him to be himself. Our routine of life is the same every day. There is no change in that. The only change here is caused by new men coming in, but these new men are soon absorbed, in fact, after a man is here a month, he becomes a regular part of the whole machinery.

. . . One can read the soul of men here as one is never able to do on the outside. We see men, for example, who tell the guards everything they see. They can be devided into two principle classes, one class who "snitch" because of hope of personal favor, and the other who do so as a sort of a sense of duty. There is still another type of "snitch" who does not know he is "snitching" at all. It is that type who like to be seen on speaking terms with an officer or guard. . . . The great majority of officers and guards have no use for a "snitch," in fact, most of them, if I see correctly, despise them. The vast majority of prisoners mind their own business and see, hear nor tell nothing. To this great mass, the "snitch" is held in absolute contempt.

Then we have that type who care only for their own welfare, who are given to "self-pity," who seem to think that every body in the world is against them and that all hope is forever gone. Nobody takes them seriously, except themselves. These, too, form a small minority.

But, the great mass! If those who make up society generally are as thoughtful of the welfare of their fellow citizens as are convicts, then there is great hope for the world. What I have seen men do here for others, the favors given and preference shown, is inspiring. It is great! It is fine! Prisoners will . . . aid one another in hundreds of little ways, which I have never observed folks on the outside do.

If prisoners are baser of soul than those who have not yet been caught, then there is great hope for the human family. Psychologically, we are O.K. There is some rif-raf, but that's to be expected. The great mass is good, very good. I've got many good friends here, they

are fine fellows. When I'm home again, I'll tell you of some things
I've experienced here that will surprise you. Then you will understand
what I mean when I say that the soul of man stands of clearer in
prison than it does on the street. Here is where you learn a man for
what he really is and not what pseudo standard he was given by the
world outside, who places value in a man only to the extent that he
makes money or runs some skin-game without being arrested.

April 14, 1919
Mrs. Cathleen McGraw Hendrie put up Sixty Thousand ($60,000.00)
and Miss Agnes Inglis put up Twenty-five Thousand ($25,000.00) in
clear, unemcumbered property. That is more than twice as much as
is needed. That ought to get me out. An equal amount was put up for
Fellow Worker Pancner.

April 20, 1919
Miss Inglis both wired and wrote me last week that there was some
technical error in the making out of the bond papers, but that she
and Mrs. Hendrie were meeting on the 17th, that was last Thursday,
to fix them up properly. My bond papers were here last week and I
signed them so there is nothing more for me to do than to wait for
the order for release.
    . . . Miss Inglis in her letter to me said that she would get me out
no matter what the obstacles were. She is surely a wonderfully fine
woman, eh? baby.

In her later years, Agnes Inglis devoted much of her time and energy to
the Labadie collection on labor history at the University of Michigan. As
a mark of respect to her, the letters, photographs, clippings, and official
documents from my father's black satchel have been donated to that
repository.

April 30, 1919
Well, baby, I'm still here, and I suppose will stay another couple
weeks.
    As you know, Inglis and Hendrie were to go Pancner's and my
bond jointly. Well here is a wire I got from Christiansen [Chris-

tensen], "April 24, the Dist Atty agreed to Doree bond but objects to Pancner bond. Reasons that Mrs. Hendrie who signed as second surety has two mortgages on her property."

Immediately upon the receipt of this wire, I wired this to Miss Inglis—"Would prefer that Pancner be the first one released on bonds." This action was hard to take but it was the only proper action because he had just finished serving a sentence before his arrest in this case and he was in jail in Chicago while I was out. I hated to do it on your account but I'm sure that you are willing to wait a week or two in such a case. I have the assurances of Miss Inglis that whatever is needed will be made up quickly and that there will be no more technical errors.

Love and don't be disappointed. I'll be with you soon, all the happier.

May 4, 1919

I was pretty nearly sure that I would be out by this time, but no such luck.

. . . I'm doing a bit more reading. It's great to read John Reed's "The ten days that shook the world." It's the story of [the] period just before and after Nov. 7th, 1917, when the Bolsheviki took control in Russia. When I read of what friends of ours did, what a picture!! I remember Trotsky as I saw him in New York on the platform. I can see him in my mind's eye, standing there before the assembled delegates, in Russia, his eyes small and beady sparkling while the expression on his face changes from [a] smile to a leering grin as different delegates interrupt his talk. And Toblinson of Chicago, the organizer of the Workers' Institute; how he pleaded for the cause of the proletariat, only later to be captured by the reactionaries and stood before a firing squad and killed. And Shatov, old Bill Shatof with whom I've chummed around, whom you know. You remember when he spoke in Baltimore? Well, the same Bill Shatov, going here, going there, urging the rebels on, on to victory. Gee, girlie, how I would have liked to have been there. You and I, baby, watching the birth of the greatest freedom of mankind, the freedom of the worker. And when I read of these old friends of mine, men who saw years in prison, men who were exiles from the land of their birth for years, when I read this, I wonder if I have the steel and sterling of their qualities, am I as willing to play my part without complaining? We must learn to suffer our part that tomorrow may be a better day for those who toil. . . . So you and I must brace up, that Bucky may never know the misery which swept the world into which he was born. Isn't it worth while?

May 4, 1919
Miss Agnes Inglis, c/o Davidow
726 Penobscot Bldg., Detroit, Mich.

My dear Fellow Worker:

One thing which I really would like to make clear to you, is that it is not my wish that you run yourself to death trying to get me released. If it were not for Ida I would ask you to drop it altogether. I feel uncomfortable when I know that I am causing folks trouble and hardship. I know what rustling bond is, it is a miserable job. . . . Please don't feel that you are under any obligation to work and work. It is not fair that you should do so. It would not be fair of me to wish that you should do so.

   Yours for Industrial Freedom, E. F. Doree

May 11, 1919

My dearest little girlie:

With this evening's mail, I got a circular letter from Christensen in which it stated that "as to Doree, an additional $15,000 in real estate is necessary, or a deposit of $7,500 in cash or liberty bonds with the Clerk of the Court."

   We can hardly expect any quick action now. It will be some time before I can get out. My reasons for saying is: the court has virtually left it in Clyne's hands to O.K. the bond, and, you know what kind of a creature Clyne is, and, because it is no easy matter to pick up $15,000 worth of unencumbered property. Cash or Liberty Bonds are out of the question now because a campaign has been started for so many of the fellows that I would now only interfere with the chances of others who are in same boat as I am.

One thing now that I do hate is the trouble I'm making for others. Were it not for you, I should ask them to drop the whole thing immediately.

Everything has reduced itself to one reason why I want to get out—as things stand now—and that's you, girlie. Some times I get such a longing for you, I would give 'most anything to just see you for a few moments. And I wish that you could see me. Sometimes I am sorry that you have not been able to visit this place, just to see it. I am not joking at all, but if there must be prisons then they cannot do much better than this one is now. When we came here, it was impossible almost to get cigarette papers, now we can buy them right in the prison, here, it used to be compulsory for an irreligious brute like me to go and listen to psalms and sermons, now only those who are interested in choice lots in heaven go, the other can go to hell if they want to, or else stay in the kitchen. Having a practical turn of mind, I stay in the kitchen. . . . As for myself, I have no complaint, but, how are you, my little sweetheart. That's my only bother.

If only it were different for you. If you could only feel satisfied. I just know that you are not. It is not in your temperament to be, nor is it in your temperament to complain.

I wish I knew that you were as happy as I am. To know that would do me a world of good.

You will never know what you are to me, girlie. While you are away from me, I feel the greatest loss I ever felt. I think that I should be beside myself for joy if I could just see you, just really know that all was well with you. I think often of you out on that farm and I have to laugh. I know that you walk around there with a long face when you should be in town a good part of the time enjoying life a bit. But what's the use, you will never enjoy life as other folks, will you? All you want is your Edely and Bucky and a place where we can all cuddle up and forget there is a world at all. Am I right?

May 18, 1919
I'm surely proud of the fine stand which you have taken. It made me feel a whole lot better to know that you can take our temporary defeat so philosophically.

. . . Baby dear, I am both happy and sorry that you wrote Feige to work for me. I wrote her last Friday and told her not to hustle bond for me till those whom she had already promised [in Philadelphia] were out. . . . Should I butt in right now, I might injure their chances.

There will be no one who can say that I haven't played absolutely fair in this whole matter. That's worth as much as freedom, yes, more. Don't you think so? It is one thing to be so easy that one is a fool and another thing to be generous enough to others to gain their respect. Girlie, it pays.

I am sorry to say that you must wait, but, I am sure you share with me the happiness of knowing that we can look all our fellow workers in the eyes and know that they know that we played on the square when it was hard to do the right thing.

May 25, 1919

Got a letter from Tom Whitehead. He has received assurances that there is a full second surety for use by either Thompson or me, whoever gets their whole first surety first. I am going to write to Miss Inglis tomorrow night asking her to save the second surety for me. I feel that I am entitled to it and am sure that she will tell Christensen to hold it for me.

Say, Nef and I had a real jolly chat today, the first real unreserved chat in a long, long time. Believe me, we were some enemies for a while, and, now, that it has gone entirely, I feel so fine. Nef surely feels better, too. Well, we had one another's goat, that was all. Well, I'm glad it's all over now. I know his weakness, he knows mine, so we will probably avoid hurting one another's feelings in the future.

It is fine that you are getting on so well. . . . Talking about feeling fine. That's me. You remember how I used to freeze and shiver, sort of chills or something. Even in the summer when a day turned a bit chilly. Listen, I'm giving a state secret, but, I haven't had on a stitch of underwear in almost two months. Never wear a coat or hat—never. Don't you know!! I don't know what it is to have one of those chills and no more colds for mine!

Today, I played handball till my shirt was wringing wet, then went to my cell and had a rub-down with cold water, than cut up a pile of bread, ate a good supper, and after loafing a while, I weighed in. Just balanced the beam at 160 lbs.

Big Bill is in the hospital. He has some sort of an ulceration in the jaw. I saw him today. His face is badly swollen but he says it is getting better. He said that the doctor thought that it was nothing serious.

. . . Yesterday the baseball team from the military prison at Fort Leavenworth was here to try to beat our white team. They were a fine bunch of players—but!!!—they had to admit that our boys understood the game. We cleaned them up with a score of 7 to 1. . . . Watching the game is fine lung experience. I got to make motions for two days after a game, no use trying to talk. Who do I root for? Who? Did you say, who? Listen and repeat this after me—For the home team. Some "home"—some "team." I say so.

But why ramble on so, well I write as I feel. I feel foolish tonight. Boose is writing a letter and he gets sore if I bother him—so I do. He looks cute as an owl when he gets sore. I get lots of pleasure out of it, and he learns to control his temper.

. . . I got a letter from mamma last week and must answer it.

Dear Mamma:

Your dear letter came to me breathing such good cheer and happiness that I sometimes think that it is I who am old and sour and you who possess the corner on life and joy.

It may be serious to you, it undoubtedly is, and I'm happy that it is so, but to me it was so humorous when I read of how you and Chiky argue as to which loves me the most. Me—Convict No. 13125—and mother and wife each contend that "I love him most." Say, who in the deuce couldn't do ten years when he knows that those nearest and dearest to him, love him most.

Now I shall settle that argument. Each one of you loves me the most, each in your way. One shall never realize or understand the love of the other. The love of a mother for her children "passeth all understanding" while the love of a wife for a convict husband "cant be understood at all." The mother is mother and can be nothing else, but the wife can choose. It is harder for a mother to disown a child than for a wife to divorce a husband. The wife has greater choice in the matter and greater freedom. It is a question as to who really loves most; the mother who can either love or hate, or the wife who can either love or forget. Either love is sublime. I'm thankful I have the great love of both of you. I should hate to ever be called upon to choose one or the other. I am positive that I should choose both irrespective of the rules. But enough of this, till some fine day I shall take you, one in each arm, and proclaim that it is I who loves greatest for I love you both with a love—there is no greater love.

Your loving kid—Ed.

June 9, 1919

My dearest little girlie:

Well, at last I know that I am coming home to you. My bond has been O.K'd but Miss Inglis, Mrs. Hendrie and Marie Kennedy must sign the bond again. So must I also. All this should be done and I should be out of here within a week after you get this letter.

June 22, 1919

My new bond forms came here last night. They seem to be all O.K. . . . There are enough official seals on them to make them good anyway.

I shall wire you as soon as I get to Kansas City and let you know when to expect me in Portland.

Tell Bucky that papa is coming home this time.

Bye, bye for my last letter is written.

Your loving Hubby,
Ed

He was free! With his railroad ticket in his pocket, he could pick up his satchel, walk out the prison doors, and begin the journey from Kansas to his parents' home.

My mother never spoke of those two years. I can only imagine the joy as summer began in 1919 when Ed reached the Rex, Oregon, farm and first embraced his wife and two-year-old son. Surely he rested, luxuriated in walking free in the country air, became reacquainted with the sisters he had not seen for years, played with his child, slept in the arms of his wife.

4

THE TRIAL

Then the judge, he went wild over me,
And I plainly saw we never could agree;
So I let the man obey what his conscience had to say,
He went wild, simply wild over me.

THE FORTY-SIX Wobblies released on bond were, of course, not entirely free. They were still under sentence. For now, they would work to raise funds, garner support, and help prepare evidence and arguments to convince a higher court that their convictions were unjust.

Let us now go back in time, to the events of 1918 and 1917, to the trial and its antecedents.

THE SETTING

In 1917, as America entered the World War, its lowliest workers, those whom John Reed called "the outdoor men, hard-rock blasters, tree-fellers, wheat-binders, longshoremen, the boys who do the strong work of the world"[1] were just beginning to taste success in their struggle for decent pay and humane working conditions. Unionization through the IWW was their weapon. Their enemies, roused to action, were ruthless and powerful.

One incident encapsulates the story of their power and reach. In July of 1917, at Bisbee, Arizona, the copper miners, all members of the IWW, were on strike. Federal authorities who were called in to investigate found no disruption of wartime industry, no reason to intervene. So the sheriff, "his captains and deputies, the mayor and the city council, the Phelps Dodge Company's top local executives . . . and leading railroad, telephone, and telegraph company officials met together secretly to plot their course of action."[2] All communication between Bisbee and the outside was cut off. The sheriff deputized two thousand men, armed and paid for by the Phelps Dodge Company,[3] who proceeded to round up twelve hundred alleged enemy aliens, Mexicans, and Wobblies, put them into cattle cars on a twenty-seven-car train provided by the railroad, take them over the state line, and dump them in the New Mexico desert. After thirty-six hours in the scorching July heat, the men finally found refuge in an Army camp, where they were held under guard for two months.[4] When the Justice Department indicted the vigilantes a year later, the Phelps Dodge company attorney defended them. The Arizona federal district court quashed the indictments, finding no violation of federally guaranteed rights.

In contrast to their corporate foes, the Wobblies had few allies. Working in remote mines and logging camps or constantly on the move from one harvest to another, they had no roots or contacts in the social life of the towns. People didn't know them. They were aliens, stinking "timber beasts." It was easy to believe anything about them.

Against this background, hatred and fear of the Wobblies was constantly, deliberately stirred up by their enemies.

It was an old pattern. False testimony was elicited by the Idaho authorities[5] in 1906 to implicate mine union leaders Bill Haywood and Charles Moyer in the murder of the former governor. (The legendary Clarence Darrow successfully defended them against those charges.) On company orders,[6] dynamite was planted in Lawrence, Massachusetts, during a 1912 textile strike to "prove" the Wobblies were violent. Now, with America at war, rumors were spread that that the IWW was burning wheat fields and poisoning the nation's beef supply.[7] The most devastating wartime accusation was that the IWW was in the pay of the enemy, receiving gold from the Kaiser. U.S. Senator Henry Ashurst of Arizona said straight out on the Senate floor, "I have frequently been asked what 'IWW' means. It means simply, solely, and only 'Imperial Wilhelm's Warriors.'"[8] The press took up and spread these accusations.

It did not matter that the charges were false. A search by a Department of Justice accountant would find no inkling of "German gold."[9] A federally sponsored investigation by Thorstein Veblen would discover no IWW disloyalty or opposition to the war effort.[10] It did not matter because in 1917 America was in the grip of savage xenophobic hysteria. People were beaten up for having German names. "Sauerkraut" had to be referred to as "liberty cabbage." The accusation that Wobblies were German agents undercut their credibility, eroded support, and made them fair game for what was to come.

The Wobblies' own irreverence and exaggerated language certainly contributed to the general public's fear and mistrust. The Wobblies were gritty, essentially artless, and, in the best sense, patriotic campaigners against injustice, but they talked revolution.

> The Wobbly program, what made it attractive to men like Joe Hill-strom [Joe Hill] was that it was no program at all. It was as reflexive as a poke in the nose, and about as constructive. We are oppressed; fight back. The other side use any means to hold us down; use any means to get up. . . . The master class has jobbed the earth; throw it out and put in its place a new master class in the expectation that under its benign rule government and class struggle and injustice will wither away. Wonderful. All it needed was harps and wings.[11]

The Wobblies scoffed openly at religion and sang parodies of Christian hymns. In winter they took refuge in warm libraries, reading European writers on anarchism, syndicalism, class conflict, and sabotage. From those writings they derived a philosophy and slogans, peppering their writings, rhetoric, and cartoons with revolutionary intent. Yet their actions were not violent. In the words of Rudolph Katz, "The American Federation of Labor does not preach sabotage, but it practices sabotage, and the . . . I.W.W. preaches sabotage, but does not practice it."[12] However, the Wobblies' espousal of radical goals and "direct action" means lent credibility to charges of disloyalty and violence.

In 1917, the immediate problem for the federal government was a drop in production figures for food, lumber, and copper—all vital to the war effort and all hit by IWW strikes. The Wilson cabinet was divided on how to deal with the labor problem. Recognizing that the companies were profiting richly from war contracts, the Department of Labor "intended that strikers return to the job only after employers improved working conditions."[13] On the other hand, Attorney General Gregory really believed that German gold backed the Wobblies.[14] In the end, "Wilson found it easy to believe reports which stressed that the IWW had struck the lumber and copper industries not to raise wages or improve working conditions but to obtain German gold and subvert the war effort. Hence the Wilson administration succumbed to the Western businessmen's anti-IWW crusade."[15] Fred Thompson has noted, "Where the IWW had already made employers take unionism for granted, as in Philadelphia, no campaign against it developed; the impetus to destroy the IWW came from the non-union fields it was invading: lumber, copper, iron mining and oil."[16]

The governors of eight western states proposed in July of 1917 that the federal government declare an emergency, intern all Wobblies until the war was over, and prohibit the press from mentioning the IWW in order to avoid making heroes of the prisoners. That plan was rejected. The course of action ultimately taken by the federal government came at the suggestion of ex-Governor Lind of Minnesota, "an ally of that state's wheat, lumber, and mining interests, . . . who met with Hinton Clabaugh, head of the Chicago office of the Justice Department, and suggested that the federal government prosecute IWW leaders on charges of conspiracy to violate the Espionage Act."[17] In August, a Justice Department official told a New Mexico senator, "something quite effective is under way with respect to the I.W.W. situation. . . . I do not think you or any of your western friends will be disappointed."[18]

When the trial began—fittingly, on April Fool's Day of 1918—everything was in place to overwhelm the IWW leaders. Their enemies were powerful and influential, the public saw them as outsiders at best and miscreants at worst, and the national government was ready to err, if necessary, on the side of protecting the war effort.

THE INDICTMENT

Seven months earlier, on September 5, 1917, federal and local agents raided IWW offices in fifteen cities, from San Francisco to Boston. As a result, all of the IWW's records—correspondence, mailing lists, receipts, etc.—fell into the hands of the U.S. government. Some of this material, evidence favorable to the defense, would never be seen again.

In less than a month, indictments were handed down in Chicago for the IWW leadership. The list of those indicted held some anomalies. Some of the most powerful Wobbly organizers were not included. Elizabeth Gurley Flynn, "The Wobbly Girl" herself, and the multilingual orator Joe Ettor had severed their cases from the others. On the other hand, the list included Vincent St. John, who had left the Wobblies and gone to New Mexico in search of gold in 1914, three years before passage of the Espionage Act. Flynn and Ettor never stood trial; St. John went to Leavenworth.

The Chicago indictment itself has been called "surely one of the more bizarre documents in the history of American jurisprudence."[19] It contained no specifics. No injurious act against any named person or organization was charged. Every "overt act" listed in the indictment had to do with writing or printing something. One of these "overt acts" was IWW leader Bill Haywood's sending a telegram to President Wilson, protesting the Bisbee incident.

The indictment contained five felony counts. In his charge to the jury the following August, Judge Kenesaw Mountain Landis (who subsequently became commissioner of Major League Baseball) dismissed one count (using the mails to defraud), then recapitulated the remaining four. His charge fills thirty-six legal-size pages in the typewritten trial transcript. (One can only guess what sense the average juror in the sweltering courtroom made of it.) Some excerpts:

> The first count charges that the defendants have conspired, combined, confederated and agreed together, and with one Frank H. Little, deceased, and with other persons to the grand jurors unknown, by force, to prevent, hinder and delay the execution of certain [wartime] laws of the United States. . . . The first count then proceeds to charge the defendants, for the purpose of executing the said unlawful conspiracy, confederation, combination and agreement . . . have done certain things which the law calls overt acts. Now follows . . . a long list of things charged in this first count as overt acts. . . . The list includes—it begins first—that Haywood, Chaplin, Miller, Lambert,

Brazier and Wiertola on April 7th, at Chicago, caused to be printed in an issue of a newspaper called "Solidarity" of that date, the pre- amble of the Industrial Workers of the World, which is then set out here. That Haywood, on August 13th, 1917, at Chicago, sent a letter to The Workers Socialist Publishing Bureau, at Duluth; and that other persons subsequent to April 6, 1917, at various times and in various places, did the various things specifically enumerated in this count one . . . each and all as having been overt acts. . . .

The second count of this indictment charges a conspiracy on the part of the same defendants . . . to injure, oppress, threaten and intimidate citizens of the United States in the exercise and enjoy- ment of certain rights and privileges. . . . The names of these per- sons so charged to have been the intended victims of this alleged conspiracy, being unknown to the grand jurors, and not set out; but being referred to by the indictment as a class of persons who intended to or desired to or had a right to furnish to the United States, various things to be used by the United States government in carrying into effect of the joint resolution of April 6th, declaring the existence of a state of war between the United States and Ger- many. . . . This count further charges that the defendants, to give effect to the conspiracy charged against the defendants in the sec- ond count, did the things I have referred to as the overt acts set out in the first count.

The third count then charges the defendants, during the period of time in question [passage of the Selective Service Law on May 18, 1917, to the day of the indictment] conspired together and with oth- ers to commit a great many offenses, consisting in aiding, abetting, counseling, commanding, inducing and procuring a great many per- sons, members of the I.W.W. organization . . . to commit the offense of each failing to register. . . . And . . . inducing . . . others . . . to desert the service. This third count then charges that the defen- dants, or some of them, to give effect to the conspiracy charged in the third count, did the things . . . which I have informed you are set out in the first count, under the heading of overt acts. . . .

Coming now to the fourth count. . . . On the 15th day of June, 1917, the Congress of the United States passed what is generally and commonly referred to as the "Espionage Act." This act contains the provision that if two or more persons conspire to violate the provisions of sections 2 or 3 of Title 1 of the Espionage Act, and one or more of such persons does any act to carry into effect the conspiracy, or to effect the object of the conspiracy, each of the parties shall be subject to the penalty provided in that Act. . . . The fourth count charges that from the date of the enactment of the Espionage Act . . . to the date of the indictment, these defendants being members of the I.W.W. organization . . . conspired together and with each other and with other persons to commit the first of the offenses which I have just referred to here created by section 3; that is, of wilfully causing or attempting to cause insubordination, disloyalty or refusal of duty in the military or naval forces of the United States while this country is at war. This count then proceeds to charge the defendants, with other persons, that the conspiracy charged in this count was also to commit the second offense. That is, of wilfully obstructing the recruiting or the enlistment service of the United States; the charges in the fourth count of the indictment being that both of these offenses were to be committed in time of war by the means set forth in the fourth count, which you will have in your hands while you are deliberating, and which you may refer to for your fuller and further complete information as to their nature, and which I will refer to generally as consisting of solicitation—personal solicitation, of delivering speeches, of articles printed and circulated in certain newspapers throughout the United States, and the public distribution of certain pamphlets."[20]

The list of overt acts was "almost laughable. They provided no instances of IWW sabotage, no examples of IWW violence, not even the name of a single union member who had refused to register for the draft."[21] The twenty "acts" consisted only of writings by IWW members. The "conspiracy" consisted of membership in the organization.

COOK COUNTY JAIL

Convinced of their innocence and feeling that they should stand as one, Haywood urged all indicted Wobblies to surrender themselves to the nearest federal agent. They did so. In his biography of Haywood, Peter Carlson provides a moving vignette involving a young fruit picker who would one day sit on the Supreme Court of the United States.

> In Yakima, Washington, nineteen-year-old William O. Douglas learned from a local newspaper that a trainload of IWW defendants was being shipped through the city on its way east to Chicago. Douglas decided to greet his beloved Wobblies as they passed by.
>
> "I went down to the railroad and waited for hours," he wrote. "The train that passed through Yakima was not carrying men on display. These were sealed boxcars carrying human beings, thirty or forty in each car. The authorities were taking outcasts through our city. There were no toilets, no food, no water, just sealed boxcars with these poor bastards inside. I walked home with tears in my eyes. I thought of all the pompous members of the Establishment in Yakima who should have been in those cars. The men who were there had only tried to increase the benefits to working people.[22]

The defendants moved from one misery to another. The Cook County jail was a hellhole when Eugene V. Debs was confined there in 1894: crowded cells, slimy floors, vermin, giant rats.[23] In 1917 it was not much different: a dark, dank, six-by-eight-foot cell held three or four Wobblies for twenty hours a day; prison fare was skimpy and nauseating. One Wobbly died; one went insane.[24] My father had been in Louisiana jails, but it took Chicago to educe the only note of panic in all his writings.

Ida S. Doree
1102 N. 40th St, City
Oct. 5, 1917

My dearest little Chiky:

I have the right to write so will use it. How is baby? How are you? I am feeling O.K. except for my stomach. It is a little bad. Chiky, write to me. You can write all you wish. Write often. Why are we not bailed out? Do you know? Seems to me that they ought to be able to get bail in a week. As soon as you get this letter bring or send down some money and send some tobacco—chewing tobacco. No one has been to see either Nef or me since Tuesday. I have had no tobacco since Wednesday. Say, Chiky get them to rush that bail. If this bunch cant get it, wire to Lever to come. His address 435 South Broadway, Baltimore. Also, you take baby and go out and see Otto Osterlund, at his drug store 4600 Baltimore St. take the No. 34 car going west. Try to get him to go my bail. You know they were great friends of the folks. Phone to [attorney] Cohen to come in to see us at once. Must see him. Tell Feige to come in to see Nef. You come again Monday if we are not out before. Bring baby.

> Your loving hubby, Ed

Don't forget to phone Cohen at once.

As the fall and winter wore on, the Wobbly prisoners organized themselves.

They voluntarily scrubbed their cellblock clean and promptly established their own institutions. They gathered a lending library composed of books donated by sympathizers. . . . The Wobblies also published their own newspaper, the Can Opener. Handwritten and passed from cell to cell, it abounded in the IWW's own brand of black humor. . . . In the mornings they exercised and in the afternoons they held educational meetings in which miners, lumberjacks, railroad workers, shiphands, and harvesters lectured on the fine points of their trades. On Sundays the Wobblies produced their own jailhouse variety shows, complete with songs, satirical skits, and short plays.[25]

PREPARING THE DEFENSE

The IWW had little choice in the matter of an attorney. Clarence Darrow was approached, but he declined, indicating that he was too busy, though he offered some staff assistance.[26] Few lawyers were willing to take on this unpopular cause in a time of such high feeling. Wobbly attorneys had been threatened, even tarred and feathered. The courageous

and optimistic George F. Vanderveer, who had defended Wobblies in
Everett, Washington, agreed to become what the press would call "counsel to the damned."

Gurley Flynn had urged separation of the cases, arguing that a mass
trial would submerge individual considerations and lead to mass convictions.[27] But Vanderveer saw the trial as an opportunity to put before the
American people the justice of the IWW cause. "Van" assured the defendants that they had committed no crime. He was confident that the government case would fail. There was no German gold. Organizing was not
illegal. The Socialist Party had officially adopted an antiwar position, but
the IWW, after debating the issue, decided formally upon a policy of neu-
trality with respect to the war. Each member was left to his own conscience in the matter of draft registration and military service. True, IWW
members had written, sometimes vehemently, against the war before the
United States became a belligerent, and a few individual members continued to object after that, but in point of fact 95 percent of the Wobblies
registered for the draft. "The IWW had never opposed conscription, nor
had any individual member refused conscription on organisation orders
or been found guilty of insubordination while in the armed services."[28]

Some of the Chicago prisoners, my father among them, were released
on bail that winter of 1917–1918 to help prepare the case for the defense.
The difficulties were formidable. Because the leaders were rounded up,
the IWW offices were now staffed by new people unacquainted with the
work. Hundreds of Wobblies were being thrown into prison all over the
country, all requiring legal defense. Financing had to be secured in large
amounts, and literature denying the charges and appealing for aid had to
be distributed. Then, methodically and illegally, the government acted to
cripple the Wobblies' defense efforts. These are the "crooked works" my
father refers to in his letter of November 24, 1918.

In 1921, my father prepared two notarized affidavits attesting to the government's actions. The first documents the disappearance, while in government hands, of evidence my father needed personally. It reads, in part:

> A defense was offered. One of the principal reasons why it was not
> a complete defense was because of the mysterious disappearance of
> many letters and documents, favorable to the defendants, between

the time of the unlawful siezure of these letters and documents from the offices of the I.W.W. and homes of the defendants on September 5th, 1917, and the time, some Five or Six Months later, when counsel for the defense was permitted to examine these letters and documents, then being held in rooms of the Dept. of Justice on the 8th floor of the Post Office Building in Chicago. . . .

I am unable to speak specifically of the correspondence of other defendants which was reported by them as missing, but I am fully able to tell of letters received and written by myself. . . . These following letters I know were on file and were seized by government officials. I have never seen them since . . . although I, personally, went carefully over what government agents declared was all the correspondence seized from the office of the Textile Workers Industrial Union. . . .

Some time in the month of May, 1917, I received two letters, one from the Peoples Council of Philadelphia . . . and one from the Philadelphia Local of the Socialist Party. . . . Each letter asked if I would consent to become a speaker at proposed anti-conscription meetings. I wrote a separate reply to each letter, each reply containing about the same subject matter. . . . I made it clear that much as I hated war, war was now a fact . . . and that I, for one did not propose to oppose either the war or conscription, that I did not believe in wasting my time barking at the moon, that I would register for the draft and would ask no man not to do what I myself proposed to do. . . . Neither these letters to me nor the carbon copies of my replies to same could be found nor did the prosecution produce them upon my personal request to them. . . . These two letters are the only ones written by me in which my position on the world war was stated. The loss of them was a most serious blow to my defense. . . . Some time in August of 1917, I appeared for physical examination before my draft board (the 50th) of Philadelphia and was exempted because of the loss of two fingers of the right hand. These exemption papers were kept in the safe in Room 507, Parkway Bldg., Philadelphia, and was taken in the raid. I was unable to locate them and the prosecution did not produce them upon my request for same.

The second affidavit spells out the government abuses more generally.

This review is made by me (one of those convicted in the Chicago
I.W.W. "conspiracy" case) because my position as a member of the
General Defense Committee of the Industrial Workers of the World
brought me into close personal contact with all phases of defense
work of the I.W.W. I became a member of the General Defense
Committee (G.D.C.) on about October 20th, 1917, and served continually on that committee until about July 15th, 1918, and was treasurer of the G.D.C. from about October 20th, 1917 to about February
20th, 1918.

. . . The function of this committee was to raise funds, secure
legal counsel, locate witnesses, give relief, etc., etc.

. . . I gave my full time as treasurer, and was at all times in personal touch with all matters hereinafter set forth.

This review is given to aid those who are now working in behalf
of the I.W.W. political prisoners now held, on sentences ranging
from 5 to 20 years each, in the Federal Penitentiary at Leavenworth,
Kansas. Without this information, one may look upon the testimony
given in court on behalf of the defendants as the best that they could
possibly produce. . . .

It is my purpose here to show that government agents, or agents
purporting to represent the government, did wilfully hamper the
defendants and their committee in their efforts to lawfully secure
funds, witnesses and information essential to their defense in court.

. . . By the middle of December 1917 moneys were coming in the
G.D.C. at the rate of about $1,000. daily. During this time hundreds
of thousands of defense circulars, papers and letters had been scattered to all parts of the United States.

. . . The first interference with publicity work of the G.D.C. was
the denial of second class mailing privileges to newspapers published by the G.D.C. The papers were then mailed at third class
rates. The Post Office officials at no time stated that the papers were
unmailable. Regular postage rates were paid, yet the Post Office
Department confiscated all defense newspapers entrusted to them
for delivery. No postage was ever returned nor did they ever refuse

to accept the papers. Only a few copies of some issues were ever delivered.

. . . Because only two attorneys could be secured to handle the Chicago Case, . . . the task of securing witnesses was largely taken over by members of the G.D.C., mostly through correspondence through mail channels. Locating witnesses for the Chicago Case was very difficult because most of the defendants tried in Chicago were brought there from all parts of the United States, from Mass. to California, from Texas to Minnesota. Information and witnesses had to be secured in all these sections. Mails had to be used as we were financially unable to resort to any other method. About twenty-five letters, concerning matters relating to the investigations and to securing of witnesses and the nature of their testimony, were handled daily by the G.D.C. in the early part of December, 1917.

So the affairs stood, when on December 17th, 1917, an army of city police and U.S. deputy marshalls, armed with an admittedly void search and seizure warrant, swooped down upon Defense Headquarters at 1001 W. Madison St., Chicago, Ill. Immediately all work was ordered stopped. The I.W.W. Publishing Bureau which was printing defense literature to the exclusion of every thing else, was completely closed, and not even a watchman was permitted on the premises.

. . . After the building had been cleared . . . the police settled into chairs and searched for nothing. Nothing was disturbed. No one was arrested. There could have been but one motive actuating this raid and that is to cripple our defense. . . . For the first ten days of the raid nothing occurred except that the stack of mail coming in grew larger and larger. The police did not open or disturb these letters.

A search and seizure warrant becomes void in ten days time by statutory limitation, and the warrant in this came became now, doubly void. Yet the police remained. It was not until the twelfth day . . . that they were compelled to leave by 4 p.m. under court order. Shortly after noon of the day a ten-ton truck was backed up to the side door of 1001 W. Madison St., and defense literature, circular letters, envelopes, contribution lists and even a vast amount of blank paper was loaded into it and taken out. Most of the literature was packed in unmarked boxes. The seizing party had no idea what these boxes contained. They took everything that looked like literature, irrespective of what message it contained. . . .

. . . Because of this raid, we got out of touch with many witnesses, and were unable to properly finance investigators and attorneys. We could not, during the raid, acknowledge receipt of moneys donated, nor send out appeals to possible contributors. We were prevented from protesting our innocence to the world while a hostile daily press screamed with lies about "German Gold."

Following the raid, a month of comparative quiet reigned. . . .

About the first of February, 1918, came the most stinging blow yet administered to the defense. The Post Office Department, without notification to the G.D.C. or without even the slightest hint as to their intention, held up all out-going mail of the defense. . . . About the 10th of February, 1918, the Chicago "Tribune" carried a news article which stated, in effect, that the Post Office Department at Chicago was holding, and would not deliver, 300 bags of mail matter sent out by the I.W.W. Then later, someone, unknown to us, and who signed himself as "P.O. Employee" caused an envelope to be placed under the door at 1001 W. Madison St. . . . He enclosed what purported to be an official notice to certain P.O. employes notifying them what particular mail to hold up. Among those listed . . . were the General Defense Committee; J. W. Wilson, secretary of the G.D.C., E. F. Doree, treasurer of the G.D.C., C. F. Payne, editor and manager of the Defense News Bulletin . . . and others connected with the defense work.

With this evidence in hand, our attorney, Mr. Geo. H. Vanderveer went to see Mr. Stewart, postmaster at Chicago, in an effort to learn the truth of the matter. Mr. Stewart denied that mail was being held up at the Chicago Post Office.

. . . Mail deposited in the Chicago P.O. on February 1st, 1918 and later, was released, at least in part, on the 26th, 27th, 28th and 29th of the following July. . . .

When it first became apparent that our mail was not being delivered, the G.D.C. began to use the services of various express companies to deliver our messages, literature and appeals. In the latter part of February, 1918, the American Express Co., returned to the office of the G.D.C., a truck load of defense material which they had previously collected. The packages were marked "Refused by the order of the U.S. Gov't." Who, representing the government issued this order we could never find out. But we had the use of no more express service until nearly the end of the Chicago Trial.

Coming as all this did in the months immediately preceding the beginning of the trial of the Chicago Case, one can readily imagine its effect upon the trial. Scores of witnesses were lost. Letters notifying witnesses when to appear to testify were generally not delivered.

. . . The denial of mail service did more to hamper the G.D.C. and attorneys in their work to secure a "fair and impartial trial" than did the intimidation of witnesses . . . the "losing" of many letters favorable to the defense . . . than, perhaps, all the other seemingly unworthy and dishonorable methods pursued by public officials to send men to the penitentiary for many years each.

THE TRIAL

When the trial finally began, it consisted mainly of the two sides talking past each other. The Wobblies tried to teach the world what they were doing and why they were doing it. They described the labor conditions they fought to change. The government tried to show that the defendants belonged to the IWW in full knowledge of its radical agenda.

My father's testimony provides a sample of this non-dialogue. His task was to describe the conditions of labor—and of attempting to organize labor—as he had experienced them in the Louisiana logging camps. Vanderveer guided him through direct testimony with questions about his personal background, then jumped directly to questions about Louisiana.

Q *Your name is Edward F. Doree?*
A Edwin F.

Q *You are a defendant in this case?*
A Yes, sir.

Q *Conspirator?*
(No response.)

Q *How old are you, Doree?*
A Twenty-nine years old.

Q *Are you registered for military service?*
A Yes, sir.

Q. *In the interests of brevity, we will skip a good many years. Did you have occasion to go down to Louisiana, in behalf of the I.W.W.?*[29]

My father's description of his experiences there fills thirty-six pages in the transcript of the trial. Another nine pages cover his direct testimony about IWW textile workers and, especially, the marine transport workers, stressing their war work.

Q *Was Philadelphia an important point for the shipment of munitions?*
A I should say it was.

Q *What percentage of the munitions handled over the Philadelphia docks during the year 1917, were handled by members of the I.W.W. organization?*
A 100 per cent. We had job control.

Q *Where were these men employed?*
A Employed from all—what do you mean? Employed on the docks.

Q *Where was the employment contracted for?*
A In the headquarters, the I.W.W. hall. . . .

Q *What percent of the seamen,—firemen,—marine firemen, sailing out of Philadelphia, are members of the I.W.W., if you know?*
A Well, practically the fire holds of all vessels.

Q *What?*
A Firemen, engineers, oilers, water tenders on practically all coastwise vessels are I.W.W.'s.

Q *Now, I want you to tell the jury whether or not, there were any accidents or explosions, or any labor troubles during the year* 1917, *on the Philadelphia docks and navy yards?*

A The Philadelphia docks, where the I.W.W. worked, there were no explosions, and we had no strikes. I believe it was the only dock on the coast [where that was so].

Q *Do you know how the water front of New York is organized if at all?*
A The docks of New York are virtually unorganized.

Q *Do you know what trouble they had with explosions up there at the same period?*
A Well, only what I read, in the newspapers. They were blowed up every once in a while.

MR. NEBEKER: I object and move to strike it out.
THE COURT: Strike it out. . . .

Q *Now, have you at any time during the year* 1917 *been identified with any strike that involved the curtailment of production in anything essential to the conduct of the war?*
A No strikes at all.

Q *No strikes at all?*
A No, sir.

Q *Did anybody ever ask you to do that in this organization?*
A No, we have not been hunting for any strikes.

Q *Has anybody conspired with you along that line or you with them?*
A No, sir.

Q *Have you ever tried to incite insubordination in the service?*
A No, not at all.[30]

The prosecutor, Mr. Nebeker, began his cross-examination:

Q *Mr. Doree, did you during* 1917, *have copies of Solidarity in the organization down where you were active?*
A I believe all of them. I believe so.

Q *And read them all?*
A Oh, I wouldn't say I read them all, but I had them all.

Q *Were they circulated among the membership down there?*
A They were circulated through our office practically to all branches of the Union.

Q *They came to you, I suppose, in bundles, did they not?*
A No; they did not come to me. They went practically from the paper to the branches and we paid the bill.

Q *Well, they would come in bundles, would they?*
A To the branches, yes.

Q *To the branches, and then they would be handed out by the branch secretaries to the members?*
A I presume so.

Q *Or sold?*
A Well, whichever the branch desired to do with them. That was optional.

Q *And was it so with the Industrial Worker?*
A We got—yes, I had a bundle order with the Industrial Worker.

Q *You have read all of the so-called literature of the I.W.W., haven't you, Mr. Doree?*
A I don't think so.

Q *Well, but you have read the various works on sabotage?*
A I believe so.

Q Pouget?
A Yes, I read Pouget.

Q *And Elizabeth Gurley Flynn?*
A Yes, sir; I have read all of them on sabotage.

Q *Walker C. Smith?*
A Yes.

Q *As far as you know, you have read practically all of the literature that is advertised by the I.W.W., have you not?*
A Well, if I did not, it was just pure laziness. I think I have. . . .

Q *Did you keep informed as to what was said in the papers from time to time about the attitude of the I.W.W. on the war?*
A I read some of it, yes, sir.

Q *Well, you knew of the general policy, I assume. . . .*
A That was, I believe the policy of the I.W.W.; keep your mouth shut about the war entirely.

Q *Even you might have very strong notions about the war, not to say anything about it.*
A That is what I think was what we should have done entirely. We did pretty well.

Q *Well, now, Mr. Doree, do I understand that from your activities down there, with respect to registering yourself, and what you said to other people about registering, that you were in favor of their registering, and that you were in favor of the war?*
A I was not in favor of the war. I cannot bring myself to favor any war or any strike, or any other trouble. I do not like trouble, I have had too much of it.

Q *Did you know, during 1917, that the I.W.W. members in different sections of the country were carrying on the activities shown by the correspondence and by those papers and documents that were read by the government?*
A I knew that they were carrying on strikes.

Q *Well, did you know in a general way that they were carrying on the various activities shown by these various documents.*

A I guess in a general way.

Q *You were spending all of your time during the same period, working for the I.W.W.?*

A 18 hours a day.

Q *18 hours a day for $18 a week?*

A Twenty-one.

Q *Twenty-one dollars a week, doing nothing else except advancing the interests of the organization?*

A To the best of my ability.

Q *During the whole of the period covered by the indictment?*

A The entire period.

Q *Do you remember of saying in that letter, dated August 20, 1917*

MR. VANDERVEER: He said he wrote it. Are you offering it in evidence?

MR. NEBEKER: It is already in evidence. I don't think it was read, perhaps. It is addressed to William D. Haywood. . . . "Going up for physical discrimination tomorrow." Do you remember that?

A Yes.

Q *What did you mean by "physical discrimination"?*

A Well, if you want to know, I will tell you.

Q *I do, or I would not have asked it.*

A I believed, following the returns of the registration, that there was a heavier percentage leaving the working class district than there were the more select districts of Philadelphia.

Q *And by that you mean that the war boards and the officers who had that matter in hand, were discriminating against men of your class?*

A I believed so.[31]

Leavenworth, Kansas, _Feb. 9_ ____191 9

Mrs. Ida S. Doree, Box 25, Rex, Oregon.

My dearest sweetheart

Your two letters which arrived during this last week were a pleasure to me. They report you all well and happy. That's fine. I also got the joint letter from Edna and mamma. I shall answer them first. But before, I got a fine letter from fellow worker J. Gaches, a colored lad, in Maryville Louisiana. He says he and the boys are more active than ever. We shall give a cheer yet for the old south. Also got a letter from Urdiss. She sent on $1.00 that someone had asked to be sent to me. She reports everything progressing nicely.

Now for mamma's letter. Thanks very much for your fine birthday greetings. I really appreciate reaching the sober age of 30 years. You see up to that age its hustle and bustle and climb, from that time on, one sits down and slides down. Its so much easier, you know. Oh yes. Don't let any more conscientious objector releases interest you so far as I am concerned. I never was and am not now, a conscientious objector. There are some good fellows among them - some, I said, a few - the most of them are

Typical page from one of Doree's letters to his wife. The prison stationery, on good-quality paper, is pre-printed "Post Office Box 7, Leavenworth, Kansas." *Photograph courtesy of Labadie Collection.*

Leavenworth, Kansas. May 4 1919

Miss Agnes Inglis, % Davidow,
726 Penobscot Bldg,, Detroit, Mich.

My dear Fellow Worker:

It is with a peculiarly mixed feeling that I write you now. I am sure that the Action of Clyne and the court has struck you far harder than it did me. I had really expected their most vicious opposition, and the news of their action struck me at a most psychological time, — I was reading John Reed's "The Ten Days that Shook the World". There I was reading of what the old Russian regime was doing — all the while wishing I were there to experience it — and, lo! and behold! I received the wire from Christensen that told me (in effect) that I must remain in prison longer, because of the vindictiveness and hatred of our masters, then — I wished no longer — I knew I was living in the "reacting" of the struggles of Russia under the Czar and Kerensky.

These are great days for the revolutionist. We are living today in the greatest period of all history — even if in prison. Much more persecution will drive the great mass to action. We must remember that the ways of the many (like the Hebrew God) are mysterious. We can never really determine what they will do next.

Letter from Doree to Agnes Inglis of Ann Arbor, Michigan, May 4, 1919. Inglis and friends posted bond, which permitted Doree freedom to help prepare an appeal of the Chicago Hundred's conviction. *Photograph courtesy of Labadie Collection.*

I. W. W. LONGSHOREMEN TIE UP SHIPPING IN PHILADELPHIA

"HOLD FAST, BUDDIE, WE GOT 'EM"

Doree cartoon that appeared in the *One Big Union Monthly* in 1920. While free pending an appeals verdict, Doree worked for the Philadelphia maritime worker's union. The racial equality depicted here was fundamental to the IWW philosophy. *Photograph courtesy of Walter P. Reuther Library.*

Doree with four-year-old Bucky, Chiky, her sister Feige and Feige's husband, Walter Nef. Taken in 1921, just before Ed and Walter returned to Leavenworth after two years' release on bond. *Photograph courtesy of Walter P. Reuther Library.*

Kansas City, 1921. IWW prisoners about to return to prison. The appeals court had reversed two of the four counts against the Chicago Hundred; but the Supreme Court declined to hear their appeal on the remaining two counts. Ben Fletcher is second from right in the front row. E. F. Doree is second from right and Walter T. Nef is fourth from left in the second row. IWW leader "Big Bill" Haywood and several others failed to return to finish their sentences. *Photograph courtesy of Walter P. Reuther Library.*

Arrest Miss Ellen Winsor and Mrs. Rebecca Evans

Clubwomen Accused of Disorderly Conduct in Their Activity at Metropolitan Opera House Meeting in Behalf of Political Prisoners

Miss Ellen Winsor, of Haverford, and Mrs. Rebecca Evans, of Ardmore, clubwomen, were arrested last night at the Metropolitan Opera House on charges of "disorderly conduct, breach of the peace and inciting to riot."

They were arraigned before Magistrate Carney at the Twentieth and Buttonwood streets station today and held by the magistrate in $500 bail for further hearing at 10 o'clock tomorrow.

The arrest of the women, who are among the most prominent in Philadelphia club circles, and members of old and prominent Philadelphia families, was due to their activity in behalf of political war prisoners who are in the Federal penitentiaries.

There has been a movement on foot for some time to obtain presidential clemency for the prisoners, many of whom are under heavy sentence for wartime offenses. Petitions have been circulated widely, and thousands of signatures appended to them.

Miss Winsor and Mrs. Evans took such a petition to the Metropolitan last night and sought to get signatures from the audience as they entered.

It was testified before the magistrate today that all had gone well until the women were asked to desist requesting signatures. They refused, it was said, and the theatre management sent for a patrolman.

Patrolman McCort, of the Twentieth and Buttonwood streets station, arrested them and appeared against them today.

Magistrate Carney explained his reason for holding his two prominent prisoners in bail for a further hearing.

MISS ELLEN WINSOR

"This is no time for disorder," the magistrate said, "with President Harding and every one else making efforts to promote peace. I feel that we had better leave the running of the country to the President and the Congress. It was for this reason that I held Miss Winsor and Mrs. Evans."

'I WANT MY DADDY,' IS CHILDREN'S PLEA

Group of 34 Youngsters Here From West Ask Pardons for Fathers in Leavenworth

WILL SEE PRESIDENT

A sober-faced group of thirty-four children from the Southwest, whose fathers are in Leavenworth Federal prison for sedition during the war, arrived in Philadelphia at 11 o'clock this morning.

The tired-looking group ranged from babes in arms to boys of fifteen and sixteen, a Children's Group for A—

They are on their way to an interview. Presi—

Prominent Philadelphians agitated for the release of Wobblies Doree, Fletcher, Nef, and Walsh of that city. Ellen Winsor and her sister, Rebecca Winsor Evans, were arrested in 1922 for demonstrating on behalf of the convicts. *Photograph courtesy of the Labadie Collection.*

AN APPEAL

In the name of

JUSTICE

Ask President Harding to pardon

FOUR PHILADELPHIANS

unjustly convicted and NOW SERVING

long terms in Leavenworth Prison

EDWARD F. DOREE, sentenced to 10 Years
BENJ. H. FLETCHER, sentenced to 10 Years
WALTER T. NEF, sentenced to 20 Years
JOHN J. WALSH, sentenced to 10 Years

Philadelphia
Civil Liberties Committee

E. Lewis Burnham, Chairman, 1400 Morris Bldg.
Edward W. Evans   Mrs. Ellen Middleton Cope
Miss Mary H. Ingham   Edmund C. Evans
Miss Sophia H. Dulles

READ THIS STATEMENT CAREFULLY
WRITE TO PRESIDENT HARDING ! !

Cover page of a pamphlet published the Philadelphia Civil Liberties Co mittee. *Photograph courtesy of the La die Collection.*

AMNESTY FOR POLITICAL PRISONERS

HEARING
BEFORE THE
COMMITTEE ON THE JUDICIARY
HOUSE OF REPRESENTATIVES
SIXTY-SEVENTH CONGRESS
SECOND SESSION

ON

H. J. RES. 60

Serial 31

MARCH 16, 1922

WASHINGTON
GOVERNMENT PRINTING OFFICE
1922

On March 16, 1922, the House Committee on the Judiciary held hearings on a bill favoring amnesty to political prisoners. Several witnesses appeared to testify on behalf of the four Philadelphians. *Photograph courtesy of the Labadie Collection.*

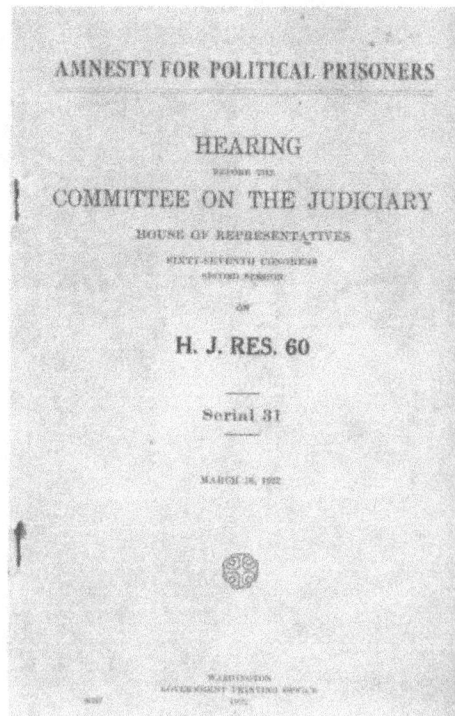

S. PRISONER PEERS
T SON NEAR DEATH

F. Doree, on Leave from Leavenworth, May Only Glance
Through Door at Child

EAR JOY MAY BE FATAL

Very still, and very white, with just
flickering of the eyelids, just a flutter
A thin chest beneath bedclothes to
ll that life still lingered, a pale little
y lay in his bed today in the Episco-
l hospital.

The door of the room was open, just
crack. Through the crack peered a
n, spectacled face, set off by a stiff
pindour wave of black hair, shot
th gray, and a heavy black mustache
pair of burning eyes looked anxiously
the half-darkened room. Then the
e softened, and a few tears fell.

And this was the culmination of days
frantic effort, of wire-pulling at
shington, of official telegraphing half
across a continent, of the opening
the doors of Fort Leavenworth pris-
in Kansas, and the trip of a wor-
d father, under guard of a U. S.
rshal, from the prison to the hospital.
All this was in order that Edward
Doree, Philadelphia I. W. W. leader,
o in 1918 was sentenced to a ten-
ar Federal penitentiary term with
orty-six others tried at once before
dge K. M. Landis in Chicago Federal
urt for violation of wartime espionage
t, might see his five-year-old son,
ddy. Buddy has just a bare chance
to live. Endocarditis—inflammation of
that inner heart membrane—has followed pneumonia, and the child is very
weak.

So weak is he, and so close to the
border between life and death, that
when the father, released from prison
for five days, arrived at North Philadelphia station today, he was told
physicians had said the only way he
could see his son was to peer through
the door at him. Should Buddy see his
father, the medical men said, the excitement, born of joy, might swing the
delicate balance between life and death,
and kill him.

So the father's impulse to clasp to
his breast the little boy he has not seen
since he was little more than a year
old, had to be quelled, and the end of
the long journey was just that minute-
long peering through the crack of the
door.

Doree's leave is to last only five days,
no matter what happens. Perhaps tomorrow, and the next day, and the
next, he may return again to peer
through the door. Or it may be that
before the father leaves, the son will be
getting well, so well his father dare
clasp him, ever so gently. Or it may be
that before he takes the train back to
the prison, the father will follow a
little coffin to the grave.

The release from prison was brought
about, the care of the boy in the hospital and the expenses of the long trip
of marshal and prisoner financed, by
the influence of a group of liberal-mind-

ted with his wife, Doree's wife, who
greeted her husband at North Philadelphia station on his arrival at 5 A. M.
with J. S. Biddle, United States Marshal, and brother of the warden of
Leavenworth. The entire party, after
the members of Doree's family had kissed him and expressed affectionate greeting, had breakfast at the station. Then

Continued on Page Two, Column Three.

In April 1922 Bucky Doree was near death. In an unprecedented action, Doree was permitted to travel, in custody, to Philadelphia. *Photograph courtesy of the Labadie Collection.*

Leavenworth, Kansas *April 12* 192 2

My dearest little sweetheart,

Well, I got back this morning, and tonight I received your letter of the 9th. Your wire was here when I arrived, and you may believe me that I was so glad to hear that our Bucky Boy is so improved. And it is so good know that you rested so well. That's fine. Very fine. We were somewhat storm bound on our road here and nearly all our trains were delayed.

This letter is the only one I shall write tonight as I'm so sleepy. I slept all afternoon and am going right away to "hit the hay" again. I expect to see the warden tomorrow and then I shall know better what I might be able to do.

Gee, girlie, I surely got a fine sympathetic reception here. When I came into the Clothing Department, the boys fairly climbed over each other to greet me with such real enthusiasm. They seemed so genuinely happy to know that our little boy was getting better. It was really remarkable how they had followed our trouble in the papers. Our pictures have been published in all sections of the country and very fine

Ed wrote Chiky as soon as he returned to Leavenworth. *Photograph courtesy of the Labadie Collection.*

If he had not been ill, Bucky would have joined with other children of political prisoners to petition the president. Instead, as the *Philadelphia Evening Bulletin* reported, the "Children's Crusade" came to see him. *Photograph courtesy of the Labadie Collection.*

PUBLIC

Published daily and Sunday, $15 a year by mail.
Entered as second-class matter at the postoffice
in Philadelphia under Act of March 3, 1879.

PARDON AWAITS CONVICT
HURRYING TO HIS SICK CHILD

The picture shows Edward F. Doree and his wife and their son
"Bucky," who now lies ill, perhaps at the point of death

Father-Love Brings Boon to Philadelphian Imprisoned
in Federal Penitentiary for Violation of Espionage
Act When Senator Pepper Learns of Man's Devotion

A father's love for his five-year-old boy has won the parent a pardon from the United States Government. The parent does not know yet that Uncle Sam beneath that grizzled exterior has granted the boon, and the man will not know it until he reaches his son's bedside at 2231 Oxford street. Edward F. Doree is the convict thus freed from serving his ten-year sentence in the Federal Penitentiary at Fort Leavenworth, Kan., where he has been imprisoned for violation of the Espionage Act in wartime.

The convict's wife believes he will reach home today.

The boy is "Bucky," who was ill in the Episcopal Hospital last April with heart trouble. The father then came East to see his son, but the physicians would not permit the elder more than a glimpse through a door ajar. Now the child is again facing death, and the physicians hold but slight hope for his recovery.

Senator Pepper learned of the case last spring. He interested himself in all its details, studied the phases of the crime that Doree, an I. W. W. member and dock-worker, had committed, and then resolved that he would bend all his energies to freeing the man. The pardon will be given him when he steps across the threshold to his boy's room, it is believed, for it awaits only President Harding's signature, and, it was said yesterday at Senator Pepper's office, that that would be forthcoming in time.

Mrs. Doree, the boy's mother, too, has been working hard for her husband's freedom, and recently she gained the help of Mrs. Charles Edward Russell, an advocate of freedom for political prisoners.

One of the decisions facing Mrs. Doree pending the arrival of her husband is whether the boy shall undergo an operation.

"How can I decide without my husband," she exclaimed. "It is not right that I should do so. They love each other so, and I think his father's right to help decide whether to risk an operation."

Mrs. Doree said she had had telegrams from Washington from Leavenworth and from her husband on his way East. He asked her to send him $50.

"I have no money. I could send him nothing," she said. "I have not a friend in the city. They are all gone. For a while I tried dressmaking, and then my health failed, and my friends have had to support 'Bucky' and me."

In late summer, Bucky suffered a relapse and Doree was again permitted, in custody, to go to Philadelphia. *Photograph courtesy of the Labadie Collection.*

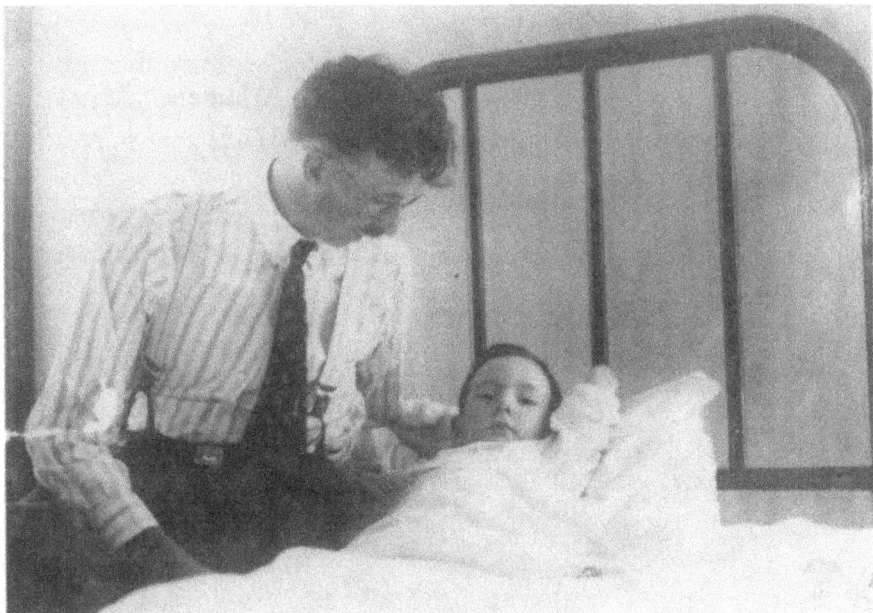

E. F. Doree with Bucky, 1922. *Photograph courtesy of Walter P. Reuther Library.*

While in Philadelphia, Doree received this telegram. *Photograph courtesy of the Labadie Collection.*

E. F. Doree's pardon, signed by President Harding. *Photograph courtesy of the Labadie Collection.*

And so it went, the defendants trying to get the jury to understand their focus on the fight for labor and the prosecution educing from Wobbly speeches and writings evidence of conspiracy to obstruct the war effort. Judge Landis permitted the prosecution to use prewar statements as evidence of wartime intentions. For unknown reasons, Vanderveer declined to make any closing argument to the jury. Following his review of the indictments (extracted above), Judge Landis's instructions to the jury set up the slippery slope.

> The defendants are . . . on trial for the offenses charged in these four counts of the indictment, as I have indicated to you their meaning. That is, having entered into the conspiracy set out in these counts, and . . . having done the things these counts charge them having done to give effect to this conspiracy. They are not on trial for anything else. For instance, they are not on trial here on a charge of having blown up threshing machines, as a separate, independent offense. They are not on trial here on charge of having driven spikes in trees or logs. They are not on trial here on a charge of having done anything anywhere save only the charge of conspiracy as I have defined the charge of conspiracy set out in the various counts of this indictment. All the evidence that has gone to you of acts and doings and sayings prior to the period mentioned in the indictment in the case was admitted by the court to enable the jury to come to an understanding of the frame of mind of the men accused here as conspirators. . . . All the evidence, all the acts and doings before the period covered by this indictment, you will consider with all the other evidence.
>
> . . . I have referred to the distinction between conspiracy to commit a crime, and the crime itself. Now, it is not necessary for you to determine, in determining this question, that the conspiracy which the indictment charges these defendants with having entered into, should have become completely effective, that is, that its objects should have been accomplished completely. To illustrate: It is not necessary that any one person should have refused or failed to register for army service; it is not necessary that any one person should have been rendered completely impotent to furnish supplies to the

Government. . . . It is enough if the evidence shows that a conspiracy was formed and that some defendant did some thing falling within the list of the overt acts set out in the indictment, to carry into effect the object of the conspiracy. Thus, having regard to the charge of conspiracy to prevent registration under the draft law, it need not be shown that any one individual was prevented by the influence or operations of the conspiracy, from registering for army service. It is sufficient if the conspiracy having been established, some defendant did a thing to induce one of the persons referred to in the indictment to refrain from registering under the Draft Law.

Landis's charge to the jury ended with these words:

Now, our industrial society is not on trial here, gentlemen. Organized labor is not on trial. The charge in this indictment is not aimed at organized labor—lawful organized labor. The charge in the indictment is not aimed at any lawful organization. The charge in the indictment is one of crime. Men belonging to what is referred to here as the laboring class have a perfect right to organize. . . . The only limitation upon the right being that they must not use their organization to accomplish an unlawful purpose; a purpose prohibited by law.
   . . . If it appears that these defendants by the processes charged in the indictment, set about solely to better labor conditions as to environment, wages, compensation, and that what they did did not contemplate anything except the bettering of labor conditions as to environment or compensation, then your verdict should be 'not guilty'; with this qualification: that men are chargeable, as I indicated before, with the reasonable, natural and necessary consequences of their acts, and they may not join together with a common purpose to intend to accomplish one object, if, in the accomplishment of that one object which may be lawful, they naturally, reasonably and rationally will accomplish another object which the law prohibits. So in this case, having reference to the count or counts that I am now dealing with, if you find the defendants did come together—that they had a common purpose,—a common understanding to accomplish an object, and that that object was lawful,

but that also there was in the situation, obviously apparent to persons of intelligence, another object which would be accomplished, it being forbidden by law, while they were accomplishing the object itself permitted by law, they should go on with that common understanding of those conditions, doing a thing to give effect to that common understanding, it would be a conspiracy denounced by the statutes of the United States.[32]

The trial had now lasted more than four months. Over forty thousand typewritten pages of evidence had been submitted. Each of one hundred men stood accused on four major counts. Altogether, some ten thousand alleged crimes were to be considered.

The jury retired and deliberated. In half an hour they returned, having found every man guilty on every count! Judge Landis decided the sentences, which were imposed two weeks later. Bill Haywood and fourteen others, including my uncle, Walter Nef, were given the maximum sentence permitted under the law: twenty years in prison. My father and thirty-two others were sentenced to ten years. Thirty-five men were sentenced to five-year terms, and twelve received a year and a day. Two were sentenced to ten days in jail. In addition, Landis imposed fines totaling $2,400,000! The brief, meteoric glory of the IWW was broken forever.

The war had created the setting, machinery, and zeal that made it possible to crush the IWW. The war had motivated Congress to pass the Espionage Act and related legislation. The war had provided the owners of mining, lumber, and grain companies with the persuasive argument that their workers' ability to strike was a threat to the nation. The war had persuaded the Wilson administration to accept the advice of Western governors about how to attack the IWW. The war had created a context of public hysteria and a general readiness to crack down on anyone perceived to be the enemy within. The war had framed the charges and sat in the courtroom.

By 1920 the fever of war was subsiding, and the men out on bond while their cases were being appealed had reasonable hope that their sentences would be dismissed. When it finally acted in October of that year, the United States Seventh District Circuit Court of Appeals dismissed the first two counts, the "industrial counts," but left standing the third and fourth. When, on April 11, 1921, the United States Supreme Court refused to review the lower court's decision, the prisoners remained convicted under the "espionage" counts.

The cage would reclaim my father and the other prisoners—most of them, anyway. "Big Bill" Haywood and eight others jumped bail, Haywood escaping to Russia, where he led an unhappy existence until his death in 1928. He was buried in the Kremlin wall.

5

LEAVENWORTH II

They go wild, simply wild over me,
I'm referring to the bedbug and the flea;
They disturb my slumber deep, and I murmur in my sleep,
They go wild, simply wild over me.

DURING HIS INTERLUDE of freedom, Ed, Chiky, and Bucky left Oregon and returned to Philadelphia. Walter (also released on bond) and Feige were living there, and Local 8, the Philadelphia longshoremen's union, was proving loyal in its support of the prisoners seeking release—unlike the new IWW national leadership in Chicago, which condemned such efforts.

A group of Quakers and other civil libertarians in Philadelphia had rallied to the cause of freeing the four Philadelphia Wobblies: Walter Nef, Benjamin Fletcher, John Walsh, and my father. These champions included the president of Haverford College and people with distinguished Philadelphia family names such as Biddle, Fels, and Dulles. Two eminent families, related to each other by marriage, took my parents personally under their wings. Mrs. James D. Winsor, her daughters Ellen Winsor and Rebecca Winsor Evans, Rebecca's husband Edmund C. Evans, and his brother Edward W. Evans became devoted benefactors, helping the Dorees in the dramatic days that lay ahead.

Following the federal appeals court decision to uphold a portion of the Chicago Hundred's conviction, my father returned to Leavenworth.

April 27, 1921

My dearest little Chiky,

This is the earliest that I could get a letter out to you. How are you? How is little Bucky Boy? And Feige? You will remember me to all the folks in Philadelphia. Let them know that we are doing well. Got a fine reception here. Treated very decently, almost considerately. . . .

[Joe] Gordon and I are celling together and am back in the kitchen. No regular job yet, just helping around, comes easy as you know all about the work, etc. Very few old faces here. We are cheerily greeted by everybody. One old man, however, had tears in his eyes as he shook hands with us.

Let me know all the news on amnesty, pardons, applications for pardons, etc. Let me know what the Philadelphia group is doing. I shall write to Edmund C. Evans tomorrow night, and will outline to him a general program which may be most operative.

Please send me my safety razor, also a looking glass. Get a different shaving brush as that one home will soon fall to pieces.

I wrote to Chicago to send you relief. Have no reply yet, of course. Now, girlie, if you need anything, let me know. I can write out and get some money for you. Don't kill yourself at the dressmaking game. Your time will be better spent meeting folks who will help you to get us out.

Was out this afternoon playing hand-ball. I'm rotten, yet I did come through with a couple winning games. Will soon be back on the winning list again.

Get out and enjoy yourself, see a show once in a while, and above all, see people. You are not in Rex now. We are both better off than when I went in the first time. I feel better at any rate.

Love and many kisses to you, my babies,

Your loving hubby, Ed

Dear Bucky Boy, Papa has gone away from his Bucky Boy for a while. Be good to mamma, my boy. Love from your pop,

Ed

May 1, 1921

Got a letter from the General Defense. They write that they will send you $12 a week. That will help you a whole lot. . . . Did you get the picture we had taken at Kansas City? They have already been forwarded to you I understand.

See that Bucky is asking questions about his dad. He'll soon get over that. Life has none of the serious aspects to him yet. Glad that you are taking this affair easily. I have got so drilled in here again that it is really hard for me to make myself believe that I was out for 22 months. Everything comes natural. . . .

. . . The Knox Resolution passed the Senate and will pass the House next week and we can figure on the President to sign as soon as the resolution leaves the House. Then we will have a technical state of Peace. The President promised to consider amnesty as soon as peace was declared.

. . . I am sure that we both are more mentally at ease now than we would be if we were yet awaiting orders to return here. It is better that the waiting is over.

Now we know that whenever I get out it will be out to stay out. We can figure and plan and do things right. We can live. This infernal "don't know what is next" was maddening.

. . . I will do any honorable or decent thing to get out, sign anything necessary except a petition for pardon. I have done nothing to ask anyones pardon for.

Have written about everything except you and Bucky Boy. But what shall I say? Can any be loved more than I love you both? Yet I find nothing to say except words which do not say what I want to say to you, and to Bucky Boy.

May 8, 1921

Girlie dear, what makes you think I am bitter? I'm not. It's true, of course, that I don't want to stay here and want to do all I can to affect an early release, but, surely one can work for and desire that end, without any bitterness at all. There is no reason to look for a very early release and we must be prepared for some months seperation.

To be perfectly plain, I realize now the real tragedy of prison, not in myself but in the other boys who were never out. They are most in good health and mentally alert, even in the finest spirits. But, they have lost 3½ years. They think of a world as they left it, in the terms peculiar to the day of their imprisonment. They do not begin to understand the outside. They reason from the premise of 3½ years ago, we reason from today. They will not believe that the world has so changed as we point out to them. They cannot understand why we say and advocate certain things. They are still nailing preambles to the mastheads. . . . It is humorous and tragic at once. When they get out they will be misfits for a time at least. Most of them will be useless.

Hope that Gurley [Flynn] and Roger [Baldwin] take over our cases. The G.D.C. will do nothing and nothing is expected of them. Pure nuts!

. . . Now for ourselves. I'm feeling fine and dandy. Haven't been assigned to any particular thing to do yet and am a general helper. Have got over the soreness from playing hand ball and am beginning to play a real game. Seem to have more ambition than when here last time. Want to be doing things all the time. I surely hope I'll get the drawing paper before long. Am sure I will be able to devote a good deal of spare time to it and learn quickly. Will have to do something when I get out and that's about all I can think of that will possibly be of any use.

. . . It seems unnecessary to say again that you must always get out and have as good a time as you can. I know what it means to you. You maybe don't realize how much fresher and finer you looked after being out to a movie even. . . .

Well, girlie dear, I sometimes wish I didn't love you so, I would miss you less. But, till we meet again, my greatest love—and many kisses.

May 15, 1921
Got a very fine and jovial letter from [Chiky's friend] Yetta. . . . Tell Yetta that I'll try to keep that date with her and hope it will be as soon as she expects. My hand-ball training should be good for me when I meet her in mortal combat. My language learned at said hand-ball may not be of the sort peculiar to Strawberry Mansion and tennis. We have no "2 Love" stuff in this game. In fact I fear that both these games carry Biblical phrasology—tennis the "love" side and hand-ball—well, you know "rules is rules" and I'm writing mail which is to be censored. However, if I can play as strong a game of tennis as the game of hand-ball I speak, Yetta hasn't a ghost of a chance.

Saw a fine ball game yesterday. The home team won. If convicts can learn from their errors, our ball team is now the wisest set of men on earth.

. . . You will have to excuse my cutting off, as they supply no more paper here. Be well, you folks, take good care of yourselves. Be happy, and of good cheer. Don't worry at all. It always makes me feel fine when I think of the fact that whenever I get out of here this time it's out to stay out. It will be over. The 5 year men have a year more exactly to do, unless—. 20 Wichita boys will go out in a few days as a result of the recent decision of the Appellate Court. Four years in jail and prison and then are told that they are innocent.

May 22, 1921

After confering with the rest here, my position is to follow their (the Phila. Group) and your advise. I shall do anything you wish knowing that none of you will want me to do anything dishonorable or that will injure any other of my co-defendants. Their interests must also be guarded. This will be for you to care for. I am sure you will. If there is anything I should do to aid this matter, I shall upon request. I am so cut off from reliable and direct information that my opinion as to what is best to do, must not be taken too literally. Things and times change, but nothing here changes. Let me be at your bidding. . . .

I see that the [IWW] convention threw out No. 8 [the Philadelphia longshoreman's union] and the Bakers of N.Y. The Textile Workers intend to withdraw, from the latest news I get. That crowd around headquarters and those at the convention are murdering the organization. . . .

What an irony. To be expelled by a movement while in prison for it's principles. I feel at this moment as though I have more of the principles of the I.W.W. at heart than the organization which is supposed to sponsor them. However, I'm out. So there we are.

You wonder what we shall do when I get out. Goodness knows. It can not, of course, be the old life. We must strike some new field. It cannot be the I.W.W. I cannot stand forever those stabs from my fellow workers. It must be something else. What? I don't know. I should much like to develop my talents at drawing. Maybe I could put that to some practical use. That's my greatest hope. . . . I have no

talent except to draw, unless it is the platform for some good movement or other and that's really no good. We must find a place some
where. But, what's the use of figuring futures, one thing is certain the
future is brighter than the past, and it will not be like the past. . . .

Well, baby dear, this won't last much longer and then think of the
joy when it is over. What fun we'll have. To live without the shadow
of prison walls darkening each day and marring its natural pleasures.
On to the tomorrow.

May 25, 1921
It is good news to hear about the Woman's committee being formed
for our comfort and welfare. However, they are making a mistake if
they send us much of anything except occasionally candy and cash.
We can buy nearly what we want and in such quantities as we desire
and can use. . . .

. . . Those who did not show up here are Haywood, 20 years,
$15,000 bond, Lossieff, 20 years, $10,000 bond, Andre[y]tchine, 20
years, $10,000 bond, Rothfisher, 20 years, $5,000 bond, Laukki, 20
years, $10,000 bond, Perry, 10 years, $5,000 bond, Beyers, 10 years,
$10,000 bond, McCosham, 5 years, $5,000 bond and Jaakkola, 5 years,
$5,000 bond. The total bond loss was $75,000.

Now to other and more pleasant topics. I am so very, very glad to
hear that you all feel fine. That's always good news. But, girlie dear,
please don't work yourself sick. Be careful. By all means stay well and
take good care of yourself. With your health O.K., what do we care?

I'm feeling so fine, I'm afraid of myself. The weather is awfully
warm. Out in the ball park in the afternoon, playing hand-ball has
made me hard as nails. Am getting thoroughly sunburnt. Stripped
from the belt up except for a cheese-cloth undershirt, a sleeveless
affair, I've been a fine target for the sun. My shoulders are bright red,
also neck, the arms are fried brown.

Joe, my kosher cell-mate, just keeps on getting redder. He is three
shades redder than a boiled lobster now. You see Joe has been in the
Clothing Business, selling suits, etc. You know the tricks of the trade,
they have big plate glass windows in front but they build walls behind
them and in front of the store proper—result, darkness. This is
brought to a confusing and mean light by a mixture of artificial light

and light (very dim) which comes thru the door transom, etc. This kind of light makes it easier to see black for blue, etc., etc. If the unsuspecting customer doesn't believe it they bring him suit and all directly into the sunlight which blinds him entirely and the sale is made. I'm sure I don't know that this is correct, but when Joe came here out of that environment he looked like as if he had been bleached in a mushroom cellar. But no more. Going to jail has improved him greatly. It has brought him out of the stifling store and given him plenty of God's sunshine. Prison is a curse to me but it seems to do Joe a lot of good. This explains Joe's good nature and my good fortune in having him for a buddy.

May 29, 1921
My little girlie, you miss me no more than I do you. That's what makes prison the miserable things that they are; it seperates those whose lives are bound together; it not only punishes those whom they seek directly to punish but those loved ones as well. But never mind, it will soon be over, not long now, and then we will drink of the cup of life. . . .

I shall try to write you more often, baby. This next week will have to write to Mr. Evans and Miss Inglis. On the week following will try to write home and a special letter to you. You see 3 letters a week doesn't go far. I shall try and manage to write you more often. By getting an extra sheet of paper I may be able to write Mr. Evans through you and in that way save a letter.

I have every thing you sent me. Many thanks, Chiky dear. There is nothing I need. . . . It would be a good idea however to see some one from #8 [Philadelphia longshoremen's union] and maybe they would send some cash monthly. . . . What we couldn't use would make a few dollars to come out with. We are entitled to that much, anyway.

. . . There's no news here, of course. That makes it hard to write—and say anything. We had a great day yesterday. We had six or seven prize-fights in the Ball Park. . . . There was a bit of crude humor in yesterday's affair. Just before Jack Johnson was to fight, the announcer got up and began to introduce a district attorney, who was to speak. When the words "district attorney" were spoken the crowd began to hoot and jeer, "boo-o-o-'s" and cat-wails were heard everywhere, and the district attorney did not speak. It was funny, but awfully crude. . . . Well, anyway, the men here, for the most part, enjoyed it, and that's more than they did when they met their last district attorney. . . .

Yeh! Yeh! Nef got a promotion of some kind. He is now "runner" or something like that at the tin-shop. Some kind of a political job. I'm still looking for a job. If they don't dig up something pretty soon, I guess I'll quit, and go home.

June 5, 1921

Was glad to get the news from you and Mr. Evans as to the activities of the group. Very fine. When I said that I would rely on your judgement, I meant it, girlie. You have more good sense than you give yourself credit with. Your last letter proved that of itself. When once you have realized that one does a movement no good by laying in jail, you have realized a whole lot. Once we were in jail for a movement, now we're in jail, that's all. You folks will determine the best methods to bring this thing to an end, without injuring the opportunities of anyone else. You understand.

. . . The other day, a party went through here and they had a kid with them who looked for the world like Bucky Boy. I felt rotten for a few minutes, but then it was to laugh. I don't give Bucky a great deal of thought. It's you, girlie, I think most of. But I try not to think much. Joe and I tell stories and crack jokes, we have a real time of it, a real time, believe me. When in the kitchen, we are pretty busy, and so it goes. Then, there is handball and sun-burns to distract one's mind, and books.

. . . If someone suggests a present for me suggest a good pipe. At the rate I'm going, I'll soon burn up these two I have up and then it will be awful.

I don't know what to say to you personally, just to you. Anything I would say is so commonplace, and doesn't say what I mean. Girlie, it's just you, and you can't be written to, one must speak to you, see you, I will never learn you. You weep when you are happy, and smile when your heart breaks. I never did nor will understand you, so how can I write and say what I mean. I want you to know that I miss you, girlie. I could be happy in prison with you, it would be hell outside without you. . . .

When Congress tires of playing football with that Peace Resolution, I suppose that we can begin to look for action. Let's hope so, more for your sake, you are too good to have your life shadowed by prison bars you cannot see.

June 10, 1921

Note that Feige was over to see Mr. Evans and that he seems to think it necessary to find out what else the Gov't may have against us beside that upon which we were convicted. They have nothing except the usual fairy-tales which are common to any newspaper reader. There are no previous convictions in any case for anything and if this administration is going to seriously consider the insane rant and ravings of the Palmer crowd then we have little to hope for. I do not think that they will. However, Mr. Turner is out as Pardon Attorney and Mr. Finch has his place. The change, I understand, is not for the good.

Some things simmer into this place, and you folks will take them for what you think they are worth. 1st. It seems very probable that this administration will set forth its policy with regard to political prisoners as soon as [Attorney General] Mr. Dougherty [Daugherty] reports on the Debs case. . . . If there is a pardon granted Debs then we may well expect like treatment. . . . 2nd I am sure that they will consider cases, not through the ordinary channels, but by and through extraordinary routes. To make myself clearer, if a petition for pardon is made in any regular form and through formal channels it will get little or no consideration, while, if the demand is made directly to the Attorney General and President some results may be looked for,— in the case of individuals, application for pardon MUST be made, upon the ground that no crime was committed and that the prisoner is innocent of the offense named. This is good in our case.

But by going directly to the Atty General or President it may also be argued (indeed that is the whole Debs case) that the war time measures were measures beyond reason, that convictions were based upon hysteria and that the sentenses are outrageous, etc. This, in addition to the fact that the offenses charged are entirely political in nature, and find the prisoner guilty of having expressed certain real or alleged opinions.

June 14, 1921

Am using only one sheet of paper this time because it takes a day longer to get the extra sheet of paper, and I am moving around. Have transfered from the kitchen to the clothing department. It is ever so much better. I have moved to another cell block and expect to move again tomorrow to a different cell. . . .

Glad to hear of the group's decision. I think that between $8.00 and $10.00 monthly will see us with everything we normally need. . . . You might so tell the committee and at the same time convey our thanks to them, also. . . .

I get to see Nef every day now. We both have the "yard" every noon. . . .

Respecting the actions of the group, I can hardly imagine of a thing they could do that would be more effective, than to see Mr. Dougherty before he makes his final decision regarding amnesty. Now, it seems to me, is the time when policy is being made and while in the making influence is certainly desirable.

June 19, 1921

I am ever so much better off now. Have a much better job. Am in the same cell with William Weyh, you know the fellow who came back with us, he with the little red-headed wife.

. . . So they cut your relief off at Chicago. I'm sorry. If things go at all hard for you financially let me know. Am sure that a letter from me would get you relief [from Local 8]. Don't forget. . . .

It is fine to hear that the Philadelphia group have definitely decided to make application for pardon in person. . . . But, I think that it is too much of a delay to wait till fall. Although one may be sure that nothing very concrete will happen before that time, yet, it is now that the administration is making their policy. Pressure now ought to be worth a lot, especially, to show to the administrative forces that violence and destruction are no issues in our case. These are connected with us in the popular mind and it is going to take some hard work to drive it out of the mind of those in official positions. They will not take the time and effort to learn the truth for themselves. We must bring the facts to them.

The Civil Liberties Union, in a circular letter to us here, states that they believe that prejudice in Washington can best be broken down by each defendant asking for a full and unconditional pardon, and by having his particular friends push it. The Civil Liberties Union will then try to bind these energies for individuals into a big move for all. The idea sounds good. I am willing to sign such papers if it will help others as well as myself. Will write to Baldwin Tuesday.

June 24, 1921

You think I am agitated. Not at all, girlie. Have had quite a time to convince some of the boys here that they are foolish in not getting their friends active in their behalf. Sometimes some of them get my goat. . . . Am feeling fine only I don't share some of the enthusiasm of some here and outside. I hope that they are right but I'm prepared to wear a warm overcoat out of here. We'll be doing fine if most of us leave here when the snow flies. That's my firm opinion, and, I think it's going to take some real work to accomplish that. . . .

It is impossible to answer your 14 sheets on one sheet. What I say must necessarily be short and dry. If it is advisable to present affidavits in Washington in support of our case, affidavits could be secured from Lever, Herlacher and Gergots which will state clearly how Nef and I stood on the draft. Either one or both of us advised them to register. This could not be secured during the case, but might be of value now. . . .

A bitter split developed and festered among the ranks of the Wobblies in Leavenworth. Some of the prisoners, with the support of Roger Baldwin of the Civil Liberties Bureau (later, the American Civil Liberties Union), felt that release should be sought on an individual basis, since the administration was unlikely to issue a general amnesty. They felt that the success of each prisoner paved the way for another. They relied on the support of local groups, agitating in support of one case at a time.

Other prisoners, by and large those under shorter sentence, were resolved that everyone should remain in prison until all were free. They signed a resolution to that effect. Their reasoning was that to accept individual pardon or commutation of sentence was to suggest either that the individual had been guilty (and seeking pardon therefore) or that the individual was innocent, although others were guilty. The national IWW leadership in Chicago supported this "resolutionist" group—whom my father sometimes referred to as the "die-hards," "irreconcilables," or "hard-liners"—and refused support to anyone seeking release on an individual basis.

June 28, 1921
It has turned warm today. . . . When I came to the cell tonight, I stripped down to my B.V.D.'s, read the "Call" which started to come day before yesterday, filled the pipe which Yetta sent and which just came tonight, with tobacco from the same source; took my pen in hand to write you two full pages. I am at peace with the world. . . .

Now, to answer your letter. My darling girlie, don't worry about me. If you saw me now, 15 pounds heavier than when I came here, wearing the smile that won't come off, you would be sorry for yourself and your tough luck. So don't worry about me, I work with a fine bunch of fellows, eat pretty well and sleep with a clear conscience. I am keeping regular habits, rising every morning at 6:30 and retiring promptly at 9:30 in the evening. I assure you I am spending no night where a self-respecting young man should not be. So lay off the worry stuff. . . .

My girlie, as hard as it sounds, yet it is better if you could get along without relief from Chicago. Would much sooner see you get it from any other source, and we can get it. . . . It is better that I should be perfectly free from all obligations when I get out. . . .

Forrest Edwards wrote to Baldwin that he was opposed to individual action for pardon and that he thought that it would hurt the movement for general amnesty. Baldwin replied very cleverly and clearly to him and pointed out that by working through and for all individuals, that they were building the best movement for all. The resolutionists are beginning to backslide already. They want to argue with us sometimes but we laughingly tell them that we are not going to try to convince them that they should try to get out, they can stay if they like. This seems to make them mad, so I guess they really would like to get out.

. . . We have some lemons and sugar and are now enjoying lemonade. Make some, it's fine. Have just read Ibsen's "The Doll's House" and "An Enemy of the People." Am now reading his "Ghosts." Also read a couple of Tolstoi's stories.

Am teaching chess to Bill Weyh. He and I play about an even game of checkers.

July 3, 1921

Mighty sorry to hear of your and Feige's sickness. . . . Am very glad, indeed, that you stated the facts so that I know. It is so much better to know the real situation.

I agree with you that it is useless to write to Chicago. Certainly will not. Now as to what we shall do. When I went out into the yard today and met Nef he showed me Feige's letter to him. It was very much like your letter to me. We talked the matter over, and, came pretty much to this conclusion.

Nef was sure that you folks had at least a couple hundred dollars on hand and could afford to rest or at least take things pretty easy for a month or so, then, we may know some thing definite with respect to ourselves. If it looked like we had to stay for a short time longer we could raise odd amounts quickly and tide you over. If, however, we might have to remain for any considerable time, we would then make arrangements for weekly relief of a fixed amount. This can be arranged all right.

What I'm not so sure of is that you have anything like the money Nef thinks you have. If you are not so fixed that you can <u>now</u> take a good rest and get well, be sure and let me know by return mail, and, I'll get busy at once. Can raise a good sum for you quickly.

See in today's Kansas City papers that they expect Debs to be released inside of a week. If this is true, and so happens, then we may expect early action also. If such is the case, it might be better if we were under obligations to no one. What makes me think that Nef is wrong is that both of you state that you are in need. Please let me know just how you are fixed. I hate to move unless it is together with the big stiff. Can you take a month's rest and still have some funds on hand?

Until I get a reply from you will do nothing, and then, if necessary, will act alone.

July 6, 1921

Your dear letter of the second came tonight. Was so very glad to hear that you are feeling so much better. . . .

. . . Am glad to know that Mr. Evans, Mr. Kane and Mr. Burnham are to go to Washington. It might be well for them to have our indictment with them. Of course, they will be prepared to present the case. It may be as well that you do not go the first time. A real drive of some proportions may be held and then your presence may be worth more.

Regarding relief, can do nothing now till I hear from you in reply to my last letter. You understand.

. . . I got my drawing material today. A fine outfit. Am sorry that it is too late to thank Mr. Evans through a letter.

Wasting a line or two to tell what goes on here. Where I'm working there is only one wobbly—Eastman from Louisiana—all the rest are just plain humans whose mistake was to be court-martialed or try to explain to a jury how it was that postage stamps were missing when they had charge. . . . They are all innocent, they have confidentially told me so themselves.

They are all quite normal except that they all suffer from one of two diseases, namely commutitis and parolitis; one Jewish fellow is simultaneously suffering from both. All being innocent, naturally they think that they should be permitted to go home, but most of them have no home,—so what's the use.

They are a most persistent lot—if they have a poor dinner, they make it worse by rehearing the menu's of some very fine dinner they once had, or maybe I had better say,—had once. None of them seem to be very well acquainted with exclusive bill-of-fares.

Our poor orthodox Jewish friend here nearly starves to death. Pork, pork—he sees it every where, and poor me, hunting for it, cant find it.

I sat beside him at the table one day when we had beans. He said he couldn't eat them because they had pork in them, I asked him to give me the pork, and, then he couldn't find any. So I went hungry because there was no pork and he starved because of the pork. And we had the same to eat. That just goes to show what religion will do to a man.

July 8, 1921
There's no news here worth mentioning. Everybody waiting to see what is done in the Debs case. . . .

With my drawing material here I drew my first cartoon, entitled "A Dutchman's Midsummer Dream" and shows a dutchman making a high-dive into a schooner of foaming beer. The workmanship surprised myself. Am trying to invent non-revolutionary ideas so that maybe I can some day put them to practical use. . . .

News, news, where's the news. I might say that we had a fine dinner today, that is, fine for prison fare, bacon, new potatoes and onions with cream gravy. Also, as they say here, bread and water, salt and pepper. As I still sit beside my Jewish friend—I got the pork and he got the onions—then I got some more onions. It's a great life if you don't weaken.

. . . In order to keep the place full, the various federal judges donated the institution 20 new men today. In the year 1921 we now have 1921 prisoners.

July 10, 1921
I got a letter from Ms. Edmund C. Evans in which she tells me that they have given you folks $160.00 so that you might have a vacation this summer. . . .

Mr. E. C. Evans wrote to Nef saying that we need not worry about your financial needs. That the people there would see that you got on O.K. . . .

It looks as if things are getting a bit better since the new warden has been on the job. The food is some better, and more general privileges allowed. He seems to want to do the square thing, something his predecessor did not let worry him.

Commencing tomorrow night we will be in the yard in the evenings. Now we are locked into our cells at 5:30—beginning tomorrow we will not be locked up till 7:30 o'clock. That's ever so much better. It is too hot in the middle of the day to play hand-ball but in the evening it is fine, and, one needs some wholesome exercise here to keep in the best of health.

. . . Have been trying to draw hands for the last two days. They are much harder to draw than faces. I'm succeeding, however. . . .

My Yiddisher friend had a great time at the table this morning. We had eggs. He ate eight of them. He will be all right for a week now. The eggs were a bit old, so he said "Old eggs for old men" and took mine, too. Might say that I don't eat these eggs. Last night I had six china-cups of milk followed by four tin-cups of lemonade. Health fine at this writing. . . .

DEAR BUCKY, AM WRITING YOU AGAIN AND I WANT AN ANSWER SOON. AM SENDING YOU A KISS. MAMMA WILL GIVE IT TO YOU. TELL FEIGE THAT PAPA SENDS HER HIS LOVE. MY LOVE TO YOU, MY BIG BOY—ED

July 17, 1921

The conviction of Sacco and Vanzetti was surely bad news. I am wondering when these "frame-ups" will come to an end. It is awful to contemplate. Yet, I suppose many must be sacrificed yet. And to me, it once more drives home the horror of this whole abysmal, atavistic system of punishment. When Sacco goes to the electric chair (if he goes) his troubles are over, but what of his wife who clings by him so loyally and his little son, who barely understands and his baby girl who knows not the tragedy,—yet. They must go on—and suffer. For what? Vengence. Those fellows did not commit the crime charged, that is certain. They are no more guilty of murder than is Mooney, but they have faced a jury of men, men who must either be liars or anti-social, men who have murder in their heart for no other kind can serve on a murder jury in Mass. Just think! A man cannot try an [individual] accused of murder unless he himself believes in taking human life. . . .

I am surely glad that you are going away on a vacation. Will do all of you a world of good. By the time you get back summer will be nearly over and then you can get on much better in town. It ought to be nice in Galeton this time of year. Everything green and cool and fresh. It will be great for Bucky, too.

. . . Girlie, many are the hours I think of you, but, I like to think of you, don't care much to think of anything or anybody else. I hope that everything will so come out that we shall soon be together with our new and happier life to be.

Don't have any idea what we can do or will do. Anyway, what ever it is, it is on a different road. We have a right to live. One can give only so much of his life to a people who don't care a damn whether they live or die so long as they can lick the dirty boot that kicks them around. One knows that some day the worker will come to his senses and learn that he has interests in common with his fellows, but to date so few have learned. I have given fifteen years of life and enjoyment to that struggle, yes, not only my energy and thought but have robbed you of many an enjoyable moment you should have had. Yet, we have yielded our best and not complained. It is not time to complain now so I wont. But this affords no reason why we should not after our struggle, try to live a while.

July 19, 1921

Say, Chiky, I am soon to write up a complete history of how we tried to finance our trial and how that work was hampered. Shall show how we tried to secure lawyers of standing and how and why they refused. Shall show why we did not thoroughly investigate many things prior to the trial, etc. etc. It will be lengthy and in some detail. I shall show how mail and express rights taken from us injured publicity and funds for our defense. These facts should be of interest and value in the work our friends are doing. Don't you think so. I have often thought to write this, but have failed so far. Will now get busy.

Nebeker is making a report on the case. It is usual for the prosecuting attorney to do this in cases where a pardon (or in this case, amnesty) is asked. . . . It would do no harm to see Nebeker if anyone goes to Washington. He will give a great story, I am sure, and, if it was possible, one of our lawyers ought to be there in Washington when he is seen. This, I guess, is impossible, but it would be a good idea for the committee to give Christensen a statement of what Nebeker told them, so that he could correct misstatements. Nebeker is rather careless in his handling of the truth. . . .

. . . Well, the Parole Board is here and "parolitis" will have many more victims. About four were up from the Clothing Department. Yes, oh! yes, my little Jewish friend was up. He has a face like the map of Jerusalem. Here is how he tells his experience with Mr. Votaw. "Vell, I go in, I see Mr. Votaw, he is such a leetle man, how should I know it vas him, and he laugh right in my face and say to me "You are a Jew" and I say to him "Sure, I am a Jew, for why shouldn't I be a Jew, can I help that I am a Jew?" and then he tells me it makes no difference anyhow, and I ask him why he ask me if it makes no difference, and he ask me "Why shouldn't I ask you, it is one of the questions" What could I say? I say nothing. Then he says, "You are in the Clothing Business and more things like that and then he stops, and what do you think he should do? He shows me a letter from Judge Landis to him, and would you believe me? The letter, I read it, Judge Landis write to him and say I should come home. And then I tell to Mr. Votaw that my lawyer and my friends seen Judge Landis and Judge Landis tell them that he does not know how the jury should find me guilty, and what should Mr. Votaw say, well, he tell me I should write to them and get Judge Landis to write a letter and say he don't think I am guilty. And he says, "You get that letter and maybe you make parole, you don't get it and you can see me again in September" Oy! If I shouldn't get that letter? For why is a parole board, if I should have to get a letter? Mr. Votaw is a gentleman, he treated me fine, but why should he insult me by smiling right in my face and asking from me, "Am I a Jew?"

And so it goes. Each with his own story, each with his tale of woe. There is one good thing about convicts, all are innocent (to hear them tell it) but they would all plead guilty if they could get out on that plea. About the only ones who don't ask parole here are the Wobblies. They want amnesty.

All this makes life interesting here. It is great to be a "father confessor" to a crowd of men. It's great to hear their stories, their alibis, their interpretations of law. The greatest masters of law are in prison, the victims of that which they have mastered.

Well, the night is short and paper soon used up, so will close. This rambling epistle don't mean much and is less but you may find some pleasure in reading it. If so, it was worth writing.

July 22, 1921

As to the Phillips matter, I am sure that you are making a mistake to take more on the list there. Boston offered to take up Phillips and Avila and they not only failed to take advantage of that but signed that "famous" resolution. . . . We cannot expect the Philadelphia group to mother the whole crowd. There are other cities in America, and in Phillips case, Francis Miller and I did take them up in Boston and had the arrangements made. The Boston people wrote them fine letters and Avila said he wanted them to do nothing in his behalf. Phillips, I understand did not even give them the courtesy of a reply. Again, I don't like the idea of Saint [Vincent St. John] writing to Flynn asking her to take it up with the Philadelphia crowd. He could have seen us here, at least. This was not done. It's not a case of money with us, we, (the Phila. Group) have talked it over, and come to the conclusion that it is bad policy to dump more on one group, especially when they are hostile to the formation of just such groups. Mahler has been after Nef. Who will be next and when will it stop? It could be done, though, we will find out who is broke and come from localities where there is no one to help them, and turn their names over to the committee and have them divide the allowance for a month to them. . . .

There are those poor devils who would like to cooperate in a sensible move. To my mind they should get first consideration. While I have said "me" and "I" quite often, the information here is that of Nef, Fletcher, Graber and myself. As for myself, I feel now as I did when, in the case of bond, I asked that those originally in the Phila. group be gotten out first. We want you to know that we do not say what we do from selfish motives, but, entirely, because we are sure that it is bad policy.

. . . Oh say, my Jewish friend was denied parole. He has a face so long that it would take a barber two weeks to shave him. He will recover in a few days and then feel better than ever. So it is with all of them.

You mustn't feel so blue. Everything will come out in the wash. Just imagine the time we will have when this is over. And it's bound to be over some time.

My mother's sister Ruchel had married Philip Weber and settled in the little town of Galeton, in northern Pennsylvania. They had five daughters, ranging at this time from five to eleven years of age. In Europe, it had been sister Ruchel, not their mother, who tended the three youngest daughters, Chiky, Feige, and Belle. Like her daughters, Ruchel's sisters found comfort in her presence.

My father wrote deliberately and clearly. His handwriting was legible; each page was full but uncrowded; he never erased. Except once, in the following letter: "We had fine chops for dinner" originally read "We had pork chops for dinner." In deference to his observant Jewish sister-in-law, Ed erased the word "pork."

July 24, 1921

Am writing this letter to you with the hope that you will get it as soon as you get to Galeton. I hope that you all had a pleasant journey and got a rousing welcome when you arrived. It has been one of my sorrows to know that you were, in a way, cut off from your folks whom you love so well. It is my most sincere hope that all the old fondness shall bind you together anew. I am sure that it will. Now, baby dear, won't you give them my love, my sincere love, for I know that I have hurt them, although, goodness knows, it was no fault of mine. When they know how great our love is, they will understand. . . .

The improvement here is marked. We had fine chops for dinner and milk for supper, this among other things. I mention these because they were unknown before. However, they are putting in one improvement here now that I can see no use for, namely, to-wit; NIGHT-SHIRTS. The only reason possible for them is that this place is for punishment and I know of no greater punishment than sleeping in a night-shirt. When society has advanced more and become more proficient in terrible punishment, then they will tear down the walls and cast into oblivion the bars, and make the violators of future days listen to a prison band by day and wear night shirts at night. . . .

In a letter received here, dated July 19th and signed by "Frank K. Nebeker," Nebeker says that he is not reviewing nor making recommendations on the entire case but only in 5 or 6 cases where individual clemency has been asked. He says that he will soon retire into private practice and does not expect to have much more to do with our case. I saw this letter myself.

. . . I just got another pair of sandals. The old ones wouldn't hold together any more. So you see you are not the only one who gets some new clothes. Or, are shoes clothes? Guess we'll have to get the New York Supreme Court to settle this, as you will remember that that court quashed the "profiteering" indictment against Woods of the Woolen Trust on the ground that "clothes" was not "cloth." And because "clothes" was not "cloth," Mr. Woods was not a profiteer. Isn't that clear? Easily understood?

Law must be a great game! They make an Espionage Law to catch German spies, and with it put wobblies in prison. Some poor diluded district attorney and a misinformed judge with the help of an ignorant jury, did send some German bomb thrower and spies to prison but ex-president Woodrow Wilson pardoned them thus correcting that terrible error. Also a Lever Act was passed to prevent profiteering. With this Act several A.F. of L. men on the pacific coast was sent to prison. When some nut of a prosecutor did grab a few profiteers the Supreme Court said that it was unconstitutional.

It ought to be easy to be a lawyer. Read a law, turn it meaning backward and you're right. Never do a reasonable thing nor give voice to a reasonable expression. Never make a reasonable argument. For instance, if a man is tried for murder, never mind the evidence, talk about his face, your expressions to be guided by whichever side pays you. It's a noble art!

Any way the profiteers are out and we are in. Thus is "democracy" forever saved!

DEAR BUCKY: I ALMOST FORGOT TO WRITE TO YOU. HOW DO YOU LIKE GALETON? BE GOOD TO YOUR COUSINS AND THEIR LITTLE FRIENDS. KISS MAMMA. A SWEET KISS FROM YOUR POP. LOVE—ED.

July 28, 1921

Now, girlie dear, I have another small job for you. Will you write to Miss Elizabeth Gilman of 513 Park Ave, Baltimore, Md., and ask her to write me if she is at home. I would write if I had the letter to spare.

She can do something for the most unfortunate of my fellows, Fred
Esmond, who went insane here. He was removed today to Washington, D.C. to St. Elizabeths Hospital for the insane. . . . He has been
improving here recently and his mind may be reclaimed if given the
very best of attention and care. . . . His wife is now under arrest in
California charged with criminal syndicalism. He must not know
this. Not now. Write Miss Gilman and give her the outline I give here.
If she will write me I shall be glad to give her greater details and let
her know what best she can do to help him. . . . You are quite a
philosopher in your dear way. You surely do go after the poor, ignorant slaves. . . . My attempted education of them has been a great
education to me. They seem to be quite willing that we should fight
for them but when we lose in our struggle in their behalf, they are
quite willing that we should remain among the lost. Unless they show
a greater reversal in form than there is reason to expect, they will fight
their ignorance without my help. I'm just beginning to realize that
I'm no longer a kid and that we both, all three of us, are entitled to
some real life. I don't know but that the I.W.W. did me a favor when
they kicked us out. . . .

　　　. . . Again Harding says that there will be no amnesty. There is
reason for this and we must make the best of this reason. The administration knows that it must make some disposition of the political
prisoners. It is to their advantage to do so. But, they have, they
believe, imprisoned a dangerous idea. The super-patriots insist that
that idea shall not be turned loose on the people. . . . The administration is not opposed to turning the men out, it's the idea that they
don't want to get away. How is this to be done? . . . The public can
be satisfied that the I.W.W. idea is in prison, while individual members are being released. For instance, the release, let us say of Ash-
ley [Ashleigh], would not be as fearful in the super-patriots eyes as
the release of the I.W.W. at once. Take six months to release them all
a few at a time, and you would find that all would be out, and, yet
these persecutors of small caliber would still think the idea in prison.
The administration, beyond doubt, has this in mind when they insist
on dealing with individual cases.

August 4, 1921

Your letters of the 28th and 29th came to me since last Sunday. There is another letter from you, I think, in Leavenworth. It was short two cents for postage. I signed for the stamp today, so I should have the letter tomorrow. Saw Feige's letter to Nef and was glad to learn that you got such a fine reception after so nice a trip. . . .

Girlie, dear, I am preparing three affidavits, one showing how we were handicapped in our legal defense before and during the trial, another, a sort of sketch of my life and labor activities covering about the same ground as was asked for by Baldwin, and a third, giving some of the discussions I had on the draft and conscription with Lever, Horlacker, Gergots and Pazos. . . .

Oh! Say, girlie, Edna says the folks at home want a picture of Bucky Boy. Can't you have one taken? I would like to have a picture of both of you once in a while, too. You must remember that I don't get to see the Buck as he grows up and, of course, want to see a bit of him, even if only a picture once in a while. . . .

For, in spite of all that may ever come, our day will come. We shall drink at the fountain of happiness. We shall know a more beautiful life yet. There isn't much happiness in this world, but we must get our share, and for tomorrow we must get more than our share for we have not had it in the past. But then, haven't we been happy, too? Hasn't our love given us many, many cheerful moments? It makes me happy now to recall the years we spent together, the many dark moments, but in that time no quarrels, no hours or even a minute of bitterness. I am sure that there are few who love as we do. . . . To me, the greatest happiness comes when you tell me of your love. Many are the times I have thanked my lucky stars that our lives came together and became one.

August 7, 1921

I let the "request man" get past me without asking for an extra sheet so will have to write you this time on one sheet. . . . It is fine to hear you say that you get along so fine in Galeton and that [Ruchel's husband Philip] Weber is so good and thoughtful of you.

You mustn't think about missing me. There are lots of other things to think about. But, when you must think, and let me come into your mind, remember, that I think more of you and your welfare than I do of myself. So let your thoughts drift to yourself, girlie, and your welfare. See to it that you keep your good health and spirits. My baby, there is but one great driving force within me and that is to be able to enjoy life and love when these days are over. We must both do our share to make it possible. By all means, girlie, take the relief. If anything ever belonged to us it is what little money they have to give in these times. By all means, take all you are offered. I've lived all my life saying "No" to dollars. I'm tired of it. So should you be.

August 14, 1921
Big Jim Thompson is now an outside trustee, that is he runs around outside of the walls without a guard. They leave it to his honor to come in to sleep. He has a big yellow star on him like a deputy sheriff's badge.

I do not know whether you have any news in Galeton about what is going on. The Phila. Ledger, Chicago and Kansas City papers have it that Mr. Dougherty will make his recommendation in the Debs' Case this month. The Chicago Examiner expects him to be released on Labor Day. . . . The "Ledger" says that recommendations on the other cases will follow shortly. . . . My belief is that Mr. Harding's signature will soon be placed on the peace treaty with Germany, and that immediately he will make some statement or take some action with regard to political prisoners.

It makes me feel fine when I get such letters as your last one. It breathes of a love, girlie, that is really rare. It is fine to have one in this world whose love is so pure and good as yours. Sometimes I wonder how we have gone through these years; poverty, persecutions and prisons have been our share. . . . Then to have those very people for whom we gave what time and talent and energy we had, turn us down. Well, I suppose that it is all part of the game, the game of life. Many, many times I have been discouraged, ready to quit, to tell them all to go to hell for all I cared, but then I know this, we live in a struggle not of our making, one that can not be avoided, that in this struggle many must suffer untold misery, why then should I, yes we, do our share grumblingly? Then I know your desires better, perhaps, than if you had spoken them openly. I have felt in my heart the anguish you often suffered. And I knew that my attitude was the greatest cause of it. Yet, what is it that calls one on? I really doubt if you ever suffered more than I did that day, when before the committee of Textile Workers, I resigned as their secretary. Every one a dear friend and a true fellow worker, they were disappointed, old Vasco Pamplona was heart-broken. His whole heart and soul in a thing which has never yielded him anything but suffering, yet with it all it is his greatest pleasure. He lives, not in the misery he suffers but in the happiness he hopes to bring to others. There is no use to argue other than that the greatest happiness and the most misery lies in unselfishness.

Maybe that is the greatest secret into our love and happiness. We have been very unselfish in our love and very quick to try to bring happiness to the other. I know that I derive more happiness from your happiness than from my own. I know that that has always been your feeling toward me. I know in my heart that I cannot seek selfishly for myself, and harden my heart against the misery and suffering of others, and still love as well. . . . You and I are very much alike temperamentally, at least in many respects. You either love or hate, and that strongly. You are even tempered, you know that I am not. I have at some time or another lost my temper with most everyone I know, except you. Of recent years I have been pretty successful in suppressing that terrible anger, but it has cost me something. I lost with it much of my former very good nature. When I quit being angry, I quit being a clown. One cannot crush one phase of one's temperament without crushing another with it. That makes me wonder. If when these doors open up and I am decided upon the point that the working class movement and I have parted company and that I shall seek for me and mine, will I be happy? More, will you be happy? Can it be possible that our misery has carried with it hopes and happiness, that made our love sweeter? Will that love be as sweet should we set out with but one purpose in life, to satisfy it, to live by ourselves with our love? I pray that we shall always love as today. I am sure we will, but, my girlie, I have never really loved you alone, I have worshipped you. It shall always be so, it must always be so. We will do nothing to quench the fire of our love. Soon I shall be with you again. Soon we shall start life anew.

August 18, 1921

I sent two affidavits to you yesterday. . . . I did not make the 3rd affidavit. I think it best that they make them out themselves. Lever's is good although he failed to mention the time when he and I went together in Baltimore to the P.O. Building and showed a couple of our seamen members where to register. Gergots will possibly remember when he and I went together to the Hungarian Branch and advised them that it would be best if they would register. He should recall some of the discussions I had with him on the draft and the war. Horlacher surely remembers that I advised him to register and appear for military service. He may recall the fact that I was with him in the P.O. in Fall River when he was notified to appear for service or examination, I forgot which. Pazos will long remember that Nef and I told him he would have to register or get out of the office. . . .

That resolution adopted here was . . . a lie on the face of it. . . . That is why I did not sign it. It is a negative resolution in that it suggests no line of action, it merely condemns a particular method and I know that most of the signers did not know what they were condemning, and, did not trouble to find out. Many have reversed their position. The worst falsity of it all is that men who signed their names were at that time, and have ever since, been doing the very thing which they condemned by their signature. Several of the signers are working, through their friends, to secure their personal release. . . .

None of those who refused to sign would ever ask for their personal freedom at the cost of others. To infer that, as the resolution does, is really rotten. The resolution says that one cannot ask for pardon or clemency unless implying guilt, while the regulation clemency blanks state on their face that clemency cannot be asked for until at least one-third of the sentence is served, <u>except on the grounds of innocence.</u> It is hard for me to understand how I could admit guilt for myself or anyone else, when I protest my innocence. Should any more such letters come to notice please try to trace back where the information comes from.

August 21, 1921

Say, my little girlie, to change the subject: I must have been asleep if I said that our past was all misery. . . . Surely we have had many happy hours. But what I referred to was all the misery heaped in between. . . . Do you think you could hide your thoughts, your hopes and your fears? You were brave, so brave. Always with a smile, but what a sad smile sometimes. There were times, many times, when I did not dare to touch you, there was something sacred in your courage. I wish I had your strength of heart. I could not have seen you go to prison, would not. . . .

Why do men sing when going to prison. I'll tell you. Because they dare not remain silent with their own thoughts and fears. Joe Hill cried "Fire" and started the steel that tore his heart out. Was it brave? Let the world have it's illusions but it was not bravery, it was more than likely shouted because he could no longer bear the strain of silence and of waiting. Had he not cried "Fire" in another moment he might have been begging for mercy. Because these things seem so clear to me, I wonder, marvel at the power of your courage. That last day at the depot! What a different one from the day we were convicted at Chicago. There you cried, there you clung to me, your courage was for the moment gone. But at the depot. You did not cry, and once you smiled. Gee, you had courage.

August 25, 1921

Am glad to hear that Belle is coming to Galeton. If she is there when this letter arrives give her my merry "Hello" and tell her to please keep her voice within the speed limits. . . .

I have some interesting news for you. Last Monday a letter was received here by the local (or prison) agent of the Dept. of Justice from Atty. Gen. Dougherty, asking that the Swedish prisoners, members of the I.W.W., convicted under war-time measures, be requested to sign clemency papers and a statement to the effect that they are willing to be deported to Sweden at once. The Atty. Gen. will recommend their release to the President. The Swedes, Ahlteen (20 years) and Johannson and Stenberg (10 years each) sent these papers away today to Washington. The Swedish Embassy has interceded in their behalf.

Yesterday, Parenti (Italian) received a telegram from his lawyer in New York saying that Pardon Attorney Finch will recommend Parenti's release and deportation as soon as Parenti deposits enough money with the Emigration Commissioner to cover the cost of his family's fare to Italy. Parenti feels certain that he can raise this shortly. This looks like as if a break is to be expected.

Then, too, the Peace Treaty has been signed by U.S. and Germany. The press keeps on insisting that early action is reasonably to be expected in the Debs and other cases. Maybe we shall soon see each other again.

August 28, 1921

Well, well, here we are writing once more. But, my little pal, it begins to look as though something is to be expected before a very long time. Of course, we can't believe everything we see in the papers but there seems to be a pretty general opinion that something is to be done for the political prisoners.

. . . At any rate, one thing is certain, there is no newspaper opposition. Even, the strongest "anti-red" papers either favor the release of politicals or say nothing at all. The Hearst papers are firmly for amnesty and many others are taking a firm stand. . . .

August 31, 1921

Of course, baby, I want to be with you, but please don't think that I go around and worry about it. If there is a "happy-go-lucky fool" in here, I'm it. I am one of those who "do time" easy. But for all that, one must think of those nearest and dearest. . . .

Sooner or later it must dawn upon us that years go by (it is odd that one should think of time flying while in prison) and that we are not as young as we used to be. Tonight I played baseball. I realized how my eyes deceive me, my muscles refuse to answer as quickly the thought as in days gone by. There comes back the days when I played in the Northwestern League, and when fielders used to move to cover a bigger field. Now I am willing, but the eye and muscles won't answer. I recall the days when I knew I could stand before nearly any man, when my fist spoke a language a brute could understand. You remember that time. To be sure, I know more, understand more, have become more settled. My little girlie, have you ever felt the desire to "get somewhere," "to really do something others cannot do as well," "to excell"? I realize now I have burned myself up in trying to excell, to get on top. Maybe it was foolish ambition, maybe not. . . .

First I wanted to be a great footracer, and became one of the best on the Pacific Coast, then it was baseball, and there I succeeded only to have fate (the broken leg) interfere, then in turn, speaker, organizer, writer, executive, and in all of them became better than the average. But to what end?

I have as fine a little wife as there is on earth, a wonderful little baby boy, as dear a mother, and a more loyal group of friends no man could ask for. I tell you what it is which captures my thoughts. I know I cannot make any very great use of what I learned yesterday. My early physical training has now weakened rather than strengthened me, and the mental development [has been] along lines which serve me no further usefulness. I am soon reaching the age where I cannot drop one activity and pick up another readily. No one knows better than I, that when these doors swing open, I must settle down to something which can serve us for the years to come. . . . But believe me, my little sweetheart, I'm not worrying nor pining away in useless longing. I know we shall make good, we shall live well and long and happily. I shall not promise you not to think about our tomorrow, nor to think often of you and Bucky Boy. That is all the pleasure and diversion prison affords. I must beg that you allow yourself to rest in my arms in my dreams if I cannot have you in my waking moments. My heart is not for me to control, nor do I want to control it, while it leads my thoughts to the happiest moments of my life, my days spent with you.

September 1, 1921
Pretty soon the evenings in the yard will give way to school. Ralph Chaplin will teach a class in drawing and I shall join in and get some real instruction.

Girlie dear, do you really think that it is a good idea to send Bucky to school? He isn't five yeas old yet and confinement will surely do him no good. . . .

I started school when I was four years old, and I can't see where it did me any good, comparing myself with other pupils.

However, girlie, you will see for yourself. You might try the experiment. If Bucky Boy complains, I should certainly favor taking him out. Four years is rather young to start, unless it is to a kindergarden where most of the time is spent playing. Another thing one must remember is that a kid so young is often bullied by older boys in the same class. I can yet remember how the larger and older kids pounded me around, and then told me if I told anyone they would beat me up some more. So I didn't tell. . . .

I am sending you $3.00. I am having a fine present made for Yetta. Please send the money ($3.00) to Gust. Johnson, No. 11600. His address is the same as ours as he stops at the same "hotel." Don't forget to put the number on the envelope. Send a money order, not a check. No letter is necessary.

. . . One of the politicals here (not a wobbly) got a letter from Dougherty, telling him that he should make out clemency papers personally if he wanted to have his case considered for pardon. Every thing indicates that the cases will be considered individually and then upon application. They seem to be working on the principle that no one wants what they don't ask for. The change of heart in Manuel Rey is good for us. In fact, there seems to be a general change of heart. Red [Doran] is hardly spoken to by any one since he boasted that he had broken up the efforts of the New York group. We can look for better judgement in the future.

So Feige has gone to Rochester, I'm glad. It is a good idea for you to be seperated for a while. Then when you get together again, all will be fine and dandy, eh?

Sometimes, when I watched my mother and my aunts Feige and Belle together, it seemed to me as though they were still small children. My mother, the eldest of the three, was conventional and wanted peace. (I suspect she was a radical only because everyone around her was, and she conformed.) She avoided confrontation, burying hurts deep inside until they burst through.

Unlike my mother, Feige and Belle were rebellious and confrontational by nature. Belle was the perpetually frustrated, angry, ineffective youngest child. She was difficult to be with—a Vesuvius of speech, telling it as she saw it, and absolutely ready to make a scene. But she was a good and giving woman who lived a conventional, if unhappy, married life with an Italian-born Socialist, Thomas Volpe. Feige, however, was totally self-centered, a bohemian, declining motherhood, making her own rules. She had two husbands and several lovers and ruled her circle of friends like a queen bee. She understood people's weaknesses and needs, and played upon them. Assertiveness appears to be salutary: Feige would live to age ninety-six, Belle to ninety-seven.

September 4, 1921
Evening has come again, and with it a refreshing coolness. All over the cell block can be heard the blare of musical instruments, everything from a mandolin to a bass horn. There's one fellow whom I could cheerfully choke to death, he's a poor fish who thinks he can play a flute or claronet or whatever it is. One thing can be truthfully said for him, however, and that is, he can make more ungodly sounds than any other human, and he is the only one in the world who can produce discord on a single instrument. Well, there are about a dozen noise makers at work, so please excuse any "boners" in this letter.

. . . I will be happy to get one of the pictures you had taken. How were you so lucky as to get the whole 12? You were better prepared than the Irish woman who went to the photographers to have a picture taken of her eleven children. She asked the price and the photographer told her $5.00 a dozen, then she said as she gathered her youngest into her arms and called the others to follow her out "Faith, me good man, an' we'll have to go now, and come nixt summer afther Patrick is born."

. . . You must tell Bucky that he is doing fine in school and that he must send me more of his lesson slips. I will be glad to get them any time, and, all the time. I'm going to save them, then he will be able to see how he improves.

. . . If I could but say those thoughts I think, what a message it would be. I can but let the written word convey my love, my fondest well wishes to you and my little school boy. You called him Lee in your last letter. Maybe I'm a fool but I think that I would always like to know of him as Bucky Boy. . . .

DEAR BUCKY BOY. MAMMA TELLS ME THAT YOU ARE GOING TO SCHOOL. THAT'S FINE. WHAT ALL DO YOU DO IN SCHOOL? DO YOU

LIKE YOUR TEACHER? I GOT A COPY OF YOUR FIRST LESSON. IT IS
GOOD. I AM GOING TO SCHOOL PRETTY SOON. I AM GOING TO TRY
TO LEARN HOW TO DRAW PICTURES. LOVE—ED.

September 8, 1921
So you took Bucky Boy away from school. It is as well. . . .

I am still in the Clothing Department. Am sort of a handy-man.
All over the place from office to stock room. May check up some book
one day, check stock another, etc. At present am given charge of issu-
ing winter clothing. All I hope is that I can remain where I am till I
leave here. Am working under one of the squarest guards, or what is
more proper, under one of the squarest men I ever met.

Your letter which came last night was divine. It was so fine to get
it, to read it, to read there your very soul laid open, to see there that
great love which is yours. You say, "In the last analysis, love is what
counts."

Let me give you an experience and experiment of my own here.
A few days ago I, as one of a committee of three prisoners, met the
representatives of a prison welfare organization, in the Chaplain's
office here. I was informed by those who are in a position to know
that 81 percent of the prisoners who come here with sentence of three
years or more, lose their wives by divorce or desertion. These figures
struck me as a poor average for love. Then I set to gathering the data
on so-called "reds" and find that of the 64 married ones located, who
had three years' sentence or more (and most of whom had been in
confinement more than 3 years already) that only four had had their
wives desert them, or, that is less than 6½ percent of their wives had
proven lacking in that love that lives. And I must say again that we
have wonderful little women, the best on earth.

And, they say that we would break up their homes, and they are
afraid. They have tried their darndest to break up ours, and can't.
They say we would break up the family and we have builded unbreak-
able families. Separate the average couple today and in three years
time, nearly all love has flown, but separate the "despised red" cou-
ples and they move heaven and earth to come together, contemplating a greater love.

September 11, 1921

Yetta's present is finished now. The job was a real good one. When you get it, press it down with a hot iron. Use a heavy damp press cloth, I'm instructed. Everything except the cloth is made in here, even the cord is hand made. The job required more than a week's time. Shall sent it out Tuesday.

. . . Am sorry to hear that any letter of mine made you feel bad. I'm sorry. I did not intend it in that light. And that you understand. Some times I have a desire to let the thoughts in my mind flow out onto the paper where you can read what I feel. But, if it ever again makes you feel bad I shall never do it again. Somehow, I felt better after I wrote it. And the price was that you must weep. I feel that in no other letter I ever wrote, was I so completely able to state in writing, my thoughts. But we shall forget that. . . . And it is out of our tomorrow and our children's tomorrow that happiness must be sought. Our yesterdays are too brutal. . . . But when this is over, girlie, . . . if all goes well maybe Bucky Boy shall not long be lonesome for a play mate.

September 14, 1921

Yetta is surely a wonderful little friend to have. I sent out the handbag last Tuesday. You should have it by this time. What do you think of the handwork? Say Gust Johnson did not get the money yet. Did you send it to Box 7? His number is 11600.

. . . The news about Esmond is fine! Great! The boys here were surely happy to get that news. I hope that they will stick with it now and get him out, for, if they cure him and send him back here, then he is apt to "go" again. Only the open world can ever give him back his full mental faculties again.

. . . Girlie dear, I smile to myself just now. In one of your letters you say that my letters make you cry, and, in one this week you say, "Your letters are beautifully written lately, every letter I get is finer than the previous one." Am I to think that you are like that woman who coming from a Jewish Theater said "I had a fine time, I enjoyed myself immensely, I cried all night." . . .

I think it would be best for Edmund C. Evans to send my affidavit to Sen. France. He knows the Senator personally.

September 18, 1921

So Bucky Boy wants to come and see papa? Well, I'd sure like to see Bucky Boy and his dear mamma. But, we shall (except Bucky) be patient for a little while yet. Much can happen in the near future. So far as Germany is concerned, the Peace Treaty is ratified. Now we shall see what the Senate will do when they get together next week. You folks will have to shape up the Phila. group about getting in the applications for pardon. I shall try to get such material together as will be beneficial to each and all the Phila. prisoners.

. . . Now, listen, some time after I get out of here, we must go to Galeton. I must see those little girls who write these nice letters. Believe me, girlie, not a thing has made me so happy as to know that you were happy there, that you were so very welcome. I'm glad. Really, I was not altogether sure till those dear letters came from those dear little girls. Then, I knew.

September 21, 1921

So you got the "blues." That's a very poor idea. What of the rain? Let it rain. Can't you say as "Cyclobs" was made to say by Euripides, so many, many centuries ago—"And when the Thracian winds blow down the rain, I crawl into my shelter, and drinking pans of milk, laughingly emulate the thunder of the high heavens, and bid the rain whirl on." So, girlie, take the advise of a great ancient philosopher and playwright, and "laughingly" "bid the rain whirl on."

Just think of it here. My Jewish friend of whom I've written before has been recommended for parole and should be released in a short time now. He was notified today. His smile was worth a million dollars. And you can imagine what a million dollars would mean to a wholesale dealer in men's garments! . . .

Am glad that you got the handbag. Am sure Yetta will appreciate it. That's all it was sent for. Am sorry that you did not send the money to Johnson at once. He has not received it yet. It puts me in one devil of a fix. If you are not certain that it has been sent when you get this letter, don't wait. Get Weber to make out a check and send a note with it telling him what it is for. Really, I can't imagine why you didn't send it yourself. The fellow is dead broke and had to borrow for the material. So, please don't wait to find out what Belle is going to do about sending out the cash.

Since last week I have received letters from Edna and from my cousin, Florence Berquist. I'm half afraid that I'm going to have to answer some of these letters. . . . I hope it will not be necessary, but maybe I'll have to steal the weekday letter from you next week. Will try not to, but really, my girlie, these letters should be answered. . . .

. . . My dear, be of good cheer and have no more glooms. Remember, you have a love as great as any woman ever possessed. . . . With our thoughts upon tomorrow, we shall not feel the blows we suffer today. Cheer up, then—and let it rain.

September 25, 1921

Today is the eve of our wedding anniversary. Today closes seven years of our wedded life. I came near saying "our life together," but, it was not destined to be so. But, all in all, it has been seven wonderful years, hasn't it. For seven years we have trials and struggles enough, your sickness, my imprisonment, and what not. Can we say that we have really known a day which did not carry with it some shadow? But, as well, those years have yielded much to us. It has given us our dear Bucky Boy, it has discovered the gold in my old mother's heart, it has given you the much cherished affection of your dearest sister, it has brought us friends whose worth has been tried and who have proven themselves loyally true.

And, between us, my little sweetheart, no matter how bitter the day nor what drear clouds darkened the morrow, all has been blissful and sweet. How many people can say, truthfully, that in seven years time they never had a quarrel nor did a bitter or unkind word ever pass between them? . . .

I'm saving the best news till last. Today the warden received a letter from Mr. Christensen telling him to notify all aliens among the wobblies of the contents of the letter. . . . The letter reads:

"I was advised today by the Inspector in charge in Chicago that the Department of Labor was requested to advise the Attorney General how soon that department will be ready to deport all of the alien defendants. . . .

Two wobblies, Olin B. Anderson and Chas Plahn, were recommended for parole and should get out next month. They were the only two eligible at this time, who made application. The parole board asked them to promise nothing with respect to the organization and they promised nothing.

September 28, 1921

How I wish at this moment I could take you in my arms and tell you what I have to say. Your letters of the 24th and 26th came together tonight. I am puzzled about them. I cannot understand them for I cannot recall just what I wrote in that letter to you. I looked up your letter to me, and it cleared matters up some. I am going to quote part of yours: " . . . I am feeling fine, cant complain. But, sometimes, especially in a day like today. It rained the whole day, was awfully dismal, not a ray to cheer one, I get so terribly lonesome. But what is the use of repeating it, some day it will be all over."

Now, girlie, there lies the inspiration to my letter, and what I intended to say, whether successful or not, was that you should do as Cyclobs "laughingly bid the rain whirl on." Try not to be gloomy, and lonesome. . . . Portions of your letter I cannot understand, it seems so distant to any thoughts I ever had, much less wrote down.

I am almost afraid now to write. I don't know what to say, lest I be misunderstood, for I'm sure you misunderstood me when I wrote before, but I must say this again, My girlie, you love too much for your own good. Your love is almost an insane love, you are jealously in love. I do not deserve to be loved so well, my dear baby. Baby dear, you are not mentally dead, your soul has not died, you were very alive when you wrote that letter—the last two. Your whole mind is alive, you lay a sorrowing and indignant soul upon your very paper and make it cry out in words of fire. God, what awful letters, what beautiful letters. Should I pray, I should pray for a soul so pure as yours, a love as great, and, with all that, I know no man ever loved better nor thought in his soul finer thought than I have.

While Im sure that you entirely misunderstood my letter and drew wrong conclusion, yet, it is well, for the wound shall soon heal, for I kiss it now. . . .

You know that I'm building my future, so far as I have power, for you. Do you think that I should quietly sink into obscurity after minions of an insane system sent me to prison for being honest, causing untold hurt to you, and certainly giving me no pleasure? Were it not that you wished quiet I should fight them to the bitter end.

But I have had my fling at my hobby, you shall have yours, it will be ours. You and I and Bucky Boy shall live to enjoy our life and love, you shall learn once more to laugh with a ringing laughter that shall be a cure to all aching hearts, and then shall we read over our letters of today, and marvel at ourselves. . . .

I must close. But before I do, please, girlie, if either you or Bucky Boy are not well let me know. My fear now is, that he was sick when you wrote, and that is largely why you wrote as you did. Not a line in either letter tells me how he is. . . . Try to think that these words were spoken to you as I held you in my arms, spoken softly to the dearest little sweetheart on earth, Lovingly, Ed.

October 2, 1921

I got your letter of the 28th and was mighty glad to see that you were in so much better spirits. That's fine. We will go to business first. Johnson got his cash from you and from Belle. That will be all right. Can square that up here. And, I guess I owe you $3.00. I got my shoes from Belle. They are fine. Really, I never had a pair to fit better, and they are good shoes. I also got some tobacco from her. Please let her know and thank her for her kindness. And before I forget someone, somewhere, sent me a fine pipe. Must have cost $10.00 and its some smoker, too. And, the picture came, it was fine. I'm going to frame it and make it liven up the cell a bit. . . .

Several of the fellows met together in here and we have decided to write to interested folks in all sections and try to get them active. We have decided to use the Civil Liberties Bureau as the center for joint activities if they are willing to act as I'm sure they are.

It was suggested that they try to get some good publicity man on the job to use the Federated Press, and, labor and liberal press, and such of the daily papers which they can reach. Also, to try to get together a group of wives, children, and mothers of prisoners and have them go to Washington. We discussed such things as picketing the White House, etc., but decided that it was not a matter for us to say what these folks should do. They outside are best able to figure what is best to do and what they can do. All we desire is that something be done now that the season is here when "get-togethers" can be held once more. . . .

Well, how does it feel to be back home?

Say, I had an unusual dream last night. I thought that I was outside these walls, in my prison uniform, strolling around, when I met you. I was surprised and asked what brought you here. You told me that you were a traveling saleswoman now, and was doing fine, and that it was fine work. I thought you told me that Bucky Boy was with Yetta and that she promised to take good care of him. I looked at my watch, and it was nearly time, I thought, to go back to prison and I said, "Well, I'll have to go now" and you said,—"Wont you even kiss me good-bye," and I thought I kissed you, and it was so good. Then you said "Goodbye" and I said "What in hell is the use going back, I've been there long enough, come, let's go," and we started off down a crooked road thru a woods, walking slowly talking about Gorky's "Exercism" and how terrible it was,—then, the bugle blew, it was time to get up. The prison bars looked cruel for a moment, but I got up and roused up Bill, my cell mate, and another day started. One Jew called to another "Good Yontif" for this is Rosh Hashonah, and the day was well on its way. So it goes. But it was a beautiful dream while it lasted, and I shall always curse that bugle which brought it to a close.

The boss over where I work says he thinks I'll be the bookkeeper in his "rag-shop" pretty soon. It's a pretty good job.

The cool weather has set in here and its fine now. The bunch were all out in their winter suits today. Tomorrow school starts with about 900 pupils. I am in Chaplins Art Class. While I don't like the idea of staying here, yet, I know that six months study under Chaplin will be worth much to me.

October 4, 1921

From your letter Feige seems set upon going to Rochester. In a way I'm sorry to hear that, and, much more so, because you seem decided upon going. . . . To tell the honest truth I am sure that it is a great mistake, an awful mistake from any angle that you might approach it from. In the first place, if it is a short time till I'm released, then we will have to start all over again, with no place to start from. Surely we will not start at Rochester. That would mean your fare there and back. Then, to sell the furniture for a song (which is all that could be expected now) would be a serious blow, too. This, in consideration of a release pretty soon. But, suppose I'm here a year more, then, be perfectly honest, could you live with Belle a year. . . . At the end of a few months you would find yourself compelled (in your own mind) to go, and no where to go to. . . . In Philadelphia you have friends and you'll never be hungry, be sure. They have assured me that, and they are real friends, too. They will feel slighted if you move away from them. Of course, you may want to move away from your present rooms. Good and well. But, we must remember, girlie dear, that it's best to have one's own roof over one's head. And you can have it, never fear, and you need ask for nothing yourself. You need not fear that you shall be living off of charity nor ever be humiliated because of poverty. Whatever you may think now will not alter the fact that you cannot go out to work. You may be able to do a little around the house but not away. You shouldn't even try.

If I were not very sure, I would not say this, but I'm positive that you can take it pretty easy and have every thing much better in Philadelphia. Your friends are there to cheer you. You will know what is going on from day to day. Rochester is as dead as Galeton.

Then, another thing, our happiness and my release are so bound together that we can not have one without the other. The release must be effected. Are you not sure that our release depends largely upon the activities of our friends in Phila? You can be an inspiration to them. There is a move now, started by the boys in here to have the families of the men here go to Washington. Then, when application is made for pardon for us, many influential Philadelphians will be needed to write personal letters to Pres. Harding, etc. This work you can and will be happy to urge on. While you sometimes may feel unequal to the task, yet, remember this, you can do so much better than you think. And,—forever get away from the idea that you will have to leave Phila. for anywhere because you cannot live properly or else be humiliated by accepting charity. . . .

But, you are outside and can see what's best, if it's best you should go, then, girlie, go and you have my blessings. But, I beg think well and seriously first.

October 12, 1921

Now, girlie, as to publicity. You must know that we here cannot write for publication. There are several of us who could ably present our cases, if we were allowed. All publicity in our behalf must be done on the outside or not at all. We are urging upon all our friends to do all in their power to bring our cases before the people.

. . . Now, girlie, as to friends getting tired, please trust me to be a fair judge of people and I want to say that The Evans; and Winsors and Kiefers, and especially Edmund C. Evans, can always be depended upon. They are real friends. Then, too, there is Yetta. There is no truer friend. . . . Mr. Evans begged me to allow him and his to see to it that all went well with you. I feel better while you are near those folks. Please don't worry about what we shall do after I get out. And don't slave to have a few dollars on hand that have been too hard earned. It's you I want, baby, you, well and happy. Be kind to yourself and you are kind to me.

October 14, 1921

I cant help but think that Feige is foolish to sell out their furniture. For the love of Mike, girlie, don't peddle ours, and if there are some things we may need of theirs and she insists on selling, get it if you can.

October 18, 1921

I see that Mr. Evans may see Senator France personally and then give him a copy of my affidavit. Good.

. . . Am glad that you feel so fine. And I surely hope that you could get a place at Yetta's or near her. Am particularly happy to know that you have decided to stay in Phila. Best for you, best for me, best all around. Thanks, my little baby.

. . . Took over the job of bookkeeper at the Clothing Dep't today. . . . It's more congenial with me and I with it; than the other jobs I've had. Work seven hours a day when I work, and I'm virtually my own boss. Then, again, it's more interesting.

October 20, 1921

Had a strenuous day today. There were 48 new arrivals and all had to be taken care of. Some job. It's my job to keep track of the money taken from them, and, it's quite a feeling to lay one's hands on a dollar again. I'm busier on my job, and, time travels far more rapidly. Today I was looking at the clock to see if I'd have time to finish before quitting time. Imagine wishing the clock wouldn't hurry along in a "pen"! Well, that's the ideal situation. Nothing is so miserable as nothing to do. And the job I'm on is good training.

Am progressing fine with the drawing. Chaplin is a wonderful teacher. He has a method that is great. Tonight we were drawing ears, nothing but ears, front view, side view, and at all angles.

I have received some very encouraging letters from Baldwin and from people in Washington. While they hold out very little hope for an amnesty, they look for early individual releases.

. . . Well, more luck in the wobblies. Johnie Pancner has been made an outside trustee. He has over five years to "do" yet, the "short way," that is allowing for his "good conduct time" which is nearly 1/3 of his entire sentence. The new deputy warden here is reported to have said that you couldn't chase a wobbly from here. He seems to act on that principle, and I surely hope his trust has not been misplaced. . . .

Bucky Boy! Chiky dear, you don't know how much I appreciate those stories you tell of him. I can imagine the little bum all covered with dirt, but it is hard to imagine that he is 3 feet & 7 inches tall. He will be big enough to lick his dad, when I come home, unless it is pretty soon.

Sure, Horlacher was going to get married just before I left. He has had time to have quite a family by this time. By Golly, if Gergots gets married, there will be an earthquake, fire or something. I doubt if the universe would go on in its proper channels, with that big stiff in a double harness.

But it happens to the best of them, so, why not the worse? Its something like the Dutchman said, though,

T'vas marriage von failure, vell now dot depends
Pretty much how you look at dot, mine friends,

Like dem double horse teams vot you see at der races,
Depend pretty much on der pair in der traces,
Unt if dey don't start togeder right off at der start
Ten times oud of nine, dey vas better apart.

But let's wish them all the best, good luck, much love and a long happy life. Please tell Yetta, who'll soon be the only one that's left, to please wait till I get out of here, for I want to dance at her wedding.

October 23, 1921
By George, I got some job when I became bookkeeper, there were 81 new prisoners this last week and I'm told that they expect 140 this next week. Believe me, it is going to be some week—some week. But tell the world, when a fellow is busy, time does fly. It whoops along. That's ideal. And, then, I'm my own boss. "The Boss" as we call Mr. Lemmer, our guard, is a prince of a fellow and so long as a fellow half tries to get along, he's running no chance of getting into trouble.

You know, when a fellow approaches most guards—it's Mr. So. and So. But when the phone rings and a voice says—"Six new arrivals," the "vic" on the phone calls out, "Hey, boss! Fresh fish!" And the boss is gone to meet them. With a fellow like that, one can "do time."

. . . Nef is foolish sometimes. There isn't any good reason to think that he will be among the last, or that the last will be far behind the first. He says so, but often I think he says it so as to prevent himself from being disappointed should it turn out true. He has no reason to think as he does. And, if Feige is so foolish as to follow his advise at this time, then, you be wise, buy up what you can that we may need. . . . If they must be unwise, you may as well profit by it as anyone else. . . .

I'm glad that you're going out more. To the movies—anywhere. That's the stuff. It will bring roses back into your cheeks, and a smile on your lips.

. . . So you know that I have ten years and that's all you know. Now Baby, you know better than that and you know it. Come, now, be honest. I'm not going to be here any ten years and you know it, don't you?

Now, I've got to tell you that I'm mighty glad that you and Bucky Boy are so well and have such good times together. Only, I don't like to hear you say that you feel so blue once in a while. Cut it out!! If you don't go out and enjoy yourself, I'm going to beat you up when I get home. Now! I bet your scared to death, eh, what? You see, I'm getting rough mixin' with a tough gang. Now you know that you'd better be careful and follow the dictates of your lord & master! So, have a good time, whether you enjoy it or not! . . . Now that I've bawled you out, let me tell you how much I love you. That's better, isn't it. I guess loving is better than fighting, so we'll keep on loving as we always have, won't we, baby? It's going to be great to love with out that love being spoiled by the checker-shaped shadows reflected upon our souls.

October 31, 1921

Yes, girlie, all the boys seem to be treated with fine consideration; they and the officials seem to have become reconciled to one another, and then, the boys have proven that they can be trusted and relied upon.

. . . You are right, my girlie, the Evans' are wonderful people. You should have seen the letter I got from Mrs. Evans last week. She seems to be in a quandary as to what she could do for all of us without appearing to be "meddling" or "trying to arrange our affairs." She would much like to help in some way, yet she fears that whatever she might do would be looked upon as "charity," and the giving of it resented, because she fears that we might feel humiliated. . . .

Folks like the Evans' are never happy unless they can be doing good for others, helping others, not because it satisfies some vanity or whim of their as is so often the case with people, but because it is in their hearts to do good. They do not extend their hand in the doing of good that people may say, "See what good folks they are." No! quite on the contrary, they prefer to give it as a thief steals. . . .

Such people are rare and to number them amongst our friends is to possess the most wonderful prize that can be gained in the game of life. Mrs. Evans was afraid that you would misunderstand her gift of last summer as "charity." I am sure that we all know the fine spirit in which it was given, you know, as Mrs. Evans knows, if she stops to reflect, that she would have been bitterly hurt had you refused to accept her offer. She wanted so much that you should understand. I'm sure you do.

Now to our case. Nef, Fletcher, Graber and I will sign the applications for pardons if the committee thinks best. I have told you repeatedly that I will do whatever you ask in this matter. Walsh says that he will not sign. It puts things in a funny way for him as he is likely to change his mind later, when it is too late. He will answer personally so there is no need for me to go into details at all. Rey has his own committee and Weinberger is his lawyer. He is trying to get deported and told me that it is his desire now that the Philadelphia committee should do nothing in his behalf. He asks me to write this for him as he does not intend to answer personally.

November 1, 1921

I did not intend to write to you tonight but the events of the day make me feel like having a little talk with you. The press generally seems to have it that there is going to be some action in our case. The Phila. Ledger of the 29th has an account, the Chicago, Kansas City, New York and St Louis papers seem to all agree that the administration has it in mind to do something. The release of Debs seems to be certain. . . .

Now there's one of two things in that report, or rather behind it, either the administration intends to start releasing "politicals" or they are trying to stop agitation on behalf of "politicals" during the armistice conference. There is no doubt but that the administrative forces are releasing those reports.

But, whatever their intentions, there should be no misunderstanding among our friends as to what is best to be done just now. If there ever was a time when an insistent demand for our release should be made, that time is now. Letters should pour into the president by the bushel. Our friends should make it clear that there is a real desire to see us freed.

We must realize that the president will be in a very uncomfortable position should he fail to act, and if he fails he has but one excuse to offer, that being, that there was no demand made by the people that he should act. This possible "out" should be made an impossibility. . . .

Did you see Charlie Chaplin's article about the wobblies? I haven't been able to get ahold of it yet but I'm told that it is good. You possibly remember that I told you of how he failed to eat a supper because one of our boys was telling him of our case. . . .

I have just read Charlie Chaplin's article. It is in the Chicago "news" of Oct. 29th. If this article does not appear in any Philadelphia papers, send for it. It is worth keeping. It is really wonderful.

November 4, 1921

The American Legion convention is over and while they adopted a resolution against granting pardons to political offenders, they also, adopted resolutions of many descriptions scoring the administration for things they did do and things they didn't do. They condemned Harding and his appointees. In fact, it seems, from what I can gather from press reports, that about all the convention did was parade, hear speeches, drink "bootleg" whiskey, shoot dice, adopt some prepared resolutions, tear up the Baltimore hotel, listen to some fine music, beat up a hundred policemen, ignore the World's War Veterans, and raise a bit of hell.

I am of the opinion that the Legion's action re. politicals, will not carry any great weight with those who are in power. However, to offset any possible attentions which may be given to it, folks ought to get busy. Letters and telegrams ought to get into Washington before the President issues his Peace Proclamation.

. . . The need of action, <u>NOW,</u> is so very plain. Believe me, my girlie, I may seem very impatient but this is not entirely true. I have had some experience in very similar cases and have some idea when the "psychological moment" arrives. I am trying to write of a line of action I should advise whether or not I was myself in prison.

November 6, 1921

Mr. Evans told me, at some length, what had been done recently and, in a general way what they had in mind to do. I'm very happy that I thought to write Christensen to go to Phila. . . . Tell Mr. Evans that I'm pleased to hear him say that Mr. Christensen told them much more clearly of the issues involved in our case than we were able to. You must let him know that I'm not in the slightest offended when he says so, for it was I who insisted upon retaining him when others wished to have other counsel employed in his stead. . . .

You will kindly let Mr. Evans know that we agree with him when he says that we must not unnecessarily irritate those who are in a position to give us favorable consideration. I have never meant any kind of a blusterous demonstration. But I can not help thinking this: if the wives of defendants were to go to Washington, see the President, if possible, see the Attorney General, Senators and Congressmen; wives of the foreign born could see their country's representatives, etc. This need not be spectacular nor in any way be offensive to the most delicate feelings of anyone, and at the same time such acts make it more difficult for those in power to fail to act favorably in our behalf. The press today would not remain quiet when such an appeal was being made, they would comment on it as well as carry it as "news." . . .

. . . Nef is getting positively too fat for anything. He blames it on this prison fleece-lined canvas underwear. I think it is caused by too much eating and an overdose of loafing. . . .

Next day:—A very pathetical incident has just fallen the lot of the boys here. An old Irish miner in California wrote a letter to Dan Buckley the other day; in it he says,—tell the boys I'm dying of consumption and cant last much longer, I've got a couple hundred dollars that I can't spend in the next world, so I'm sending it to you to be divided among the wobblies there. See that these war-horses get it. Sorry I cant hang out long enough to see the better world we've been fighting for. Give my best to all of them, and, Dan, if you hope to have me read your answer, please write it at once for I'm slipping fast.

. . . The memory of him, who as he toddles into the great unknown waves back a salute, and who in his last breath calls back a word of cheer will live long with me, yes, all of us.

Was out in the yard today and the most of the boys are unreasonably optomistic. They all see themselves going out pretty soon. . . . The Swedes have been told that it is merely a matter of a few days now till they start back to Sweden. I don't know how true this is, but they say it comes from very reliable sources. We shall see. Letters coming from Senators, and particularly from Sen. Owens of Oklahoma, indicate early action is expected.

Whatever else there may be or may not be, one thing is certain, that the air here is charged with expectation. . . .

Now, maybe I'm foolish, too, like the rest of the fellows here, but I'm confident that we are within reaching distance of the end. . . .

With such men as H. G. Wells in Washington, to say nothing of the many representatives of powers which have long since released all politicals, it seems highly improbable that the administration can afford to go on record as being determined to hold its politicals much longer. . . . To make it more probable all pressure should be brought to bear now, letters, telegrams, and such.

November 9, 1921

Yesterday I was moved into the new cell block, the cells are about 10 by 20 feet and we are four men to a cell. Lots of room, a heaven compared to the cells I lived in when here before. For cell-mate I have three fine fellows, checker players, or, should I say, would-be checker players. I'm champion at present by a small margin.

. . . I was just thinking how foolish all this whole thing is, how foolishly serious we are over small things, and to what awful ends small things can lead.

Does anyone in a serious moment think that 148 men, who make up the army of politicals in prison, are so terribly dangerous? What must be the mental state of the representatives of one hundred million people when they think that they must protect that vast multitude of people from the words, the sentiments expressed by 148 men, men largely unschooled in the cunning and trickery which has meant the success of most enterprises in this land?

Does Morgan, Rockefeller, et al, admit possible defeat in their money schemes if "Bill Smith," the lumberjack or "John Jones," the longshoreman is released from prison? Does Mr. Harding think that the political institutions of the U.S. are unsafe if 148 politicals are released? If so, what must he think of the institutions? . . .

But let us hope that this is soon over, I'm sure . . . so far as the activities in the labor movement, of this group is concerned, it is also over. I do not think that it is over because of their imprisonment but rather because of the passage of five years of time. Had no arrests been made at all, it is in the nature of things that a vast majority of those now in prison would be out of the labor movement, at least actively. Where are those, let us say, in Chicago, who were not arrested? Mostly retired. . . .

Debs would hardly have been heard of today if he had not been sent to Atlanta. Today he is a national and international hero of workers and liberals. If those in power heed history they will drop this bunch and turn them loose to be forgotten, they have made a god of Debs and they are making the erstwhile despised I.W.W. respectable.

Armistice Day 1921
The Peace Treaty is hung up somewhere and ratifications have not been exchanged, so, necessarily there was no Peace Proclamation issued today as was expected. . . .

. . . It's my love and longing for you that causes every shadow here. There isn't a privilege given to a prisoner inside these walls that I haven't got. And what is worth yet more, the confidence and respect of both officers and prisoners.

November 13, 1921
Caroline Lowe was here today and saw some of the boys. She can't see it any other way than that there will be a general release on Thanksgiving day. Hope she is right. The Chicago papers have it that the attorney general is preparing a sort of a proclamation for the president which will call for the release of all those convicted of acts which would not have been a crime in peacetime. Your committee, using your best judgement, will do much to convince Mr. Harding of the rightiousness of his act of releasing politicals. . . .

I got a letter from Edna last night, a fine lively note. She is a great little girl when it comes to writing. She has real snap in her words and phrases. Lots of pep! And I really don't know where she gets it, it doesn't run very thick in the rest of the family.

She writes that mamma and all the rest are quite well and busy. Frank is still in Skagway and seems to intend to stay there. He is working on the Daily Alaskan there. Al is home again. They're fixing the place up in great shape, wiring the house, putting in an electric pump, more chicken houses. Hilma and Alvin have oodles of rabbits now. They all seem to be coming on very well. . . .

You must not forget to tell me what Bucky Boy has to say to Mr. President. You must remember that. Stop to think of it, Bucky has had some experience for a little boy, hasn't he? . . .

DEAR BUCKY. I GOT YOUR DRAWINGS. THEY WERE FINE. AND YOUR LETTER. I WILL TRY TO COME HOME TO YOU SOON. KISSES TO YOU XXXX ED.

November 18, 1921

Saw in the press that ex-soldiers who were decorated in the service have made protestations in our behalf. We surely appreciate it all.

How absurd it seems that all this agitation should be necessary! Even a cursory review of our case would show how outrageous were the sentences, to say nothing of the conviction. Of course, the conviction was to be expected in those days. . . . No jury would dare to find a verdict of "not guilty," that is, if they expected to ever live in peace again. That Judge Landis should inflict such frightful sentences at that time is not at all surprising for two very good reasons, he hated us and all we stood for, and he has an overwhelming mania for publicity. We, being helpless before him, offered him a wonderful opportunity to satisfy his personal hatred and at the same time gratify his insane craving for the limelight. Evidence they had none and needed less. Scores of men on trial with me did not even mention the war let alone oppose it. Some of them got twenty years. . . .

But now, the guns have been silent a long time. . . . We have good reason to expect something now, that the people have sobered up sufficiently to see the injustice of our continued imprisonment. No good purpose is being served by it, frightful punishment is being meted out, not only to the principals in this, but to their families. You have suffered much and Bucky Boy is of an age now that he understands this tragedy. It made me feel badly when you wrote of his saying that he "was ready to go to Washington to get papa." It hurts me when, in his crudely scrawled notes, he asks me to come home. . . .

. . . We have been held here for quite a long time. You will notice that at one time we are all optomism then all pessimism. The sameness of everything here causes the mind to lose all sense of proportion. I am conscious of this, but yet realize that I am a victim of it. . . .

Can you imagine this? Every day the same exactly as every other day. Not a particle of change except in the weather. The same routine, the same work, the same play, all is so alike. . . . Prison robs one of the best uses of his mind, that mind capable of analyzing and understanding proportions.

If our friends could realize this, they would be far more urgent than they are in getting us out of here. We have committed no offense against any man, but we shall not cry much about that. We were sent to prison because a nation got mad much as a very big man might get mad, and to be pummeled around during that madness we figured a part of our lot, but then, when the nation has sobered up from its debauch it looks but reasonable that it should try to repair some of the damage it wrought in its frenzy. . . .

. . . The matter of our freedom is out of our hands. We are not permitted to write for publications. We cannot conduct meetings. We are limited in the number of letters we may write. Our mail is subject to censoring. What we may do is not much.

. . . Saw Feige's letter to Nef. She has the right idea. Some ONE should be put on the job to act as a center and direct all forces into one in channel. The men in here should be told what to do rather than have their opinions asked about anything. Go ahead, you folks on the outside, never mind our opinions.

November 20, 1921
I was really surprised to hear of the War Veterans going so strongly to the front for us. . . . It was very good of Mr. William Allen White and his committee to see the president about our release.

November 22, 1921
On picking up the evening paper I see where the president has given out a statement to the . . . effect that he has ordered the attorney-general to submit to him a review of the cases of all political prisoners with the view to an amnesty proclamation which he expects to issue. He states that he will release all those convicted under war-

time laws and acts, but will not release those against whom a conviction was secured because of "overt acts." . . . Under the Espionage Act, it was an "overt act" to say almost anything. Surely he does not mean that. Those who were convicted of acts of violence, such as bombing ships, bridges, etc. have been released long ago. Now, there may be some reason or motive for ringing in "overt acts." . . . There is a possibility of the president releasing some and saying that he was holding others because of some "overt acts." The I.W.W. has a reputation. They may choose to take advantage of that fact. This is merely a surmise.

The facts are that we were charged (in the first count of our indictment) with having conspired to do certain things, thru and by violent methods. This count failed to stand in court (on appeal) and the sentence and fine were taken off. The same for the second count. . . .

We are in jail today because of a conviction under the 4th count (we have served our time under the 3rd count—Violation of Draft Act). This count (the 4th) charges a conspiracy to violate the Espionage Act, "thru and by means of public speeches personal solicitations and the distribution of certain literature." On this count alone are we serving time,—on this count alone are we held in prison. Everything else, real or imaginary, on any other count is dead.

THIS SHOULD BE MADE CLEAR.

Thanksgiving Day, 1921 [November 24]
We had a wonderful day today. Music along with breakfast, the King sisters sang in their wonderful contralto. A picture show this morning, for dinner we had chicken, cranberry sauce, celery, mince pie, etc. After dinner, a very fine whirly-girlie show, lots of good singing, some dancing by the chorus, and the very good comedy. A good act that would be good anywhere. This was followed by a feature movie. Supper, more chicken, cake and tea. Some day.

How fortunate we are in our misfortune, little girlie. While at the table I remarked to the lad next to me that I'd sooner be home to dinner, and if I was, I'd possibly be out to friends with my wife. I told him you'd been invited out by friends. He said, "I reckon I better wish my folks was here, they're starving at home." He told the truth. I spoiled his dinner by mentioning home to him. His desolate home nearly spoiled mine. Just think. He's here and his family feels disgraced and are starving. No one does a thing for him or them. I'm here; that fact alone has made me many friends, it has given you friends who are happy to be your friends. And, many hundreds are clamoring for my release. We may feel proud of my imprisonment, while they, like my friend here, feels disgraced.

Tell Mrs. Evans that the warden here, Mr. [W. I.] Biddle, is a Philadelphia Biddle. He was born upstate, but his people come from Phila. I would suggest that she drop him a line. He is a prince of a fellow.

December 6, 1921

There isn't a word that I could say regarding our case that would contribute anything, even a suggestion of what ought, or should, be done.

However, the biggest thing seems to be rather poorly done, that is publicity. Several of us have taken this matter up with people who could adequately do this work, but somehow they do not seem to be able to get anything in print. The capitalist press has carried as much as the so-called liberal press and far more than the would-be radical press. . . . I have seen nearly every issue of the "Industrial Worker" and to read it you would not know we were here at all. . . .

. . . A lawyer serving time here for "Espionage" violation, brought to my attention a possible course which we might persue and expect results. I shall try to make clear his proposition so you can show my letter to the lawyers and ask their opinion.

December 8, 1921

Your very fine letter of the 4th came last night and I was surely tickled to get it. Was so glad to hear that you are well and Bucky Boy is getting on so well.

. . . I must make a confession to you. I'm getting so infernally lazy that even if I get home I'd be useless. For some reason I stopped taking exercize. I go to breakfast in the morning and immediately afterwards climb up on my chair and sit there. And sit there! And sit on whether I have anything to do or not. At noon I do give my jaws some exercize on dinner, and then, I can have over a half an hour to play hand-ball or something like that, but, usually, I crawl back to the "rag-shop" and stretch out full length and half snooze for that time, then up on the chair once more. It's awful how lazy I am getting to be. And I'm picking up weight too. I now weigh 172 pounds. . . .

Oh yes, Dan Buckley, the now-emancipated Sinn Feiner is celling with me. Since Ireland has become free, he doesn't know he is in jail.

December 11, 1921

Say, girlie, I'm full of kosher roast pork and can't think, so you're going to have to be satisfied with a very rambling note this time. . . . It is a wonderfully fine day. From my cell I can look out over a wonderfully wide stretch of rolling country. Every thing looks like early winter, the hills in the distance look grey and desolate, the trees have shed their last leaves and the bare limbs are swaying in the breeze, and while the sun shines brightly it does not seem to light it up, somehow it seems to throw a bright glare over it. All this I see through an interlacing of two sets of bars. It is all so close—yet so far away. And funny, too, for if I was outside I know I wouldn't roam among those barren trees and dull brown grass. I should seek pavements and plate glass. Why do I care to roam through them now? I don't know! Why should a person wish for the things he doesn't want? But so often we do.

I guess, my girlie, that these sparce trees here somehow recall the little timbered canyon at Rex, where we so loved to roam. What wonderful nights they were! There was something in those nights which I never knew before. Really I think it was the healing of broken hearts and we may rejoice again now, for that wonderful experience shall be ours again.

December 14, 1921

Chiky, you must understand this, all of you outside, that there is no agreement in here. We get along fine so long as we don't try to agree on any policy. . . . Spring any plan for agreement on anything and you start a squabble here. These men have been in prison too long. . . .

Read carefully what you have to say regarding application for pardons and the work which they intend to do toward that end, and how they expect to present it. I rather doubt the advisability of a test case, principally for this reason: the administration is either going to deal with classes of cases or with individual ones. If with classes of cases, then it is surely better to simultaneously present all the cases, at least from one locality, at one time. . . . However, if the powers-that-be decide to go over individual cases, then the action in one case would have little or no effect on the other, although it may pave the way. That's a question.

But if the committee think that it is best to proceed upon the lines which they have chosen, then Nef's case is the best from the purely war standpoint. There is nothing against him and his "pro-ally-ism" is well established. Fletcher's case is also a good one, in some ways better than Nef's. But, there are no bad cases from Phila. . . . of course always bearing in mind that . . . to some degree those who will come forward as "character witnesses" for us will be different persons.

I want to feel that what is being done in my behalf is reflecting the good of all the rest. . . . We must not forget those here who are without powerful friends, that wouldn't be right. To my mind we should appear as individuals only as a last resort. . . .

December 18, 1921
See that Bucky Boy is to go to kindergarden. Fine. That'll be good for the boy. Mamma, I've drawn a Santa Claus in charcoal. I shall try to send it to Bucky in a day or two. I will have to make a tube to send it in. . . . I'll address the picture to Bucky himself. Be careful when you take the picture out of the tube as charcoal rubs off very easily, and, don't touch the picture. Better tear the tube from around it.

December 20, 1921
I hope that Bucky Boy will be entirely well when this letter comes to him. You must explain to Bucky that these letters are to both of you. He must know that I think of him often. . . .

Yesterday, a fellow who has been here 12 years and 2 months was told that his sentence had been commuted to expire on Dec. 21st. He was serving a life sentence. When he was notified and for an hour afterwards, the sweat stood out on his face in huge beads. He trembled and could not stand still. What happiness he suffered! It was a Christmas pardon.

December 22, 1921

Last night I got packages from Ellen Winsor, H. P. Mallery, and from home. As you know everything is opened and inspected before I get it, and, is delivered to me in paper bags. The outside wrapper of the package containing the address is put in the bottom of the bags. Things became so mixed up that I don't know what one sent from what the other sent. Anyway there were 2 cakes (one of them from mamma) some nuts, candy, dates and figs. A lot of everything. I'm playing Santa Claus in this cell. . . .

. . . There will be no school over the holidays here. We have had two shows already this week. Last night we saw a movie of the White Pass & Yukon Railway, Skagway was shown. That place has not changed a bit since I left there. It showed so many scenes of my kid days. What memories it brings forth. There's something about the old home town that clings. Some day we'll go up there. What do you say? As Bucky used to say "When we get rich."

. . . Mrs. Evans writes that she wishes you all out to their place for christmas feast, as she well puts it, that they have a whole turkey and as she is a vegatarian, Mr. Evans is going to need some help. She says Bucky's stockings are waiting for him at their home. What good folks they are!

Christmas 1921

Christmas is here and we have had our cheer. This morning Albert Prashner, Jack Law, Ed. Hamilton, of the Chicago Group went home. So, too, did John L. Murphy of the Sacramento Group. Charles Ashleigh and John Baldazzi will leave for deportation abroad either tomorrow or Tuesday. That makes six gone. Each had ten years except Murphy who had five. The ice is broken. The dark clouds have commenced to part and a shaft of sunshine strikes to earth, the great madness has begun to recede. . . .

. . . Mr. Evans . . . asked if there were any here who wished to present their case and had no one to do it for them. I know one and will ask the Phila. Folks to kindly handle it. I refer to my cell buddy, Dan Buckley. He has had his pardon papers ready quite awhile but has no one to present them so that there would be any likelihood for action. He is getting well on in years and is altogether too fine a fellow to be overlooked. His case is one of the most favorable amongst us. His misfortune is that all his life has been spent among migratory workers, largely among miners and construction workers. You will let Mr. Evans know that I have taken the liberty of asking Buckley to forward his pardon papers to you. . . . Buckley merely wishes that they present the papers and let the powers-that-be know there is some one interested in him. I'll tell you how I feel about it personally, if I had only myself to think about, I should very frankly tell the committee to drop me and handle Dan's case. There isn't a squarer fellow on earth than Dan. . . .

Baby, did you ever see the movie "Over the Hill"? We saw it today. It's a wonderful picture of mother love, wonderfully acted. Well, two-thousand convicts looked on and I swear one half of them had tears in their eyes and many wept like children. Then there are those who speak of hard-hearted convicts, criminals, social outcasts. They speak of men without hearts. By God, they wore their hearts on their sleeves today. I wish I could write with a pen of fire that would sear into the hearts of all mankind this fact: convicts are no more criminal than the rest of the human family, they are merely in prison because of misfortune. If laws were strictly applied and all violators apprehended, I firmly believe that there would be less people "outside" than are now in prison.

December 29, 1921

Bill Wehy's wife and sister are here. He is in bad shape, I understand. Every effort should be made to get him out <u>at once.</u> Am sure it means his life. . . . Cook County Jail has done it's work. The warden here is doing everything in his power to help Billy, most unusual care is given.

On Christmas Day President Harding authorized the release of Eugene V. Debs and twenty-three other political prisoners, as my father alludes to in the following letter.

New Years Day 1922

Today I received a wire of New Years Greeting from the Italian Workers Educational Circle of Phila (or something like that) very fine greetings. If you know who they are and where they are located, please extend to them, on behalf of the boys and myself, our warmest thanks for their well wishes.

. . . I must let you know of our home now. The hotel here is getting crowded so we have to live six in a cell, so Buckley and I have moved. In together now are McDonald, Thompson, Chaplin, Buckley and I with a very fine lad named Bahl. Our cell has been dubbed "Wobbly Headquarters." . . .

My little sweetheart, don't worry about when I get out nor about work. Whenever I get out, Uncle Sam will pay my way home. I have somewhere around $50.00 in the office here and that will grow as time passes. Unless you want to buy a farm, I'd suggest you let work drift easy and mind your health very carefully. Health is what counts.

. . . I saw in the press that Debs made a couple speeches, one in Washington and one in Indianapolis but saw no mention of his saying a word respecting political prisoners. I think he missed a wonderful opportunity. . . . [Last April] millions of people did not know what amnesty meant, the press denied that there were any political prisoners. Now everyone knows what amnesty is and the press either openly or covertly favor amnesty and all admit that there are political prisoners. With each day the I.W.W. cases are better understood by a greater number of people, and unless they wish to reveal the whole horridness of war-time frightfulness, [the attorney general] had better act quickly. Those who opposed the war are released, those who did not are yet in prison. These facts will out, and soon. Upon this issue people will listen, I'm sure. Debs should have made that clear before now.

January 5, 1922

It was so good to hear that you are feeling so well and the ringing tone of your letter assured me that you are in fine spirits. . . .

You must tell Yetta that I got her candy but that McDonald ate most of it up. He lays awake o'nights eating candy, so you see how it is. I guess I got my share, though. In this cell what's mine is everybody's and what's everybody's is mine. Mac asks me to let my friend know that if she is as fine as her candy, she's a very fine girl. I assured him that she's much finer than that, and I'm not knocking the candy, either. Aren't you jealous now?

. . . Caroline Lowe and Mr. Shields were here. I had all afternoon with them and it was very pleasant. . . . The fine method in which our visitors were treated was most pleasing. We met them in the warden's office and were permitted to speak with them privately. No guard was about at all. . . . I am glad to know that we are now considered absolutely trustworthy. The present administration is the only one we have had here who seem to try to understand us. I am sure that it will make you happy to know that this is so. It surely makes life far more pleasant here. There is something paradoxical about this administration here, they seem to have fallen upon a scheme by which they are simultaneously able to more strictly enforce rules and yet allow more liberty. I cannot explain it.

January 10, 1922

I think that the group made a happy choice when they selected Nef's case as the one around which to center their preliminary fight, but I do think they are making a grave mistake when they separate the cases at the outset.

. . . What I'd like to understand is, why the committee does not desire to present our applications at the same time. . . . Their present action has made Nef feel mighty badly and uncomfortable, more so than he is willing to admit. They ought to give him some explanation.

. . . The principal reason I have against further delay is that unless we are released by May, we can figure to remain here till next winter. There is never anything doing in the summer time. . . .

You say, "Ed, leave it to me and Feige that the things we are trying to do are the best." Be sure I shall, and be glad to. If I couldn't confidently and lovingly leave anything to you two to decide upon, then whom on earth should I rest my head upon? You're a pair of darlings, and <u>what you say goes.</u> Now, I've made myself perfectly clear.

Buckley is writing you tonight. He got a letter from Gurley yesterday and she says that they have just the right crowd in N.Y. to see him through. You see they have only the case of St. John left now. I should do as Buckley suggests, and send the papers on to Gurley.

I wont see Nef till tomorrow and then I'll show him your letter. He seems hurt because of the turn things have taken. He told me today that he wished they had chosen someone else instead of him. The committee's choice is a wise one, but Nef is sensative, and he wants to see the whole group go up. That's what I want, too, if it is possible.

January 18, 1922
Poor Bucky and his cold. Tell Bucky that he shouldn't hide anything from his papa, even his cold, yet one cannot help but admire the splendid sympathetic nature shown when he wishes that I should not be made to feel sorry.

My little sweetheart, were it not for the misery you suffered, I should be inclined to be funny regarding your letter of the 12th. I did say that "personally I am unwilling to be a party to leaving the other boys behind." I mean that, but—get me right, if any wish to stay, or can get any glory or self-satisfaction out of their petty heroics, I am the last who wishes to interfere with their foolishness. If Walsh does not care to have friends act in his behalf, that's his business, not mine. In that case, he's the party to leaving himself behind, I am surely not that party. But, then, with Fletcher, for instance, he . . . is willing to do all he can personally, in a case such as his, I feel that I am bound by every tenet of honor to be with him in his struggle.

. . . By George, I'm getting on with my drawing. Its just reached a point where I don't want to stop. Imagine, I'm six days working on one face and get more interested in it each day. I can close my eyes and see that face, every line and every shadow. Funny thing, too, did you know that there are dozens of shadows or "planes" in the face that none of us thought ever existed? Well, there are.

January 24, 1922
The big stiff wants to get out, and that badly, too. He is kidding no one but himself. He's about 90% strong character and 10% baby. He hasn't got that kid face for nothing. This baby side must be taken into consideration whenever dealing with him. Nef is least safe in his own

hands. He would fight for the world with reckless abandon and then when he must fight for himself, he is little short of a coward. He has always been so. This must be held always in mind, and, with it in mind, you can go ahead.

But, here is a whole phase I cannot understand, why put the cart before the horse at all. The issue of what anyone intends to do, is not yet an issue. Why not wait till it is reached. Let the people at Washington ask the question and then you answer it . . . Just let the other fellow make the issue.

Experience proves that it is useless to concede too much to anyone voluntarily. Begging is usually the poorest way to make a fortune, it commands the least respect, and generally is paid for in contempt. If the powers ask respecting future intentions of anyone, then its time to reply. You may reply then with force and dignity. Why not wait. If, in any case, you haven't time or inclination to refer a matter to us, go ahead yourself. Nef's philosophy has always been,—do it first, explain it afterward. Adopt that rule.

To be sure, you assume a great responsibility. All of us have futures in which we must live, there is such a thing as buying today what we cannot pay for in a life time. It would not pay to leave here if tied down by a hundred strings. . . .

. . . If they choose to make our promise a law for all future conduct, then life wouldn't be worth living, because, if they have a string to hold on to and choose to use it, they can make themselves mighty miserable. You've heard of frame-ups before now. . . .

I have no faith in any politician's word. Neither have you. Feeling sure that you never had in mind any proposition to bind us to any conduct other than we may choose for ourselves, I feel perfectly at ease in leaving everything in your hands.

January 27, 1922

I saw in the Kansas City "Times" of yesterday where the Senate had adopted Borah's resolution which demands that the attorney general show what evidence he is supposed to have against war-time espionage and conspiracy offenders. I am wondering what the motive is behind this move.

Had quite a talk with the big stiff yesterday, and, I'm sure that he is quite in accord with all that has been done and will go a long way to help in securing his release. But he seems correct in this: he is not ready to promise that he is through and that he wont belong to a labor union, or the like. On that score I think he is correct. . . .

We have some lessons on the futility of promises here. Phin Eastman has quit the I.W.W., renounced his fellow prisoners, is willing and has promised everything, his wife is an invalid with no hope to live, Eastman is in bad health himself. He applied for executive clemency. . . . He, you might say, wore the buttons off of his vest crawling up for mercy, and, today, he got a flat turn-down, Why? Can you imagine? Because it was feared that he would be a menace to society!!! He is done with all revolution, all movements, everything, he wants only to be left to go into a restaurant business, care for his wife whom he loves very dearly. But no! he's dangerous. His promises were not worth a damn. Moral, don't promise too much. A man who stands upon his "rights" commands the respect, not only of his friends but his enemies as well. . . .

Evening has come. Say I completed the portrait I have been working on for the past three weeks, and it's fine. Ralph told me that I should be able to get a job as a "spot-knocker" that is to say commercial artist with three or four months actual practice at the work.

January 30, 1922

By the way, I suppose that you know that Bill Weyh has been commutted and is gone from here. Elsie (Mrs. Weyh) was here all the time since he took sick. She was allways smiling and pleasant, with a spirit of cheer about her, till Bill was actually "dressed out" then she broke down and cried.

I saw Bill about 15 minutes before he left. How bad he looked! Skin and bones. Maybe the desert climate of New Mexico will help him, but we all doubt if he can survive. We can only hope, no more.

To the local administration must go the credit that Bill is alive today. Every tender care was taken of him. When the commutation came, all the machinery was set to work to get him out as soon as possible with all excitement avoided.

When I knew that he had his release papers here, it was noon-hour. I secured permission to see him and when I came in Bill was up and alone. He was nervously fiddling around with his effects. He asked me to sit down which offer I declined, asking him to rest himself. He said he was all right. He didn't look it! I asked him if he was compelled to promise the government anything for his release and he said "No." The only thing he was required to say to them was that he would be law-abiding (!) and hold himself ready to be deported to Germany when his health would permit.

As we were talking, the warden and Chief Clerk came in, together with Elsie. Elsie told Bill to sit down and conserve his energy and when he said he was all right, the Warden turned to him kindly and said, "Now, my boy, do as your wife asks you"—he paused a moment and said—"She knows best."

It really was not what was said but how it was said. When it came time for me to go, I bid Bill "good bye." He was almost playful, but something told me that I shook Bill's hand for the last time. I think Elsie knew that, too, for she had a quiver on her lip when she said "good-bye" and there seemed little hope in her smile.

February 1, 1922

It was especially fine to get all the news of the doings of yourself and Bucky. I bet he is a proud boy, now that he is going to school. You must let me know what he learns there, what there is to do, and how he likes it, more particularly the other children.

. . . I see in Feige's letter to Nef that Mr. Kane says that Washington is making their fight on Nef, that they are raking up some old articles left over from the dark ages. It is well to force them to show their hands. When they have been compelled to show what they think they have then it will be easy for us to rebutt them.

So far we have not learned what steps have been taken to present our cases fully to those senators who have secured the passage of the resolution. The attorney general's office, we may be sure will drag to light all the junk that the wild imaginings of Palmer caused to be placed on file. Most of this stuff is the worst kind of lies. It will have to be combatted. I shall try to talk over this phase of the matter with Baldwin and Flynn.

February 3, 1922
Mr. and Mrs. Edmund C. Evans:
Ardmore, Pa.

My dear Friends.

I have Mrs. Evan's last letter before me now and I wonder if you know or realize how much cheer there is in one of them. You can't know what the mail man means to us here, he means all that is left of outside.

There are six of us in the cell, and when mail is delivered we are all attention,—he calls 13-1-04, and it's "here's yours, Ralph" and then 13-1-19, "Hey, Dan, been writing to yourself again?" then 13-1-45, "Well, Jim's got his tonight." I'm waiting,—then comes that 13-1-25, "That's me, bet it's from home." When two letters come it's a treat. And, the poor devil who gets none, gets sympathy, It's "better luck tomorrow, old man."

Then again there are letters and letters. Some full of love, some of bitterness, some of cheer, and then those who see the humorous in everything.

Your's are the cheery sort. One feels better for having read them, the world seems brighter, and, the outlook more hopeful. They give one greater courage. We are all politicals in this cell and I'm sure you don't mind that I read your letters to them. . . .

From my sister Edna, I get letters, humorous and satyrical. She is a second Mark Twain. All I have to say "Fellows, I've got a letter from sis." and the air seems electrified. The boys are too polite to ask me to read it, but at least two will inquire as to what she had to say. I read, and the fellows enjoy wit and humor seldom found in letters.

The truth is, letters give us more real pleasure than all else combined.

. . . Ida has often written me telling me of the many good things you have done for her and Bucky Boy. I wish I could adequately thank you for all this, but I fear that you would feel offended if I tried to, so I shall say but this,—I appreciate it more than I am able to tell you, and if you are able to realize, even in a small measure, how much good your kindness, in one way or another, has done for my dear ones and me, you will feel repaid.

Roger Baldwin was here today. I saw him for a few moments. . . . Fom what I could gather from stray bits of talk among the boys tonight, it is very likely that they will accept his proposition, namely, that all shall make application for executive clemency, and the A.C.L.U. fight on behalf of all, especially those who have no local groups working to secure their release. I surely hope that the boys have the good sense to accept this suggestion.

. . . I'm doing fine here. Have a good job, good food, a good bed, and the best of health. There's many a poor devil tonight who would gladly share my comfort. One wants to get out of here as one wants to get out of a hospital. It's the confinement that hurts, the keeping of one from those near and dear to him. That's the punishment.

Please remember me to your mother and sisters, and, with all good wish to you, I am, your friend, Doree

February 5, 1922
My dearest little Chiky:
Was just thinking that tomorrow is my birthday, and the 33rd milepost will have been passed. It reminds me that I'm getting old and yet just a kid.

. . . So my Bucky Boy must be vaccinated. I wish he didn't have to, but if he must I guess he must. It seems to make no difference whether one goes to prison or to school, he must be vaccinated.

February 9, 1922
Gee, I'm glad to hear that the Friends [Quakers] are sending a committee to Washington. They are the one group who have influence. I hope that they see the president himself. . . .

I saw Dougherty's reply to the Borah resolution. He says that he has not got the evidence, etc., against the politicals, and that it would take considerable time and expense to gather it together from the records in the hands of district attorneys all over the country. Borah replied that he did not want any great expense or loss of time, but if the department of justice at Washington submitted what evidence it had in Washington, he (Borah) believed that the spirit of the Senate Resolution would have been complied with. The attorney-general's reply to the senate was awfully weak.

. . . Now, my little sweetheart, I guess the circular you sent me must be great. I am not yet permitted to have it. I was up to the mail room today and the matter of whether I shall ever get it was turned over to the warden. Please do not say anything of this to the Evans as yet, as I'm quite sure that Mr. Biddle will let me see it. . . . The reason I do not wish to say anything to the Evans' is this: they may feel inclined to take it up as an issue, and, if this is done the warden will be possibly held to blame and this is not true, and, because he has done so many fine things, as in Bill Weyh's case, I would feel a scoundrel if anything I said or did should reflect the slightest ill upon him.

The whole thing has struck me rather as funny. Just think of such staid old dyed-in-the-wool Americans, of Lord knows how many generations standing, being charged with writing "radical" literature.

Chiky wrote Ed to say that she was tending to Bucky and Feige, both of whom had fallen ill.

February 13, 1922
On returning to the cell this evening I found yours of the 9th awaiting me. Am sorry to hear of your hospital but hope that you've closed up before now.

I'm glad to hear of the visit of Mrs. Cope. What did she say were her intentions specifically, that is, in what way do they propose to aid you. To tell the plain truth, I'm sure it would be ever so much better to feel morally obligated to folks in Philadelphia than in Chicago. . . . They, the Chicago bunch, feel that they are doing us a great favor while our bourgeois friends feel it an honor to be of service in these hours thru which we now live.

February 15, 1922

My dearest Bucky Boy:

When this letter reaches you, you will be celebrating your 5th birthday, and I hope you have a very good time, and when your next birthday comes we will be all together and then we will have a real time, wont we?

. . . Who was the sickest? You or Feige? I hope that you are both well and feeling fine when you get this letter.

. . . I am sending a whole world of kisses and love for your birthday. You must hurry and get well and then have a nice picture taken so you can send one to me.

I must write to mamma now . . .

. . . I'm very happy to hear that your patients are much improved and on the road to rapid recovery. Nef was considerably worried till he heard from Feige last night.

. . . I shall write the rest of this letter with difficulty as there is so much noise here now. Buckley is telling of his experiences in getting jobs in the "wooly west" and what he heard, said and did at the Frisco earthquake.

February 17, 1922

By George, I think I'll stay in jail. It pays, doesn't it? You'll be rich yet. You mustn't deny yourself or work too hard in order to gather a few dollars together. We shan't starve even if I do eat a whole lot. And, you cant tell, I might go to work myself. Had you never thought of that? You know these "hoose-gows" makes one foolish and, they say that only fools and mules work and a mule turns his back upon it. . . .

Gee, I feel foolish tonight. I could have a great time now if I was home and we had a gang there. I think I could tell stories and made them all laugh,—as in days gone by.

February 21, 1922

I was mighty sorry to hear that Bucky Boy is sick abed. Let's hope that he'll soon be well again. I'm glad that I'm to hear often from you so long as he does not feel well. I do so much want to know how he is getting along.

. . . Do you think it wise for you to write to Chicago at all? Wouldn't it really be better if I did? . . . If the situation would become such as to permit, I should prefer to break with them.

The whole affair in Chicago has degenerated into a tragic joke, a mess so sickly that I'm really disgusted with it. It seems that with each succeeding month they go lower into the mire of their own making.

Sometimes I am almost ashamed to be called one of them, and when I think that more men and women are being sacrificed for such fellows, I feel sick at heart.

I shall not burden you with what this is all about, not yet, anyway. I hope not to be compelled to say anything till all the politicals are out. That would be the best. This much I can say, they are not only crucifying the men who largely made the movement, but the very movement itself. I guess I've hoped against hope, so far as that organization is concerned. Perhaps I shouldn't say this now, surely it must not be known what I think till we are all free, but the sooner that it is possible to cut the string with the official bunch, the better.

February 24, 1922
The 5 year men leave here May 14th of this year. When they are gone, harmony will be more possible than now. They are "brave" and "hard-boiled" now that it is perfectly safe for them to be so.

February 26, 1922
I am very happy to hear that you are all well once more.

. . . There was quite a discussion regarding asking for clemency today. They agreed to disagree. What a bunch of men! Just like so many children. It's all too bad but I suppose they'll have to sleep in the bed of their own making. I shall not sleep in it with them. It is one of the privileges of men to be foolish, but I cannot see why they should abuse the privilege!

You must know what wonderful weather we are having here. This morning we awoke to see the beginning of a gentle snow storm, while at breakfast it turned to a most wonderful snow, flakes like giant feathers, one would imagine that they would be so soft to lie down in. It is just cold enough to hold the snow on the ground, and, now, as I gaze out of the window over the hilly landscape I yearn to be out there, if for only a few minutes. If one must be in prison, it is better that he should see no beautiful things, his mind should be always on prison, it's walls, it's noises, it's silence, it's smell. There should be only a vague outside, lost into the past like some sweet memory mellowed with time.

March 2, 1922
Your letter of the 25th came some days ago and nothing since. I rather expected a letter tonight but the mail man breezed merrily by and left me out of the race.

    Before I undertake to reply to yours, I have a message to deliver. Nef asks me to ask you to ask Feige to send him some money to have his teeth repaired. The cost will be about $100.00 (one hundred little round iron men).

    . . . So you have again gotten relief from Chicago. That's good. All were cut off for a while for "lack of funds," I'm told.

The mailman had "breezed merrily by" without delivering a letter from Chiky because both she and Bucky were now hospitalized with influenza.

March 5, 1922
I shall wait impatiently for something more definite from Bucky Boy. I should much have liked it if he could have been in the same room with you, but maybe it is for the best.

    . . . I'm sure glad to hear that you are treated so well by those in the hospital. Stay as long as you can and see to it that you get thoroughly well. Please do that.

    . . . I suppose that you know that the Judiciary Committee of the U.S. House of Representatives has set March 16th aside to hear arguments on Meyer London's amnesty bill.

Under the chairmanship of Congressman Andrew J. Volstead of Minnesota, the Committee on the Judiciary met on March 16th to hear testimony from fifteen witnesses, all urging support for H. J. Res. 60, Congressman London's proposal that Congress recommend to the president that a general pardon and amnesty be granted to 113 federal political prisoners, ninety-five of whom were convicted in the IWW conspiracy trials in Chicago, Wichita, and Sacramento.

    Albert De Silver of the American Civil Liberties Union was the first to speak, emphasizing that these were "political" prisoners in the sense that they were convicted of no overt act other than expressing opinions. He cited Civil War precedents for amnesty and the fact that, before the end of 1919, amnesty had already been granted to all Allied political prisoners in Europe.

Wobbly attorney Otto Christensen appeared next, focusing on the Chicago case. He was met with rude skepticism:

MR. WALSH (of Massachusetts). *They have had their day in court upon that question?*

MR. CHRISTENSEN. Yes.

MR. WALSH. *And the court of appeals has upheld the conviction, has it not?*

MR. CHRISTENSEN. It has upheld the conviction, yes.

MR. WALSH. *Now you want us to say that the court of appeals, in upholding that conviction, erred?*

MR. CHRISTENSEN. No; I do not. . . .

MR. WALSH. *Then you want us to say the jury erred?*

MR. CHRISTENSEN. I do not want you to say the jury erred, but I will make this observation, that the jury returned, in this case, 400 verdicts in 25 minutes, in a trial that lasted more than five months; so that it is quite apparent individual consideration was not given to the cases of these defendants as to whether they were participants in this general conspiracy that was charged . . .

MR. WALSH. *Suppose there was one verdict that took 400 hours, what difference would that make?*[1]

Soon after, Alexander S. Lanier of Washington, D.C., gave his statement. As a captain in the Military Intelligence Division of the General Staff of the Army, Lanier said, he been assigned to summarize the evidence in the Chicago case for the information and use of that division. It was his testimony that, although a member of the "capitalist class" who stood "uncompromisingly against the I.W.W.," after reviewing the case he decided to come forward, feeling "a grave public duty on my part to expose the great injustice the record discloses."[2]

March 7, 1922

Got a letter from you today and yesterday and was so awfully glad to
know that you all are progressing so well. You inquire of my health.
Why, girlie, I always feel fine and dandy, always. There has been a
good deal of sickness here but they all miss me a mile. I'm commencing to think that I'm sick-proof.

. . . I suppose that it is unnecessary to mention, but perhaps it is
well. Will there be any one from Phila. to appear before the House
Judiciary Committee on March 16th when they have their hearing on
amnesty?

. . . When you see Bucky Boy, you must tell him how much I hope
that he'll soon be well and about again. . . . Give my love to Feige and
my hope for the early return of her health.

And you, my little darling, I'm glad you're so much better, now,
by all means be careful, so very careful, get good and strong again. . . .

Some one from Philadelphia did appear before the Committee. Dr. Frederick Edgerton of the University of Pennsylvania spoke "on the case of
four members of the I.W.W. from Philadelphia, who were convicted in
the Chicago case."[3] He stressed how the longshoremen of Philadelphia,
under IWW control and Walter Nef's leadership, had in wartime loaded
munitions without accident or strike. He introduced character references
from Nef's former employers, an editorial from the *Philadelphia Evening
Bulletin,* and a pamphlet, "An Appeal in the Name of Justice," endorsed
by eminent Philadelphians, including Mrs. James D. Winsor. That pamphlet reviewed the charges, presented evidence that these men were not
guilty, and included passages from my father's affidavit detailing illegal
governmental interference with the defense.

At the end of his testimony, Dr. Edgerton was asked whether he had
any connection with the IWW. When he answered, "No," he was asked,
"Why do you take particular interest in this matter here?" He replied,
"Because it seemed to me it was a case of flagrant injustice in the cases
of these men."[4]

March 10, 1922

Miss Winsor tells me that they sent Bucky Boy a picture book for him
to play with. I can't help but wonder what he thinks away from you.

In a letter a few days ago, Mrs. Evans said that she thought it would be well if you and Bucky Boy would be able to get away from town for a while and take a good rest. She says she was sure that it would do Bucky Boy a whole lot of good. . . . While I'm sure Mrs. Evans did not intend it, yet she made her appeal quite pathetic. She pointed out how they could be depended upon to carry on our cases with all vigor even if you should leave the city for a while; she assured me . . . that it was a pleasure to them to know they were prepared to send you $25 a week for months to come.

Maybe it would be well for you to go to Ruchel's, but, if my opinion be asked, you should not go till you are thoroughly well, as you know from experience that there is no such a thing as a doctor in Galeton. Until you are completely well, dont you think it best to stay in town?

I asked Nef about his teeth and suggested that he try to wait till he gets out, but he says his front teeth are worn down so that he cannot chew on them any more. He has no back teeth. That's the situation.

March 12, 1922
I'm glad that you are well enough to go home.

. . . I'm so sorry to hear of Bucky having been so sick. Somehow, I sensed that he was quite sick. The flu seems to have made quite a general attack in this country, but the doctors seem to have learned how to handle it, and the death rate was not great this time. . . .

Every precaution was taken here to prevent an epidemic. School was stopped, likewise church and picture show. No one died and those who are still in the hospital are on the high road to recovery. All danger is over.

. . . As to Nef and his teeth money, it can wait, must wait till the health on the outside permits taking care of it.

I'm sure glad that you are able to be home and can but hope that Bucky Boy will be as well soon. Was surely sorry to hear of Mr. E. C. Evans troubles. That flu has been raising Cain all over.

March 15, 1922
Last night brought me two letters and tonight another from you and one from Mrs. Evans. I'm so glad to hear that Bucky Boy is so

improved. And, needless to say, I'm might glad to know that you and Feige are well once more.

. . . It is good that you said nothing to the folks at home about your illness. Mamma is getting pretty old, too old to stand too great a shock. It is much better that she should hear of all this after it's over.

. . . You must not forget to tell Bucky that I've thought much of all his trouble and have hoped so hard that he would get well and be able to go home and get so big and fat again that he can have a fine big picture taken and send to me. You must tell him, too, that I'm proud because he was a brave boy and could stay away from mamma for so long and be a good little boy. Really, mamma, I think that you should see him. It's hard to say what he may think has become of you. If you think it is risky otherwise, take a taxi. It's worth a couple of dollars.

March 19, 1922

We just read a long account in the New York Call about the hearing in Washington. Must have been interesting to say the least. It seems that a very fine appeal was made for us. The local papers had quite a write-up on it. I am sending you a clipping from the first page of today's K.C. Star. . . .

. . . Before I go further, I'll tell you that I wrote Grady today at Chicago. . . . I said, "My wife is reminded that funds are hard to raise, and, on that score we shall be glad to aid. She and I are of one accord in this matter, stop the relief, also on my account, if anything is being sent to me, stop that, too. Anything further sent will be returned. From now on in case of extreme need we shall rely on personal friends.

"You may depend on my wife's cooperation in the amnesty drive. . . .

"Just now she cannot do much as both she and my baby have been down with the 'flu,' my wife is still confined to her room while the boy is yet in the hospital. As soon as strength permits, the amnesty movement can rely on her to the fullest degree. However, she does not wish to have it thrown up to her that "WE expect the co-operation of everyone, especially those closely concerned." . . .

There's a whole lot more, where I go on to tell about how we have seen the movement go to smash. . . .

I surely hope that you shall not suffer because of this move. To tell the truth, I'm mighty happy that you were able to take this stand, because, for one thing, when I get out, I'm sure that we'll both want to feel free to build as we choose, that no one shall hold a hand over us. Also, it frees you from the talk of idlers now.

March 22, 1922

It is fine to get such fine news that Bucky is getting better and all that.

. . . I saw in today's paper that 50 Congressmen have asked Pres. Harding to release all the political prisoners. It seems that the press is pretty well all in favor of amnesty, that is all except the small country papers.

. . . It seems to me that the demand for amnesty is ever growing. I am wondering if the president can face all this music and still do nothing. The Dept. of Justice's misrepresentation of fact has not done them a bit of good it seems.

So Feige is to go to Washington. I suppose if health permits you will be there, too. Also Bucky, if he is well enough. It would be fine if everyone is well enough, but surely you are going to take no chances, and in that you're right.

Bucky was too ill to participate, but Feige went to Washington in company with the Children's Crusade for Amnesty. Twenty-five children, most of them from western states and ranging in age from three to nineteen, traveled together to ask President Harding to free their fathers, all political prisoners in Leavenworth. Under the charge of Kate Richards O'Hare, they made stops in several cities. In Terre Haute they called on Eugene V. Debs and inspired some of his subsequent articles.[5] In Philadelphia, driven in automobiles furnished by Mrs. Samuel S. Fels and other prominent women, they were taken to the Episcopal Hospital to visit Bucky and give him flowers.

March 24, 1922

Gee, Bucky Boy must have had quite a bad case. I'm so awfully glad that he is so much better. . . .

With Nefs papers in the hands of the people at Washington and mine in the last stages toward the securing of my signature, things look good. We got a long letter from Mr. E. W. Evans tonight and he told us, in detail, of the hearing on amnesty in Washington. . . .

I didn't know that Fletcher had the "flu." I wouldn't know it now, if I hadn't heard it from you. I haven't seen him in several days, may be weeks, now that I come to think of it. You see, he eats on a different mess, cells in a different cell house, and unless we happen to meet in the yard on Sundays, we don't see one another at all. You must know that it's easy to miss one man among 2350. But I must confess, I had not heard of him being sick at all.

March 27, 1922
I wrote to Edward W. Evans today, merely a one page letter. It is indeed sad that his little girl is so sick. It's a shame that the angel of death must hover over the homes of such fine folks, when it passes completely over some of the most miserable types on earth.

March 30, 1922
Gee, I was so glad to get your last letter and hear that you had seen Bucky Boy and found him so much better. It makes the world seem so bright after so much darkness.

One thing struck me hard, and that was when you wrote of Bucky asking you if you would come and see him every Saturday and Sunday. I cannot overcome the idea that he sometimes feels as I do here, that time is endless and only certain things in a dim distant future counts. . . .

I was sorry to hear that Dad and Florence had the "flu" but it's surely good news to hear that they're well again. It's good news to weak ears to have it reported that mamma and Uncle Gus are on the job. If a bit of noise comes from outside of Philadelphia it will help some, believe me.

. . . Regarding the trip to Washington. It seems that the "Children's Crusade" is becoming quite a success. They seem to be able to enlist quite a number of women and children. I should judge that it will be the 1st of May nearly before they reach Washington. Maybe by that time both you and Bucky Boy will be perfectly all right again.

An article on the front page of the *Philadelphia Ledger* of April 5, 1922, read:

GLIMPSE OF SICK
SON ENDS CONVICT'S
RACE WITH DEATH

———

Federal Prisoner Comes 1270
Miles Under Guard for Brief
Look at Boy in Hospital

———

CHILD TOO ILL TO TALK
WITH FATHER, DOCTORS SAY

———

A 1270-mile journey from the Federal prison at Fort Leavenworth, Kansas to the bedside of his son, in the Episcopal Hospital, ended early today, when Edward F. Doree, Philadelphia I.W.W. leader, now serving a ten-year sentence, stood at the partly opened door of the child's room and gazed upon him unseen.

So serious is the condition of "Bucky," the five-year-old boy, that physicians would not permit the father to make his presence known to the child, in fear of the effect which it might have upon his greatly weakened heart.

The father tip-toed to the door, followed by United States Marshal Biddle, in whose custody he made the journey, and looked cautiously through the crack, which was just wide enough to reveal the wasted form of the boy lying quietly on the white bed.

As Doree peered into the room, a smile overspread his thin face, pale from two years within prison walls, and his tall, emaciated form was pressed against the wall. He took off his thick-lensed spectacles and wiped them.

Is Content to Wait

"How I would like to hold him, so," he said to his wife, who was at his side, and he held his arms as though enfolding an imaginary form. "But if it is better that I should not be with him yet I will not go in. Perhaps later I can be with him."

. . . Doree arrived at North Philadelphia station on the Manhattan Limited at 7:29 o'clock. He and Deputy Marshal Biddle stepped from the train more in the manner of two friends than as prisoner and captor, and looked about them for those that were to meet them.

"How is my boy?" were his first words, and in an instant he was holding his wife in his arms, after a separation of two years. Then others came forward to greet him—Miss Ellen Winsor, of Haverford, Pa., who was instrumental in securing permission for the journey; Mr. and Mrs. E. C. Evans and Mrs. Walter Cope, who are also interested in the case, and Mrs. Walter Nef, whose husband is now serving a twenty-year sentence for the same offense, that of sedition.

Doctor Takes Precautions

After some delay at the station the party set out for the Episcopal Hospital, at Front street and Lehigh avenue, where "Bucky" occupies a private room on the third floor, through the generosity of friends of the family. Mrs. Doree herself, left without support since the imprisonment of her husband, was unable to afford this luxury.

They walked south on Broad street to Lehigh avenue, and there boarded a car, which took them to the door of the hospital. After being admitted they proceeded upstairs at once, where they were met by a nurse, who explained the condition of the child in whispers to his parents.

"The doctor said that you might go in while Bucky is asleep," she said, "but he is awake now and resting quietly, so all I can let you do is to peep in through a crack in the door so that he will not know you are here.

"He has endocarditis," she explained, "and any little shock, such as seeing you again, might affect his heart fatally."

The child became seriously ill following an attack of influenza and pneumonia, from which his mother and Mrs. Nef also suffered.

His condition had been so critical that it was thought that he would die before his father could reach his bedside, but this morning his temperature fell from 104 to 101, with a better pulse and respiration. At the present time he is thought to have an even chance for life.

[Post Card]
Altoona Pa
April 9, 1922

Dear Girlie:

Will leave here early tomorrow. I may not get your special delivery letter before I go. Will go straight on from here. Wire me at Leavenworth how Bucky Boy is. Be of good cheer, my baby, and keep a smile
on your face. My love to Feige and all-all. I will kiss you bye-bye now
and send on a letter as soon as I can write it.

    Lovingly Ed

    Please tell Bucky if he asks for me that I'll be over to Phila pretty
soon again.

    Love—Ed

[Post Card]
April 10, 1922
Just a line before I leave Pittsburgh. . . . I take it for granted that
Bucky Boy is coming along all right, or else I should have gotten a
wire from you. I saw this morning a Phila. Record and it reported no
change in his condition. Therefore, I can but hope for the best.

[Post Card]
April 11, 1922

My dear Chiky:

Leaving St. Louis in a few minutes. Have followed the papers carefully and seen no news. It will be good to hear from you and hear that
Bucky Boy is better. I am going to get added writing privileges at once
and try to get in touch with all the people I can. I am convinced that
a release must be effected as soon as possible. So, if at any time you
can suggest a thing that I can do, please say so. Girlie dear, give my
love to Feige and to our poor sick Bucky Boy. Be well yourself and all
will be all right. Loving you tenderly—Your fond hubby—Ed.

April 12, 1922

My dearest little sweetheart.

Well, I got back this morning, and tonight I received your letter of the 9th. Your wire was here when I arrived, and you may believe me that I was so glad to hear that our Bucky Boy is so improved. And it is so good to know that you rested as well. That's fine. Very fine. We were somewhat storm bound on our road here and nearly all our trains were delayed. . . .

Gee, girlie, I surely got a fine sympathetic reception here. When I came into the Clothing Department, the boys fairly climbed over each other to greet me with such real enthusiasm. They seemed so genuinely happy to know that our little boy was getting better. It was really remarkable how they had followed our troubles in the papers. Our pictures have been published in all sections of the country and very fine articles written in all parts of the country. It really caused the biggest stir of anything recent. But, what does it all matter, our Bucky Boy is getting well again.

I had quite a talk with Nef. He was surely happy to hear of the general improvement among all of you. He, I thought, showed signs of worry. But, I think, I was able to cheer him up a bit.

Will write to the Attorney General tomorrow when my sleepy head is a little more clear. . . .

Somehow I cannot help but let my mind wander to one subject,— what fine friends we have, what real and wholesome friendship they are showing. Friends here, friends at home.

April 14, 1922

Last night and tonight I got letters from you telling me of Bucky Boy's improvement. Gee, how happy that makes me, you can just imagine. . . .

I was up today for physical examination. You know one is called up for such examination after application for pardon is asked. It seems to me as pretty quick action. . . .

I shall write home to mamma on Sunday and let her know of our trouble. It will be better than if she should hear of it from other sources. She may get a garbled story, and that would be terrible. It is impossible to think that she will not soon hear of it because the story has been carried in nearly all of the papers. Our pictures were shown in newspapers all over the country. . . .

Am sending you enclosed a copy of my letter to the attorney general.

I take this occasion, upon my return to prison, to convey to you my warmest thanks for the privilege you extended to me when you permitted me to go to the bedside of my little boy who is critically ill.

The doctors now have hopes for his recovery although it will be a very long uphill struggle. . . .

Just before returning here, our physicians told me that if my boy recovers he will be compelled to remain confined in bed for at least three months after which he will have to receive the very best of care, perhaps for years.

My funds are long since gone, and my wife and boy are now compelled to rely entirely upon the aid given them by our friends.

I have applied for executive clemency. I have presented my case to the proper authorities. I know that it contains merit and am sure that whenever it is given full consideration that the President will allow me to go back to my family who needs me so badly now.

I feel that I owe it to those nearest and dearest to me, to urge upon you to give my application an early and very serious consideration, for I must go to them soon. They need me as I long for them.

Thanking you again for the kindness you extended to me, I am,

Very Sincerely Yours.

This is the full copy of my letter to the Atty. Gen. sent April 12, 1922. Ed.

April 16, 1922

Dear Folks at Home,

Perhaps I should have written sooner, but Bucky Boy has been a very sick youngster, and I wanted to save you the pain of knowing it while his condition was critical. He seems now to be well on the road to recovery.

As you know, about two months ago, he took down with pneumonia. He had not quite recovered from that attack and was still in the hospital (Chiky was sick in another part of the same hospital at the time) when the "flu" got him. He was very low with this and, I'm told, was very near death. However, he seemed to be getting well rapidly, and two weeks ago last Thursday, Chiky expected to take him home from the hospital and both should go on to Atlantic City for a while to regain their strength. But, on that day he was started on the decline with an illness settling in his heart. On Friday he was worse, a specialist was called in and Bucky was moved to a private room in the hospital. On Saturday, the doctor said that he had no chance for recovery. That night a move was started to get me home to his bedside. On Sunday it was hard to connect with the officials at Washington who have the power to grant such permission.

On Sunday, Bucky Boy was putting up what appeared a hopeless battle for life. His heart beat was 185 and his fever was 105–106. Frantic efforts were being made by friends to get me home. On Sunday afternoon about 5 o'clock I was informed by wire of Bucky's condition and of the efforts being made to secure permission for me to go to my boy.

On Monday, Bucky was still clinging to life but his condition showed no improvement. On this day, I was allowed to start home with a guard. Mr. [J. S.] Biddle, brother of the warden here went with me. I was treated with every courtesy that could be shown anyone, at no time was I hand-cuffed and no one knew I was a prisoner. I was placed upon my honor and both Mr. Biddle and I knew that a guard was absolutely unnecessary. He gave me all the freedom he possibly could and tried very diligently not to make my position embarrasing to me or mine.

On Wednesday morning, I arrived home. Chiky and Feige and several friends met me. Also a crowd of newspaper men whom I was not permitted to interview.

We went directly to the hospital and found Bucky Boy very low. I was not allowed—by the doctors—to see him as they feared the shock would be too great to one so weak. Nor did I see him the next day, except through the crack of the door. However, Thursday a week ago he began to improve and I was allowed to see him Friday. Chiky told him in the morning that I was coming and when later I came into his room his whole face lit up in a smile, his little hands worked spasmodically, and he tried to talk but was too weak. But he laughed, he was so happy. I joked with him and he quite enjoyed himself. But he is so thin, so weak, the fever had burned him to a mere shadow.

Soon after I talked with him, he went to sleep and slept soundly. Later I had another talk with him, he again smiled and shook his head slightly as a reply to my questions. I saw him again next day and he was much better and the doctor took on great hopes for his recovery. Bucky is now suffering from inflammation of the inner membranes of the heart. The doctors say that he will have to remain in bed for at least three months after which he will have to have the best of care for months, years perhaps.

Saturday, a week ago, I started on my way back here, just as soon as the danger point was believed past.

Chiky is well now, as am I. Bucky is coming along better than was expected. Friends of mine feel confident that they will have me a free man before long, they say very soon. Had it not been for them Chiky and Bucky would be dead before this time. Bucky has the best care that money and love can secure. Our friends are paying over $100 a week for hospital alone, and they had the best of specialists to attend Bucky. Beside this they are caring for Chiky, and then, working hard to get me out of here. Mrs. Evans was so pleased with your letter. Let me know how all of you are. Love to all and a sweet kiss to my mamma,

Lovingly—Ed.

April 17, 1922

My dearest little Chiky,

I have just finished a letter to Ellen Winsor, and will be able now to write you but a single page. My little Sweetheart, I got your letters each day and was so glad to get your good news. It's so fine to know that Bucky is improving. I guess we must expect some slight set-backs. Surely Bucky will be a bit irretable at times. Two months in bed is enough to make any one fitful at times. . . .

The warden has allowed me six letters a week for a while now. . . .

. . . The fact that Bucky's temperature is normal once more, speaks well for his chance to completely recover. The recuperative power of a child so young as him is wonderful and if all goes well for a short while now, all will be well. . . .

. . . Say, girlie, could you write or see Mr. E. W. Evans and give him our word of condolence and sorrow because of the death of his little child? If you can, please do. Maybe Miss Winsor or Mrs. [E. C.] Evans could help you frame a fitting letter.

April 20, 1922

It was great to hear of how Bucky Boy is coming along.

. . . It is possibly a fine thing that Bucky makes no mention of me. Maybe he thinks I played a mean trick on him by leaving again. I sometimes wonder what he really does think anyway.

. . . I must agree with Mrs. Cope, Bucky Boy should not be moved until asolutely all danger is over. Another set-back would surely prove fatal. We cannot be too careful now even after he is much stronger. . . .

My dear little Chiky, please think twice before you write Chicago. I should have spoken to you about it in Philadelphia. You have no idea of the amount of back-biting from them. What they give in cash they collect from one's soul and spirits. I know that it is a great financial burden on the good folks in Philadelphia, that I realize, but must you sell your soul completely? You haven't heard what I have, and don't want to.

. . . See that preparations are under way in Philadelphia for the "Children's Crusade." That's fine. It ought to awaken considerable interest in some people who never cared before.

April 23, 1922

So Bucky Boy is coming along nicely. . . . Am sorry to see the nurse go, but happy, oh! so happy, to know that Bucky's condition is such that she can go. Yes, I wrote home and was glad I did so. Last night I got a letter from Edna dated the 16th. They did not know a thing about our trouble when she wrote, as she made no mention of it at all. They should get my letter in a day after she wrote.

It is well that you wrote to Mr. & Mrs. E. W. Evans. I know that it is hard to say just the right thing, but no matter how poorly it is said, I'm sure that they will appreciate the spirit of your message rather than the words.

You did not mention Chicago in your last letter. . . . Guess what they did to Mrs. Chaplin? Mrs. O'Hare asked the bunch in headquarters for Mrs. Chaplin's address. They didn't send it. Then Mrs. O'Hare went up and asked them directly when she was in Chicago. What do you think they told her? They said that it was useless for her to get in touch with Mrs. Chaplin as she was not the kind to do anything. Imagine that! And that after she had run her legs off getting signatures to the General Defense petitions and helping all she can otherwise. I can't imagine what they feel they have to gain by their blackmailing of the wives of the men in prison. Gee, how I want to be independent of that crowd when I get out of here. I'd like to see them all in hell, that's the way I feel about it. So much do they care for the politicals that they have no one with the Children's Crusade to secure signatures for their petitions. They make me sick!

Say, girlie, there is a vacancy in Nef's cell. I have put in a request to move there. I hope it is granted. You'll know in a couple days.

. . . By the way, did you try yet to get all the clippings for that week I was in Philadelphia? Some day we will prize that as nothing else in the world. A wonderful history of a terrible week. Please try to get this, if it has not already been done.

Something tells me that soon we shall be together again, and, then we want to start to live as we never lived before. Give my love to Feige, and a big bunch of kisses to Bucky Boy, and to you that love that only we understand.

April 25, 1922
After acknowledging the good news from you, I must tell you that I have moved down into the same cell with Nef and we are buddies with Miller, Pancner and C. W. Anderson. We are quite a family.

April 26, 1922

My dear Mrs. Evans,

First, I must tell you and you must tell sister Ellen that I got her letter and check for $19.03. Really I didn't expect that. Don't you think it is stretching generousity rather far? You folks secure the privilege for me to come home, stand all the expense and then, when I spend a few dollars previously given by you, then I have it refunded? . . .

The Children's Crusade seems to be coming along nicely. Here's hoping it every success. . . .

I wrote, at some length, to Miss Ellen regarding the "irreconcilables." Some are non-understandable in every sense. There are a few who won't even talk to me, so it is hard for me to tell them anything. . . . For most of them, I'm genuinely sorry, especially a poor devil like Quigley. In the name of "Solidarity" he is committing suicide. I talked with him today. He will not be convinced of the foolhardiness of the attitude he has taken. He has been coaxed, cajoled, and threatened into taking his present stand. Those few who are responsible, will be nothing short of his murderers. Surely they must know this. I can't see where anyone finds it his duty to keep his fellows in jail. . . .

Fletcher and Walsh received their clemency applications last night. Fletcher signed his and returned it today. I am told that Walsh returned his unsigned. That is as I expected. I have always felt that it was useless to send it on to him. He is a funny sort. He'll sign those papers some day, mark what I say, so please have them saved for him unless his brother or some one else signs them in his behalf. If he sent a "warm" letter with his papers, please ask that a copy of it be sent to us. It may help us in the task of taming him. He'll come around all right one of these fine days. There's only two things that bothers him here,—he must stop eating to sleep and stop sleeping to eat. He's one of these carefree types who really don't care. Nothing is very serious with him. He would like to be out, though.

Yes, I'm sorry I wrote my first letter to Ellen Winsor after my return. I felt awfully blue just then, but all that's over now, I feel fine and dandy. Nef and I are celling together. . . . We get just twice as much news now and can talk things over in great shape now.

Believe me, I'm so glad that Ida and Bucky Boy are coming along so nicely. And for all that, I know whom I have to be grateful to, and I hope I shall live to see the day when I can do as much for some other poor devil. . . .

Yes, indeed, those editorials were fine—great. All going well, I'm coming home with my pals here, and, I'm going to take the dearest burdens in the world off of your hands. Till then, they are in your tender care. Warmest greetings to you and Mr. Evans from all of us, and especially from,

Your Friend,

E. F. Doree

April 28, 1922

My dearest little Chiky:

I'm so very, very happy that Bucky is coming along so well and that you feel so much better. . . .

Before trying to answer your letters, I shall write concerning the others I received. First from Ellen Winsor. My trip to Phila. cost $319.03. The warden sent this statement on to her, and lo! and behold! She sent me a check for $19.03 or the amount over $300 which we spent. . . . Their kindness knows no bounds, but it can reach a point where it makes me uncomfortable. I asked her to please use everything on you and Bucky Boy, and try to forget me in any financial sense. . . .

I see that you got $50.00 from Chicago. That's all right, girlie, you're the cook, and, it is you who must figure to make things meet. I cannot feel different than I do toward them but shall say nothing about it. Only the devil had better help them if they ever mention what they did for me or mine after I do get out. You are right, we paid that bill in advance.

. . . So the Children's Crusade sees our Bucky Boy. He will enjoy it, I'm sure. And while at this point, please get the newspaper clippings on that, too. . . . Think what it will mean to Bucky to have them in years to come.

. . . Oh, yes, I must tell you. Fletcher signed his papers and returned them. Walsh returned his unsigned. The group ought to write to him and tell him that as much as they desired to see him out, that if he prefers to stay, they are sorry that they did so much already in his behalf . . . He has acted the part of a cad if ever a man did. He will get over his hard-boiled stuff yet, believe me. Did I tell you that I made out Clyde Hough's papers? He tore up those sent in to him about a month ago. Then the people in Rockford told him unless he wanted to be sensible he could go to the devil. They only wanted to get those out who wanted to get out. Then he changed his mind.

April 30, 1922
From today's papers we learn that Pres. Harding refused to see the Crusaders. I am sure he made a great mistake when he did so. What do you think?

May 2, 1922
I just got your letter of the 28th. It is too bad that you are not feeling good. . . . I wish Bucky would improve more rapidly, then besides all else, you would have a better chance to thoroughly recover your health. His health and your's, I fear, will go together. . . .

Say, the demand for amnesty is surely growing. . . . The editor of the Baltimore Sun had written to the Attorney General about our case. . . . I read today an editorial from a recent issue of the Boston "Globe" where they refer to our continued imprisonment as a crime and an act unworthy of a free people. They minced no words whatever. It was a splendid editorial. Then, too I suppose you saw the Feature Editorial in the Washington, D.C. "News" where they speak of the children and Pres. Harding's refusal to see them. For all eastern sections it seems as though the papers are much in favor of our release.

. . . Beginning last night we are allowed in the yard from suppertime to half past seven. The fellows are all in the yard now but I stayed in to write. It is so nice and quiet now. When the fellows get back, it's talk, talk, talk like a lot of old women, so it is hard to think of what one is writing.

So you had the crusaders at home? I saw in the papers where they were out to see Bucky Boy but you made no reference to it. Did he see them, or them him, or neither, or both? How did Bucky Boy like it? You didn't tell me how his stomach is coming along? How I wait for such news, girlie, you must know. Remember always that I cannot call up the hospital and find out, so please let me know in each of your letters, won't you, sweetheart?

Sometimes I wish those who hold us here could change places with us for a while, what a difference it would be, eh? To be guilty of no offense, yet be held away from loved ones and have loved ones to worry and struggle, makes one bitter at times. Surely there is no good in feeling bitter, but I guess we're human, no more.

Don't get the idea that I'm going around harboring grudges, for I'm not. What I say is merely a passing thought, such as goes through one's head for the moment, nothing more. Somehow, I feel awfully confident that we shall soon come together again and rebuild out nest. Of one thing I'm sure, prisons hold no place in our future, the entire stupid, thoughtless working class isn't worth the price. . . . What spineless creatures! Even when the children of imprisoned men are paraded before them, they are indifferent. It seems a tremendous shame that the capitalistic newspaper should champion the cause of our release with stronger spoken words than do our own fellow workers. . . .

It has taught me this one lesson, they shall buy their own freedom with their own blood, time and freedom, not mine.

May 7, 1922

I am surely glad to hear that our Bucky Boy is coming on so well. That is fine. Girlie dear, please do be careful about taking Bucky from the hospital too soon. I know the cost is great and that it's very tiresome for you, and all that, and I know how you want to have him with you all the time, but, please be careful. He is surely better off where he's being continually watched by those who know what he needs when some trouble arises.

. . . Gee, I surely like your idea about moving to Fairmount Park. That's great. Just what you'll need for the warm weather. Bucky Boy will find it hard to stand hot weather this summer and he should be where he can get the best of air and plenty of park. I should suppose that it is not so very hard to find rooms now, and you will want to be all fixed up before you move Bucky Boy at all. Yes?

News has come in here that Nef's and my case are now being considered in Washington by the pardon attorney. This word came to some of the boys here who have had word directly from their families. . . . Have the group heard anything about when they will be given the hearing they have asked for? I know that it is not advisable to tell me all that they are doing, yet I go on asking questions. . . .

I got letters from mamma and Edna last night and answered them today. They were quite worked up over Bucky Boy and all his and our troubles.

May 10, 1922

I am sure that the doctor is right about moving Bucky Boy. It is surely best to take no chances at all. It is surely fine to learn that you feel that he is improving. The fact that his fever is gone and that he seems more at ease mentally, and that he is playful, is a mighty fine sign that he is on the right road. Just a little more time and we may have an entirely different Bucky Boy. . . .

I did not know that Ellen Winsor paid the money for the trip herself. She told me, if I understood her rightly, that several people did. Truly, the Evans and Winsors are wonderful folks, few friends like them are ever found anywhere. How fortunate for us that we had them in these past few months.

May 12, 1922

My dear Mrs. Evans,

At last we have struck upon one thing upon which we can disagree, and disagree thoroughly. After all due apologies, given and accepted, I still hold that nature is a blundering fool, a poor doctor and a cruel murderer. . . . The law of nature is not a law of love but of hate. That the great pine tree may live, grass and flowers must die; that the wolf may live, sheep must die; the trait developed most strongly in animals (and human beings) which survive is cunning and trickery.

The poor savage is to be pitied, not glorified. If he contracts a sickness or an epidemic crosses his path, he goes to "kingdom come" by express, charges prepaid. If he breaks a leg he is gifted by nature with a crooked, weak leg, etc.

Nature is to most people what lumbering is to lumber-jacks. A stranger goes into the woods and remarks upon the health and physical fitness of the lumberjacks, and therefore draws the conclusion that lumbering is a healthful occupation. The fact is, 30 out of every 1000 die violent deaths annually, and the sick are expelled from the camps, and only husky young men can do the work, and then for only a few years and, he is done for.

Nature planted the "ague" in the soil of Indiana, man took it out; nature filled the air of Louisiana with malaria bearing mosquitoes, man drove them out; nature filled the waters with typhoid, man filters it out, nature makes boils, man cures them, nature creates poor optic lenses, man corrects them. . . .

Of course, there is the other side of the question, nature's marvels, nature's beauty, and all that, but, one of the most beautiful creatures is the gila monster of the desert. From the design on his back the Indians got their pattern for the Navajo blanket. The gila is beautiful and he is the most poisonous of all living things. So with all nature's products, there seems to be a "rider" in all her plans. In all things she is a paradox, a complex, a combination of good and evil, a "picnic spread" with ants on it, a pleasant moonlit evening with ankle gnats at work, life with health and vigor at play with death.

Perhaps I am wrong, I am a cynic, I admit that! Elizabeth Gurley Flynn used to tell me that I was the most optomistic pessimist she ever met and the most altruistic cynic on earth. I never could really figure out what she was driving at, but, her view may help you to understand my perverted notion on nature.

. . . Please tell me, what will we have to think about when your dear mother will be well, and Bucky Boy in good health and the fellows out of here and home once more? What will we do? For one thing, we'll settle this argument on nature. What do you say?

May 12, 1922

My dearest little Chiky,

I cant say how happy it made me feel to hear that the doctor says our boy is so much better. . . .

I see in the paper that Ladd of North Dakota introduced an amnesty bill in the Senate and Griffin and London introduced a similar bill in the House yesterday. . . .

The crowd in here is now in two camps, the "clemency hounds" as they call us, and the "die hards" as we call them. We are as far apart as the two poles, except that we win a convert once in a while, they never. Sunday, before you get this letter, nine of the 5 year men will be gone from here. Within a month 5 more politicals go, one a Socialist. That will leave 97 politicals in Federal Prisons. Under the hundred mark. Slowly but surely we get out. And when we do, <u>it is all over,</u> that's the great big thing.

May 17, 1922

My own dear Bucky: My dear boy, do you realize that you wrote me two letters in the last two days? Gee whiz! But that's fine. That's the boy, hurry up and get well, won't you? No, I never saw a panorama picture. What is it like? I'm going to look around and see if I can find you some kind of a toy. There arent many toys here, but I'll see what I can find. Say, Bucky Boy, you surely do write a very fine letter. Where did you learn how to write? Tell me that! I am sending you so many kisses no man can count them and more love than there is in the world. Please write to me once more—your dad.

May 19, 1922

Somehow, I cannot understand the administration at all. Surely the primary election in Indiana and Pennsylvania should show them how the political wind is blowing. The temper of people is surely not what it was in the war and people are inclined to be more liberal and tolerant. They want to be rid of war hysteria and get some real peace.

May 21, 1922

I see that you have gotten rooms opposite the park. That's fine. The rent is pretty high but a porch is worth all of it. Where is the porch, on the 3rd floor? And what other facilities has the place. Let me know from sink to bath. You must be getting something for $45.00. . . .

Yes, I'm glad our number has become less, for two reasons, that the number is less and that the most of them were "irreconcilables." I have heard that one or two may come to Philadelphia. If they do, watch your step. They will be . . . likely to have a few uncomplimentary things to say about the Winsors and Evans. Say nothing to them (The Winsors & Evans) but keep your eyes open, and, unpolite as it may sound, your mouth shut. . . .

It is needless for me to say that I'm so happy that both of you continue to improve in health. I couldn't feel better. The big stiff has the upper part of his face fixed now. A good looking job it is. He has the bottom row of teeth to get fixed up now. I have a good mind to get my teeth fixed up. It does not bother me at all but my teeth seldom bother till they have to come out. . . .

Girlie, I got a letter from a M. Hirshberg whose address is 503 Boardwalk, Atlantic City, N.J. He writes that he wishes to send me a book and asks me what I want. Would you write him and tell him that I am grateful for his offer and if he has "The Cooks Wedding and other stories" by Anton Chekhov, I should be very happy to get it? I really cant spare the letter to write him myself. You might explain to him that books sent to any of us are eventually read by all of us.

May 23, 1922

It's very fine to hear that you and Bucky Boy are so well and that he seems to have passed the point of danger entirely.

. . . So the police revoked their permit to secure amnesty signatures? One must expect such things, I suppose. Mrs. Evans writes that she played herself out trying to get signatures. How good of them to be always on the job!

I guess you saw by Nef's letter to Feige that Joe Gordon and two German agents were commutted and released yesterday. Gordon had ten years and was out on bonds for two years. I was surely glad to see him make it.

May 23, 1922

My dear Mrs. Evans,

A couple of the "fierce ones" may come to Philadelphia and you may have a chance to see them. Maybe you will be able to put some sense into their heads. If you can, you will have accomplished more than I and the rest of us could. But, what ever you do, don't take them too seriously. I'm sure that if you meet them, that they'll be very nice to you, so don't be frightened, they're not half so fierce as they write.

. . . I had quite a shock yesterday. Just as I was returning to the office of the Clothing Department, where I work, after being to dinner,

the phone rang. The guard answered, in something of this manner,—
"Clothing Department . . . Yes . . . That's him talking now . . . yes . . .
yes . . . commutations? . . . yes. . . . what's that . . . Yes . . . I've got
you . . . thirteen. . . . yes . . . one . . . Yes . . . twenty . . . what? . . .
twenty two? . . . thirteen one twenty two? . . . yes . . . Commutation . . . At once? . . . yes . . . alright, give me the next one . . . " (My
number is 13125, and believe me I was waiting for more as he went
on) "Hello, . . . yes . . . sixteen . . . yes . . . etc, etc"

Well, there were two more commutations. The first, 13122, was
one of the I.W.W. boys convicted with us, and sentenced to ten
years. . . . The other two who were commutted were german agents,
spies or something like that. They served a few months of a three
years sentence. . . .

. . . Now, I want you to know that there is a large group here who
do appreciate what all of you are doing. You have a good sized family
of trusting children in here, looking upon you and other good folks
like you as our liberators. Listen, you will never know or realize what
you've come to mean to me. I could worship you and love you as I
do my mother, because of the great good there is in you. You won't
be discouraged because a few "fierce ones" can't understand, will
you?

May 27, 1922

My dearest little Chiky,

I am glad that you found such fine rooms. . . . I'm so glad that Bucky
Boy will soon be able to go home. Isn't that fine? Especially now,
when you have such a nice home for him. It is going to be a lot of
hard work for you to move, and you must take care that you don't tire
yourself out. You'll surely get someone to help you.

Charlie Plahn got a good jolt from the Chicago bunch today. His
wife is with the Crusade and while gone, her rent and payments
on furniture go on, and she needed $55.00 to meet these bills, so she
wrote Plahn and he wrote Feinberg and that gentleman wrote Charlie that they could not pay those bills. . . . What do you think of that?
This, too, after Mrs. Plahn had worked steadily to keep herself and

girl, and keep up payments on furnitures, etc, with no relief from anyone. Then, too, Chaplin's father gathered signatures on the 20th in Chicago, and he reported that no I.W.W.'s were out with petitions,—only society women and some other folks. Believe me, if they ever catch me with that crowd again, I'll be tied hand and foot, that's all.

Say, girlie, the "irreconcilable" ones coming east are Ted Fraser and James Manning. They are sent by the General Defense Committee, so watch out. I write this as a warning. They are going east for no good. Neither of them have the least use for three of us from Phila.

May 28, 1922

I'm very, very glad to hear that Golden and McNamara or Lever will take rooms at your new home. That will be very fine for you if it isn't too much work. You know how careful you must be, don't you girlie? . . .

Bucky boy will have it fine at home in such a nice place. I'm glad that he will be in a position to get air and rest. There is no car line on Oxford street, is it? Your closest car is at 33rd and Columbia, isn't it? To be that far from the noise is worth something too. Your apartment faces the south, doesn't it? That for the sun that Bucky Boy needs.

Girlie dear, I shall not expect so many letters now that you are so busy. You've been so awfully good about writing. Your letters have meant so much to me.

. . . Say, listen, little girlie, the laugh is on you. Here I am expecting to hear that I'm to go home most anytime and you fill the house up with a pair of roomers. Is there a place for me on the roof? . . .

My dear, dear own Bucky Boy: I got your fine letters. . . . You bet I am glad that you will have such fine rooms to move into, and that mamma paid for them right away. So you are going home on the 1st of June? Maybe you will get this letter at home. Wouldn't that be fine? Really, Bucky Boy, I don't know how soon I can come home, but I'll come just as soon as I can.

. . . What do you think Nef is doing now? He is playing dominoes.

. . . Mamma wrote to me and told me that you have a new bed. Let me know how you like it. You live in bed, don't you?

May 31, 1922

We have two new guests in our apartment in this hotel, St. John and Dan Buckley. They moved in with us today. Now we have a full house, all right. We have some crowd. They are a good bunch of fellows.

. . . You are right, girlie, it is none too pleasant to have to run to a hospital every day, especially with so many things that must be done. It's been awfully hard on you. I can imagine your struggle. Well, if all goes as it now looks, I will be home pretty soon to give you a hand with all that you have to struggle with. That will be better, won't it?

June 1, 1922

My dear Mrs. Evans,

What do you say? Shall we let the irreconcilables rest? One of our boys, when asked what he thought of something said or done by one of the "fierce ones," said, "I'm not here to discuss other people's insanity, and that's all there is before the house." The bitter attacks upon your sister, Roger Baldwin, Gurley Flynn and others can be attributed to nothing else than "prison simpleness."

. . . I had a little treatise on Scripture here in our cell the other day. One of my cell-mates was in line to sweep out the cell in the morning but was slow about arising, so he was reminded of his task. He yawned and drawled out, "Say, fellows, I'm a politician not a street sweeper." Another popped in, "I suppose you think that you're better than Christ himself, don't you?" "No-o-o, but what has Jesus to do with sweeping a cell." The answer came back, "Well, when he was in jail he didn't renig." "Renig, what do you mean, renig?" "Don't the Bible say that 'Jesus swept,' what makes you think that you are better than he was? The story produced the desired effect.

Illness is an odd thing, isn't it? Had I not broken my leg in 1908, I should not be here today. I should be playing baseball. I was good at the game and was rapidly going up. Then a horse fell with me, then eleven months in a hospital, and, well, hard work and hard times,—

an agitator, a convict. Illness you say made you turn from a life of pleasure seeking to a life of usefulness. A crushed leg changed the flow of my life from ball-field to prison cell. . . .

The many disappointments are offset by the few victories we secure. It is the old story, we must weep that we may know laughter. And, then too, it stirs one's gambling instincts to always bet on the under dog. I have always bet on him—and lost, but I'm sure that the race was just as exciting to me, while it lasted, as it was to the winner. Like the challenger in a match, I never had a championship to lose, always all to gain.

June 2, 1922

My dear little Chiky,

Your letter of the 30th came to me just now. Girlie dear, I'm a little bit afraid that your worry and trouble is getting the better of you. Your last letters seem to show signs of nervousness.

Maybe I should not trouble you about so many things, often I am a bit careless, I must confess. It is altogether possible that I do ask you to do too many favors. I shall try to write to the other folks as you suggest.

It will be nice for you when Bucky Boy is home. Of course, you will be tied up to the house pretty much, but it will surely be better than to run to the hospital each day. . . .

. . . There is talk in Chicago of expelling all members from I.W.W. who have made, or will make application for clemency. . . . Six die-hards have been sent to the six centers where there are groups working for individuals, for the purpose of breaking them up. All six of them were five year men recently released. A couple of them are clever, the others have no ability. I am sure that they can do no harm. The thing I hate is the idea of anyone attempting to injure anyone's chances to secure his release from prison. . . .

I am sorry to hear that you are so short on money. I was sure you had more. Should you get too close, let me know and I'll possibly be able to help you a little. . . . You'll let me know, won't you?

June 4, 1922

I have had no word from you since I wrote last but I'll try to give you some of the latest news as we have it here. Pancner got a letter from his wife at Washington in which she says that Mrs. Clark and Mrs. Reeder saw the president on June 1st and were to see him again on the following day. Just wonder what will come out of their visit.

. . . I hardly think that it would be wise for you or Feige to see the M.T.W. about money, but it is my duty really to call their attention to your needs. . . . I've done a whole lot of work for the local there that I asked nothing at all for, and, now you ought to have all you need. But before I write to them I ought to know what and when you last got money from Chicago, and if you received anything from them after you last wrote them asking for help.

. . . The ball-game Saturday gave me a little rest. It was a very fine game,—a game between the two home teams (you know we have two teams here, one of colored and one of white players) and it was wonderful. The final score was 5 to 4 in favor of the white team. It was a 10 inning game, and did I holler? Say, you should have seen me, jumping like a crazy one, yelling like a savage, and a wild man generally. It was far the best game ever played here.

Gee, isn't this nice to write to a poor little girlie who has to stay in the house with her sick Bucky. I am ashamed of myself, but really I can't help it. I did have a good time for a couple of hours. . . .

Some fine day, girlie, when this is all over and when Bucky Boy is well once more, and when we have solved the struggle for existence for ourselves then you shall learn to appreciate baseball because Bucky and I are going to drag you along to the games until you'll want to drag us, then we will all go together. How will that be? . . . See that Manning is in Phila. Keep your eyes open for false moves, he is dangerous, if sober.

June 6, 1922

I am told that Mr. Harding saw some of the women and told them that he would do whatever the Attorney-General recommended, no matter what it was. He himself refused to take any initiative in the matter. It is hard to really know what he means by that attitude, whether it is one of defiance or one where he "passes the buck" to the other fellow altogether.

. . . We have some fine crowd in this cell now. We have a great time, a really good time. Everyone seems to realize that good humor is the most needed of all virtues in here and acts accordingly. St. John is a great story teller and he knows a whole world of humorous stories and has a very fine way of telling them. He has a laugh for every occasion. Then, too, we have our stories of life and experiences and they take a bit of time to relate.

You see there are eight of us to the cell and there is only one wash bowl so we have quite a time of it in the morning to get all cleaned up. So we have a program. St. John gets up first, then Anderson, then Pancner, then Nef, followed in rapid succession and in this order are Buckley, Miller, Falksted and then yours truly. I'm nearly always the last and I hardly ever get a chance to sweep out. This makes me sore as you may imagine! I guess not!

June 9, 1922

I have your letter of the 5th. I shall send you a copy of my letter to the attorney general next Sunday. I have no permit for an extra sheet with this letter. Girlie dear, I often ask you to transmit messages because I haven't the letters to write these other people at this time.

I see that you have some money. Yet you say nothing about what I really asked you. Shall I write to the M.T.W. and ask them to do something? . . . Also I should like to know when and how much Chicago sent you last and whether or not you wrote them last before or after that time.

We are not expelled yet that I know of. All that I know is that they are talking of doing so. Hope they do, will save the trouble of telling them to go to the devil.

. . . I am sure that I'm not taking the "die-hards" too seriously, but it is poor policy to underestimate an enemy. If they are able to do any harm, we must of course, do all to head them off. To be sure, Manning wont be sober after he learns where whiskey is to be found. That's much in our favor.

Am awfully sorry to hear that Bucky Boy is bothered with side pains. Hope they will pass off soon.

June 9, 1922
Mr. Daniel Kiefer
The Seabreeze House, Deep Brook
Ann County, Nova Scotia

My dear Mr. Kiefer,

I am just now able to acknowledge your letter of May 14th.

Perhaps you have heard that Godfrey Ebel has been recommended for parole. I hope he makes "the grade" and is soon on the outside. He is a splendid fellow, a real fine chap. Rice, one of the 10 year men in the Chicago Case, was also recommended as was Phineas Eastman, who was sentenced at Wichita, Kansas, to serve 7-1/2 years. . . .

I am most greatly interested in Eastman. Since he came to prison his wife has gone insane. I knew her ten years ago in Louisiana. A remarkably fine woman, one of those tender hearted loving kind. She and Phin were as fine a pair of pals as I ever met. Today she lies in bed, partially paralyzed, and wholly insane, while Phin. here has nearly lost his mind in worry and sorrow. He did every thing but turn traitor on his fellows to secure his release, he quit the organization, did everything, and, I cannot and do not blame him. It is asking a whole lot too much of a man to ask him to stand defiant when agony grips his heart day and night. I shall never forgive those officers and members of the I.W.W. who cut him and his wife off from financial aid because Phin quit under such circumstances. It will stand to their everlasting shame. God! I hope he gets out. I learned in the last few months what it was to suffer the torments of hell and the acme of such suffering is a prison cell while dear ones suffer and die.

Ida reports that Bucky Boy is coming on splendidly. He is home now, although yet confined to his bed. They have rented a second floor apartment at 3231 Oxford St. They write that it is a splendid, sunny, airy place.

June 11, 1922
My dearest little Chiky,
Am sorry that Bucky Boy has those pains in his side. . . .

Am very glad to know that you are better fixed financially than your recent letter indicated. I shall do as you say, do nothing in the matter at least at present. I must have about $75.00 here. I bought a fine pair of sandals. Got them yesterday. Paid $2.75, and they are worth it. Now I'll get some socks and if I have to put in the summer here I will be well fixed.

. . . So Golden and Lever have moved in. That's very fine. Give them my "hello."

June 15, 1922
It is a bit cooler tonight so I have stayed in from the yard to read and write. I'm getting to be awfully lazy. Should I have to stay here much longer I shall be useless, perfectly so.

. . . Was surely happy to hear that Jack Lever was put on the job to work for amnesty. He, I am sure, will make good. I see that the Philadelphia folks seem to think that they will have results almost any day now. . . . I have not heard that our case has gone to the Pres. as yet. You know, they can spar for a whole lot of time in Wash. They are great at that. Anyhow, it makes me feel much better to be told that the end is in sight.

We were told here that Manning reported that since he came to Philadelphia the movement in our behalf has been stopped entirely. There was great rejoicing over this by the "die-hards." Of course, we had a good laugh ourselves, but it does seem awful to laugh or rejoice over a fellow man's imprisonment. But then, too, it is great to have a saving sense of humor.

I have felt ever so much better since Bucky Boy's improvement has been so apparent, and since you yourself seem to be getting on so nicely in health and spirits.

. . . Now, listen, send no more candy or cigarette papers in here, and ask all who may do so, not to. This same rule for cigars, too. This rule has been made so as to prevent the smuggling of "dope" into the prison. There are hundreds of dope addicts here, and they use every conceivable means of getting the stuff in. We can buy all of these things, cigars, cigarette papers, candy, and the like here, so we shall not suffer at all for lack of them.

June 20, 1922
Believe me, I was more than pleased to hear that Sen. Pepper had seen the president and attorney general in our behalf. That should aid us a whole lot.

. . . Now listen, I've got a good one for you. . . .

One of the Sacramento boys, Godfrey Ebel has applied for and been recommended for parole. As all who were released on expiration and those who were commutted at Christmas time, received $50.00 each, Ebel asked them (the bunch in Chicago) if they could help him, also, when released, because he is without funds. For reply he got the following letter under date of June 16th, 1922.

"I cannot send you relief money in view of the fact that you have requested parole. It is our understanding that you renounced the organization and did not stand with those who refused to make application for parole.

"Money coming into this office is to be used for general amnesty purposes and not for those who have taken individual action. The Civil Liberties Union of New York, I understand helps those who have made application for parole. It may be to your advantage if you write to them. Signed: Harry Feinberg"

For rottenness that is about the limit. Ebel has repudiated not an ideal he ever held. He joined the organization in 1907 and was a paid up member ever since: His record is absolutely above reproach. He must leave here broke unless some one lends a hand. What a tragedy! . . .

Feinberg talks of principle. Here in my cell are seven members, who have made application for clemency, (or are we former members?) two are charter members of 1905, two joined in 1906, one in 1908, one in 1912, and one in 1914. All were active and respected in their day, and I guess are now by decent people. Any way we were good old truck horses once, we builded with sweat and blood, gave of our time and energies, saw few victories and many defeats, yet, we went on, loyal as we knew how to be, some to untimely graves, others to prison. But now, when our many days in prison shall have been ended, we are paid by those whom we made possible, no cash, but only in the bitterest of abuse, and this, after we had gathered that very cash. . . .

What a mockery. I was the first treasurer of the G.D.C. I handed out $131,000 in an effort to help my fellows, and this in an hour when it took guts to stick on the job, now my invalid baby cant have a generous nickle. Damn them. It would be humiliating to have to touch a dollar they had fingered.

June 25, 1922

There is an empty bunk in our cell now. St. John left us yesterday on commutation. Gee, I was happy to see him go, and Clyde Hough went also. St. John is going east and will likely be in Philadelphia shortly. I gave him your address and he will surely see you if he comes. He intends to straighten things up with respect to Fraser, Manning & Co. That's one reason for coming east at all. You'll be much surprised at some things you are to learn. He can let you know how much poison there is in the Chicago crowd, and he will.

. . . Now listen, It's impossible to write, Nef and the barber are playing dominoes, Dan and Pancner are having a lively discussion on hair tonics, and Miller, for no known reason, is reading the paper out loud. So what am I to do? Quit? You're right.

June 27, 1922

Note that Manning is doing some pretty good work outside. So long as he goes that way, all right, but watch for the turn. He has back-bitten most of his very best friends at different times and the organization has never known just where he stands. He is the type that may as readily be your friend or a spy from the enemies camp. . . . He is this way, he may speak highly of me to people in Philadelphia, where and when he thinks that attitude is most advisable to his purpose. Then, write Chicago and tell them how he has been able to turn every one against me, and then, should he meet me personally he will rush out to greet me with all show of friendship.

If, however, he finds a loophole where he can knock me, he will be in highest heaven while doing so. . . . Of all types on earth, that type I dislike most. If he is sincerely at work for general amnesty then he has double-crossed the crowd in Chicago, and to double-cross even a cur-dog is mean and despicable.

I shall not waste further time on him, and, I shall be glad to hear that the Evans & Winsors have left for Europe before he crosses them.

Lever and Golden will be able to see into any fake moves he may try to make later on. I may have been fooled in lots of things but I have seldom been badly fooled in my judgment of men.

. . . You mustn't mind my raving tonight. I eat too much supper, and I have seen three men commutted and one paroled in three days. Too much for my weak nerves.

My little sweetheart, so you don't care to go out. What a lucky boy, our Bucky is to have such a fine, good mamma. He doesn't understand how fortunate he is, does he? What he does not know or understand, or appreciate, his papa does.

June 30, 1922

Well, girlie dear, it looks very much as if we were nearing the end of our great trouble that had for so long burdened us. During the past week six politicals have been released from here. . . .

Such effort as is being made by the Balto. Sun will help greatly to force the issue, I'm sure. The administration surely prefers to work in line with public sentiment and newspapers are public sentiment to a wonderful extent.

July 5, 1922

It's too bad that it is so warm back in Phila. It's particularly bad for Bucky. It's got a habit of getting so hot here that they bury their dead in overcoats to keep them from catching a cold. . . . The "A" cell house where Nef and I are is far the coolest. We have had a blanket over us nearly every night. . . .

Yesterday was a wonderful day, clear with a cool breeze. It was splendid. We were called from the arms of Morpheus about 45 minutes earlier than usual, so at 8:30 in the morning we were all in the grand stand watching the beginning of a ball game. Our white team beat the colored team 5 to 4. Then to dinner, boiled ham, creamed spuds, pickled beets, cake, coffee and ice cream. We were allowed a time to rest our vocal organs, and the gong rang to start us off for the afternoon ball game, this time it was a contest between our white team and the "Apex" team of Kansas City. We (our team) cleaned up the visitors to a tune of 11 to 2. Some day. Supper was chiefly pie and lemonade. For the rest of the day we played at dominoes and told stories, and I wrote a letter to Flynn. So it went. It was a splendid day, inside or out, but I guess I'd sooner have been with my girlie and Bucky Boy.

. . . Girlie dear, pity your poor husband. Here he sits and writes while the rest are out in the yard playing. Already this evening I have shaved and fixed up a little repair on one of my sandals, and as soon as I get through here I shall have to darn up some holes in a couple pair of socks. And I haven't had a thing to drink but lemonade. . . .

MY DEAR BUCKY BOY: YOUR LETTER OF JULY 2ND CAME TO ME TONIGHT . . . IT WAS AWFULLY FINE OF JACK TO MAKE YOU THAT BED WITH WHEELS ON, SO YOU CAN GO TO THE PARK. HE IS A FINE FELLOW, ISN'T HE? I AM SENDING YOU MILLIONS AND MILLIONS OF SWEET KISSES—YOUR ED.

July 16, 1922

Now, girlie dear, can I have a little talk with you now? Surely I can. I realize that you are under a terrible mental strain just now, and what can I say? But I think, my little sweetheart, that you should try to make the best of it for a while anyhow. Both you and Feige have been under a frightful strain for several months now. Bucky has been a great burden, and it has had it's effect upon both of you.

It may be that while so worn out and under the strain of awaiting our release, you both lost your patience and let your tempers get the upper hand. What shall I say, or how can I make clear what is on my mind.

It would have been easy to pick a very unpleasant quarrel with me here while Bucky and you were sick. I know what it is to be locked up with others in a small space where small differences become great grievances. You and Feige have lived too close, especially with your temperamental differences, and this flare up, what ever it was, has not come to my ear unexpectedly. Had not Bucky been sick you would have parted long, long ago, I'm sure.

You have asked me not to take too seriously those here and elsewhere who have come to disagree with me, and who, I am sure, did a lot to injure me and my chances for an early release. I have done as you have asked, just for the sake of harmony. Will you try to do the same for me, girlie dear?

I'm awfully glad that you did not mention your trouble to me. That was splendid of you, and I appreciate your wonderful consideration for my feelings. That was so much better than to have complained. You are a wonderful, wonderful little girl, and how I do hope that your troubles will soon, very, very soon be over. That is my hope and prayer, no more can I do now.

Please, please try to make the best of your present difficulty. Won't you please do that, girlie dear? The big stiff has asked Feige to do the same. No matter what it was, maybe both of you can forget it for a little while. I don't know, I don't know, but I do hope so. God! What a world. My heart bleeds for you, and, damn it, even though I am innocent of crime, why couldn't I alone have been punished?

I must close. I send you the tenderest, sweetest love, and so many many long clinging kisses.

July 19, 1922
Yesterday Phin. Eastman (Wichita 7–1/2 years) was released on parole. His release was hastened by the death of his wife at the Cook County Hospital at Chicago. She had been ill for two years and became insane some time ago. When he was released he was penniless, and as he could secure no aid from any where, we made up a purse for him here of $50.00. As I had more than that amount here (and as funds cannot be transferred from prisoner to prisoner) I sent the $50.00 to Phin's "First Friend"—the party who reports for a man on parole—from my personal account here. Other of the boys here who will stand their part of this will send the money to you, and you will keep it "to home." I don't need it.

. . . Shall not write to Bucky Boy this time as I must hurry and finish this letter . . . before the lights go out.

July 21, 1922
Before covering the news in your letter, I shall give you the news from here. Stanley Clark was released today. The president commutted his sentence last night. C. H. Rice left today also, on parole. That cuts more from our crowd.

. . . It is good that you have written to Mr. Finch. This is the only way to get information—go directly after it. Those who have gotten out are those who have had some one right on the job all the time. You cannot do that, of course, but a single trip would possibly do some real good.

I had expected the petition to carry little or no weight with the official family. I dare say that only a lunatic would start a drive of petitions on Washington in the month of July, the deadest of all months.

The papers in this section had practically nothing to say about it and not a word about it's presentation—not a word! As a publicity stunt it surely made no hit here. Three months earlier or three months later would have been the time, the real time to get something accomplished along that line.

. . . So mamma sent Bucky Boy $5.00. Isn't that fine? What is he going to say to grandma, when he writes to her? Has he written to her yet?

Girlie dear, I had a day's work today, we released 33 men on parole, one on expiration of sentence, one on commutation of sentence and one died. It kept us going to beat the band all day. But it has the elements of pleasure in seeing men leave here. They come and go, but the most nervous are those who go. Clark nearly shook himself to death. Gee, but he was happy to be gone from here. I wonder shall I be so nervous that I can hardly write? When men are released here, the last thing they get is their personal property, their tickets money and postage stamps, etc. They sign the final receipt for them, and some of the poor devils take up the pen (a hard stub especially for them) and scratch a signature that in most cases one wonders what it is.

Can one blame them? How many days, hours, years, minutes have they counted? What tragedies have happened in their lives? Some that have happened since they came here. Some have been deserted by wives, some by family, nearly all by friends. Most have less than ten dollars when they leave, and to all practical purposes no clothes. Yet, with all, the great outside looks wonderful.

I shall leave here happily to meet happiness, to meet the finest little wife in the world and a fine Bucky Boy, and many loyal friends, and surely the whole family have stayed with us truly. It's better than eating green apples; the pleasure comes first and the pain afterwards.

August 1, 1922
Well, Munson and Danley, Oklahoma politicals, were released today on parole. This afternoon saw the release of Risley and Powell, Texas politicals, by commutation of sentence. That cleans up the Texas cases and there are only two Oklahoma cases left. . . .

Also, two wobblies were commutted on condition that they agree to deportation never to return: Tanner (5 years) to be deported at once, and Parenti, after release on bond for 90 days so as to close up personal and family affairs. So you see our family here is getting smaller all the time. Soon, and it will be our turn. Eh? What?

. . . Now, as to going to Washington. If it were left for me to judge the wisdom of the move I should certainly say that you should go, and, if possible both of you. I say this to you for this reason, girlie, you can get a statement from the doctor as to Bucky's condition, go there and present these human facts. If it could be arranged (and I'm sure Mrs. Russell or Congressman Burke or someone else would be happy to make the arrangements) so you could jump down for a day and see Mr. Dougherty and maybe the President, if not the latter, at least you could see Mr. Christian, his secretary. I am quite sure much good would come of such a move. The only question is that of leaving Bucky for a day, but surely someone can be gotten to stay one day, someone who can be depended upon. It is not a question of what they tell you but of what you tell them. See my point?

Of course it would be a good idea for Feige to go. The squabble at home is making it hard to do many things. I have waited to see if your wounds would not heal up at least enough to make it possible for you two to consider and plan action in our case. I hope the situation is such that you can soon call an armistice, and if I could feel that such were the case, I would humbly suggest that you try it. . . . Perhaps if you were to start speaking over our case to one another that would ease the atmosphere. . . . I can't talk except from the clouds when I don't know what all the trouble was about, but, Lord knows, I wish it were not so and that there was peace and happiness at home once more. Isn't that possible again between you sisters who have suffered so much. . . . Understand me, dear, I am saying the best things I know. You will understand me, won't you?

Mamma says all are well at home and in the best of spirits. She sent me a picture which I am forwarding to you. Mamma mentioned about her sending the sewing machine to you. Girlie, why not let them have it? They have been good to us and things, materially, have not been the best. We can get another easier than they. Also they gave their old machine to a poorer family. Let's do that for the old folks, what do you say? It will make mamma happy.

August 2, 1922

I suppose that Feige is in New York as she wrote Nef that she is going there for a day or two. As everything is as it is, it is better that you seperated, at least for a time. . . .

You don't know how happy I am to hear that Dora [Oleve] will stay with you and help you out. Isn't that splendid of her? You must let her know how much I appreciate it.

. . . Am certainly happy to know that Bucky Boy is getting on so well. . . .

I am as optomistic as ever as to our release. Nearly half of those who made application have been released already. The most of those applications were in months before ours. . . . Time drags with us but really it has not been so long as it seemed. Cheer up, our day is near at hand. . . .

P.S. The big stiff is quite troubled over the squabble but takes it philosophically. He seems sorry.

August 10, 1922

Am glad to hear that you continue to feel so well and that Bucky Boy is making such splendid progress. I am feeling fine and dandy. Just a bit impatient for action.

. . . Am very glad to note the manner in which you wrote mamma about the sewing machine. Why not keep the machine you have. Surely we can scrape up the dollar a month. You have $16.00 in the machine already. Why lose that?

. . . Now, girlie, on last Tuesday all special extra letters, over the regular 3 a week, were revoked, so I lost three letters a week. I shall not ask for any more extra ones, but it may cut you to 2 letters a week, so you'll understand.

. . . Buckley is surely tickled to know that his papers are in the hands of the President. I'll surely be glad to see him go from here.

August 13, 1922

The letter from Dr. Edgerton is so fine in spirit and written in such a splendid manner that I am reluctant to write as I now do, but it is really necessary, very much so. We had hope that this word would not have to be sent out of here, but I see no way now to avoid it. We feel that the G.D.C. and the Paterson P.C.C. [Prison Comfort Committee] have pulled this latest move over the Penna. Com. with no other object than to draw further relief and support from the group here who have made application for pardon. Several of the boys who have applied are broke or nearly so, and we have not asked the Penna. Com. to aid them because we did not want to draw that committee into our internal squabbles . . . but this latest move is freely heralded in here as a victory for the G.D.C. and the "irreconcilables."

The Penna. Com. has been the only group sending any thing to those who have made application for clemency. A great number of P.C.C.'s about the country (largely controlled by the G.D.C.) are sending money to the "die hards." . . . The "irreconcilables" are fairly well supplied by these agencies, and when released from here they receive 1– $50.00 in cash from the G.D.C.; 2– a suit of clothes from the Phila. "Harlan" group; 3– transportation to points further than allowed by the Gov't; and while here, the G.D.C. allows them extra money for repair of teeth, eyes, etc., and their families secure relief from the G.D.C. NOTE: all this is denied those who apply for parole or pardon.

On the other hand, from the funds we have received we are compelled to help one another with tobacco, fruit, etc, and, as in Eastman's case, relief upon release. When the "clemency" group leave here they leave broke; for example, Tanner was commutted last week to be deported, never to return. He left here in a prison suit and $6.80 in cash to carry him to Finland. Parenti is to leave here tomorrow. He has a family of five. He has to pay his own fare from here to San Francisco. Neither the $50.00 nor the suit was sent to him.

Of those recently discharged from here, the following received nothing from any source upon release or afterwards, Rice, Plahn, Anderson, Clark, St. John, Gordon, Hough, Eastman and Tanner. . . . These men left here with an average of less than $10.00 each, while the "die hards" released on expiration this summer had well over $100.00 in cash and a new suit of clothes each. One "die hard" who left here this year possessed $3,000.00 in cash which was willed to him while serving sentence. Never-the-less, upon release he got a suit from Phila. and $50.00 from the G.D.C. beside other money.

While this sort of a situation obtained, Mrs. Miller, wife of Francis Miller, was ill for a period of three months and is now in need of an operation and is unable to work. Miller asked the G.D.C. that she be given relief. She got $30.00 and that two months ago. She has received only $115.00 since 1918, while other families, less needy, are kept supplied regularly. Mrs. Eastman was allowed to die in a charity hospital in Chicago without a cent's worth of aid while Phin was in prison. What was her crime that she should be allowed to lie ill for two years and then die a miserable death in abject poverty?

I appreciate the splendid effort of the Penna. Com. to create harmony here but it is impossible. The further the Penna. Com. keeps away from our squabble the better for all.

August 16, 1922

I have come in from the yard and taken a fine shave and feel great. Am in the finest of spirits, too. Was a little disappointed not to hear from you tonight, but am sure of a letter tomorrow.

Your letter of the 11th came since I wrote last and shall first answer it, then to other matters. You are quite right, the Baltimore Sun article was all that could possibly be expected. It was splendid.

. . . I shall drop the discussion regarding you going to Washington. I realize the difficulties attached to it, and also the great need for you to be with Bucky Boy, nor am I unmindful of the fact that you have a great deal of work to do, with no one to help.

The New York "Call" in a recent issue stated that 52 of the wobblies here were soon to present a letter to Pres. Harding stating why they would not make application for clemency. Several of us here have inquired of some of the "die-hards" and none know a thing about it. Evidently, that is more of Mr. Feinberg's works. Some of the die hards are sore about it, too. In case mention should be made about this, or any letter published, you will all know that it did not come from in here but some one is acting on the outside without authority of the 52 non-applicants in here.

In my next letter or on Sunday I shall send you a copy of a letter turned over to me by one of the "enemy." It is self-explanatory. Show it to Lever and I think it would be advisable to show it to Dr. Edgerton and Mr. Bernham [Burnham].

When you have finished with it send it on to Gurley, by all means. She will see to it that the Saint and Roger get it. They will know who wrote it, for the real name is not signed. My guess is that it is from Wetter. However, they in N.Y. will know. . . .

. . . The coal strike seems to be on it's last legs and the rail strike seems on the road to settlement. If these strikes come to an end, it might be that Mr. Harding will be able to give our cases a thought.

August 20, 1922
Before all else, let me say that I am awfully glad to hear that Bucky Boy is coming on so nicely, and is now able to wear overalls once more. Isn't that fine? . . .

. . . You say that you are asking me to do the impossible when you ask me to give up the game and the class struggle. Why the impossible? You may rest assured that I'm done with the I.W.W. After their treatment of you and me, do you think that I would so much as walk across the street to do them a favor? So far as I am concerned, they can go to hell. Is that plain?

Any movement that becomes dead to human emotions, is as dead as it can ever become.

. . . The I.W.W. has chosen a course harmful to the workers and dangerous to its members, why then should I further tangle up with it? I shall not! The only reason I have not said this sooner, is because some people would not understand and would say that I say so merely to get out of prison merely because I was afraid and cowardly. I want to leave here as I came in, but the I.W.W. has my last dues and my utter contempt now. All this which I have said is private, between you and me. When I do get out I shall probably make public a statement as to why I quit the organization.

. . . Let me say finally that you shall win and the I.W.W. lose so far as I am concerned. How's that?

August 25, 1922

Your wire came just now and what a relief it was! For the love of all that is good, girlie dear, wire me when Bucky's condition takes a serious turn. The wire this afternoon from Mr. Dougherty granting me permission to come home, nearly drove me mad. It was just luck that your night letter was delivered tonight.

How on earth did it come that I got permission to go to Philadelphia? Do you know?

Gee, I do hope that Bucky gets better quickly. Please keep me posted, won't you dear?

My poor sweetheart, what trouble you do have. God, if it would ever end. Isn't it possible to bring pressure at Washington to secure my release?

Let this be plain. You or our friends are at perfect liberty to promise, on my behalf, any action on my part that could reasonably be asked of any honorable man. As for the I.W.W. I'm done!

If that fact will help, use it!!! I have not wanted to take this step prior to my release, but my likes or dislikes cannot enter where the life or happiness of you and Bucky Boy are concerned. I do not want to take a cowardly position, but I feel it cowardly to stand loyal to those who have turned traitor to me, and still more cowardly if I failed to stay loyal to those who have been so loyal to me.

The I.W.W. crowd have turned their backs on you and me. Bucky suffering means nothing to them. Why the devil, then, should I say I'm with them when in my heart I hate them for their brutality or at best, their indifference.

You and my friends in Phila. have been so loyal and true that I am deciding to leave my destiny entirely in their hands, and, above all, in your hand, my little mamushka.

What wouldn't I give to be home tonight? Half my life.

August 28, 1922

I just got your letter of the 25th and, in a way, it was a world of relief to get it. These last three days have been awful to me in that I got absolutely no news whatever.

First, on Friday I got word of the wire from the Attorney General. This came from a clear sky, I never thought that anything was wrong at home. I waited for a wire from you stating what was wrong, and how poor little Bucky Boy was. None came. Then I wired and just by luck got your night letter that night. Then no more word till this morning when the warden called me to his office and read me your wire to him. He also had wires from the "North American" and the "Ledger." There was also a long distance phone call from Philadelphia, I don't know who from. All these messages asked if I had been released yet. I didn't know and don't yet know what to think of it all.

You may be sure it brought cheer to me to know that Bucky Boy is not so low this time as he was when I was home. Good God, girlie, how I hope he will soon be better and that you will stay well. Please keep me posted. . . .

I have . . . written to Mr. Dougherty asking him for early action because of the situation prevailing at home. My appeal to him was directed to his heart. I assured him that he would be given no cause to regret having released me. . . .

Mr. Biddle has been very good and is sympathetic. He wishes to see me able to go home with my Bucky Boy and his mamma. He cannot do a great deal however but will do all he can to help. All he can do is give the Department my record here, and that is excellent.

Now, girlie dear, please let me put myself at your direction. Whatever you think I can do or say to make you and Bucky Boys position better, call on me. In this crisis, I am permitted to write a few extra letters. I shall do, say, promise anything you like. I shall leave nothing undone that you may suggest. Please call on me for anything. You and Bucky have suffered enough, too much.

Now tell me, what seems wrong with Bucky this time? What is his ailment? And, how are you?

It was awfully good of Belle to come to you. I hope she is there long before this time.

. . . It is nine o'clock now and no wire has come so I shall have to close. Just now no news is good news, so I take it.

August 30, 1922

Because of lack of news I wired you this morning and I guess I shall hear from you in the morning. I surely do hope so for I've been awfully out of news, particularly as to how you are and how poor little Bucky Boy is coming on.

Girlie dear, please remember that it is very, very hard to know there is trouble at home and then not know how things are progressing.

Please, please keep me posted. A wire now and again doesn't cost much, certainly, dollars, so few of them, are worth so much less than heart-ache.

Fortunately Ben gets the "Ledger" here and I saw the Saturday and Sunday stories. The Saturday papers says Bucky was a bit better, and also from the same source I learned that Belle had arrived. From the paper alone, I learned that Sen. Pepper was interested in the case and that it was expected that the President would sign the papers. There, too, I learned of the activities of Mrs. Chas. Edward Russell. . . .

But, my dear girlie, what I want to know, is the condition of Bucky Boy. This I do not know. I don't know whether he is home or at the hospital, whether he is desperately ill or whether he is showing some improvement. All this plays havoc with my mind. . . . I notice that the Phila. Ledger seems certain that I will be freed. Their word is reported to have come directly from Sen. Pepper's office. If I knew something of these developments, I could possibly help along in this line, too. But, never did I feel more helpless and ignorant.

. . . I pray, girlie, that all this trouble may soon end, that Bucky Boy shall become well and strong once more, that you shall soon have real health and happiness once more, and that we shall soon be reunited. . . .

Your ever loving hubby — Ed.

Suddenly, on September 2 he was on his way again to Bucky's bedside.

Chas. P. Hill

c/o Mrs. E. F. Doree

You are authorized to extend Doree's visit five more days.

WESTERN UNION TELEGRAM

1922 SEP 9 PM 4 54

GB825 27 I EXTRA

   LEAVENWORTH KANSAS 9 328P

EDWARD F DOREE

   3231 OXFORD ST PHILADELPHIA PENN

PRESIDENT HAS COMMUTTED YOUR SENTENCE TO TERM
ALREADY SERVED YOU NEED NOT RETURN HERE STOP MR
HILL IS TO RETURN HOME STOP ACKNOWLEDGE RECEIPT
OF TELEGRAM

BIDDLE WARDEN.

EPILOGUE

⁖

Will the roses grow wild over me
When I'm gone into the land that is to be?
When my soul and body part in the stillness of my heart,
Will the roses grow wild over me?

3231 Oxford St.
Philadelphia, Pa.
September 22, 1922

Dear Mamma,

It feels splendid to be free once more, to come and go at will. Bucky is getting better. His heart seems to be improving as well as can be expected and his general condition is considerably better. We have real hopes now. He eats well and is always in good humor. He reads splendidly. He is especially fond of poetry and likes Poe's works and is taking more than ordinary interest just now in Service's Poems.

As for the rest of us we are quite well, perfectly so. I'm looking for a job, am trying to get on one of the newspapers here. Don't know with what success yet, but have several friends plugging for me.

. . . The whole thing has taught me one thing, that one cannot affort to deal all the cards to the other fellow, one must deal a few to himself occasionally. I shall get a master and deal some of the material things of life to myself and mine.

No boss could possibly treat a slave with greater indifference or contempt than the I.W.W. treated their politicals. But nothing is gained by this talk. For me it is over. We are bending all our energy to get Nef out now, and hope to succeed shortly.

Chiky and Bucky Boy join with me in wishing you the best life holds and we all send our love to all of you. I kiss you bye, bye for this time. Please excuse brevity.

Your loving kid,

Ed.

There remains no information about the months immediately following my father's release from more than two years' imprisonment. Eventually he found congenial employment as a field accountant, an "accountant-on-horseback" as my mother put it. He had a head for numbers: he had managed monies for the textile workers' union and the prisoners' defense fund and kept the books in the prison "rag shop." My mother told me that he learned accounting in prison. He was probably self-taught out of the thick, black "Principles of Accounting" book that has come down to me.

A construction firm hired my father to keep track of inventory and costs on the work site. The little family moved with each project—from telephone line to oil rig. One letter survives:

c/o Day & Zimmermann Camp
Robertsdale, Pa.
Mar. 11, 1923

My dearest Chiky & Bucky Boy,

You will likely not get this letter before Tuesday. I'm sorry, but we left for camp immediately after landing at Saxton with no chance to write.

The mail is a poor proposition here, we are 13 miles from town. I don't think that I will be in this camp long. Rather hope I can stay for there is a fine bunch of fellows here. Was over the job today. It looks good. Am feeling fine.

How are both of you? I hope the doctor let's Bucky use the chair. This is a hurried note as I want to send it to town now.

Love, much love to each and both of you. Your loving Pop.

Kisses, kisses, kisses to mamma & Bucky Boy.

Two weeks later, on March 27, 1923, Bucky's fight for life ended. The extraordinarily intelligent and perceptive child was gone. His little body was cremated and my parents kept his ashes with them always, wherever they lived. My father probably found some distraction from his sorrow in the tasks and people that came with his job. My mother, I know, was unconsolable. She would grieve for Bucky all her life.

In 1924 my parents were living in Oil City, Pennsylvania, and my mother was pregnant with me. She suffered from high blood pressure and, as she phrased it, "was in bed for months, swollen like a balloon." I was born in November, a post-term infant weighing less than four pounds. The doctors told my mother never to have another child. In deep post-partum depression, my mother decided that my father would be better off without her. On the pretext that she was not well enough to care for me, she persuaded him to send for his twenty-three-year-old sister Florence, who quickly made the trip from Oregon. Then my mother tried to kill herself.

My mother told me that, after I was born, she "swallowed something" in an effort at suicide. Aunt Florence said the "something" was rubbing alcohol. It did not kill her, but it made her dreadfully, pitifully sick for some time. Her mental breakdown was my father's nightmare come true. In pictures of him holding me as a baby, he looks like an old man.

My mother was in her own world for weeks. She did not participate in naming me. My father, unaware of the European Jewish custom of not naming children after the living, named me Ida Ellen. In time, my mother rejected the name Ida; although it was hers she never liked it. I became, and remained, Ellen. The Ellen was in honor of Ellen Winsor of Philadelphia, to whom my parents owed so much.

Florence stayed in Oil City for three months, caring for me, full of trepidation at my size. My fingers, she said, were like matchsticks. She formed a deep attachment to me and, even after I became a gray-haired grandmother, Aunt Florence would continue, occasionally, to sign her letters with, "Goodnight, my little red-headed baby." When she was in her eighties, she shocked me by confessing that she sometimes fantasized about how things might have been had my mother's suicide attempt succeeded and she, Florence, raised me herself. That was particularly poignant because, despite a happy marriage, Florence never conceived a child of her own.

Gradually, my mother recovered physically and mentally. My father continued to work for Day & Zimmermann, and life for my parents became normal, even boring.

P.O. Box 274
Saxton, Pa.
Nov. 26, 1925

Dear Folks at Home:

Thanksgiving day!
We did not work today so I shall definitely let you know that we are very much alive and kicking. Little Ida Ellen has just passed her 1st milepost in life and she is having just a great time running around the house, from one room to another like a runaway train. She is a great little one. Chiky is having a time keeping her away from the stove in the kitchen.

Well, how are you all? And how is everybody. I havent written nor heard in so very long that I suppose we both rely on "No news is good news!" . . .

Letter writing is made difficult for us in that we really have nothing to write about. Life here is very unromantic. We rise and go to work at 8 and return at 5. Well, we live about 2 miles from the job but I drive back & forth. In the evening we play chess or the Victrola and retire early as a rule. . . .

The only news, which might be called news is that Day & Zimmermann, Inc. has organized a new company known as Day & Zimmermann Engineering and Construction Company. It is by this new company that I'm now employed. The formation of this new company was brought about so that construction and engineering capital would be more readily available, thus permitting D. & Z. to cover a larger field in construction work. Just in what manner this will operate I do not know, but it is intended that they spread into the South and West. And according to their present plans, should they be successful in expanding into the newer territory, I will be sent as cost engineer. I would like to be sent west but not so sure that the south would appeal to me. So that's the news. The Nefs are in Pittsburgh. He is working as foreman for Day & Zimmermann in the erection of a power plant in Braddock, a suburb of Pittsburgh. They are well. We expect to have them with us for Christmas, also a girl friend from Phila. a Yetta Kaplan. Now, positively, that's all the news. . . .

　　Your kid,
　　Ed.

In the Fall of 1926 the anticipated job relocation did come about, and we moved to Texas.

607-1/2 W. 21st St.
Amarillo, Texas.
Nov. 7, 1926

Dear Folks at Home.

I realize that I should have written before now, but we have been awfully busy lately, awfully busy. As you have already noted, we are in Texas, and have been for two weeks. We drove down in our car. 1700 miles in eight days. We had pretty good roads the whole way except the last 200 miles.

We are in good health and spirits. The baby feels fine now after resting up from the trip. Chiky is all right except that she picked up a bit of a cold. I'm feeling a whole lot better. This higher altitude agrees with me.

I am still with D. & Z. Have charge of accounting on the construction of a power plant here.

We are now in the richest and newest oil field in the world. There seems to be no end to the field here.

Amarillo is a boom town. A year ago it was 15,000 population. Today it is more than 3 times as large . . . and growing. The housing problem is a tremendous one. We are paying 75.00 a month for 4 rooms & bath, and we are 1-1/2 miles from the business district.

. . . We hope that good health and much happiness is your lot. And further hope that our next job will be further west, so we can visit you. Gee, how I wish we could visit once more. . . .

Well, supper is ready and they want me to eat, so I shall.

Love from all of us to all of you.

Your kid

Ed.

My father did not know when he wrote this letter that my mother was four months pregnant. She did not know it, either. As they jounced and bounced their way down from Pennsylvania, my mother was aware that she had stopped menstruating. But she was forty-two years old; she assumed that she was entering menopause. The "menopause" turned out to be my younger brother. Without any of the difficulties of her previous pregnancy, she produced a son on April 6, 1927.

Their happiness was complete. Life was really, finally, good.

1116 West 10th St.
Amarillo, Texas.
April 8, 1927

Dear Folks at Home,

You will pardon a hurried note as I'm writting many short letters telling of the arrival of a 6-1/2 or 7 pound Texan into the Doree family.

This, I suppose, comes as a surprise to you, but hardly more of a surprise to us. Up to an hour of the baby's coming, Chiky slept soundly and peacefully. The pains she felt in the last hour were so slight that she could not believe them birth pains. I however had gotten up and dressed and called the doctor and a neighbor and run the car to the door. In this time Ida rested quietly and up to the moment the baby was born we discussed our foolishness for disturbing the doctor.

Our neighbor came and we all sat and talked when suddenly came the moan and cry of the birth. Ida had been sitting up talking and chatting. I had just time to reach her and hold her so that she could properly brace. In a few seconds the baby was born. There are 12 families in our apartment house and only one person heard Ida cry. There was only one cry and that of but a few seconds duration.

After it was all over the doctor came. All was well.

Ida feels splendid. She sleeps soundly, eats well and is happy. The baby is a strapping little youngster. We have named him Ivan Lee.

Ida Ellen had her tonsils removed a week ago last Saturday. She feels fine again. She was never sick but as her tonsils were badly infected we thought it best to have them out.

I'm happy—very happy. If all goes well we shall have the family I've always longed for, a boy and a girl. I feel confident of being able to provide for them whether I live or not. Those provisions are partly made and very nearly completed. That was my only fear and that seems to be quite well solved.

I hope that you are all as happy as I am tonight. . . .
Your kid
Ed.

April 8, 1927

My dear Yetta:

Hear ye! Hear ye! His Royal Highness has arrived.
Announcing:

IVAN LEE DOREE
6 1/2 pound Texan,
at 3:20 a.m. April 6, 1927
at the home of his parents.

His arrival was so sudden that it was impossible to get Ida to the hospital nor the doctor to the home, so, with myself as doctor and midwife he came into the world. And quite successfully. Ida is doing splendidly. It is nearly impossible to believe that she was so recently the mother of the babe beside her. She feels great, sleeps soundly, eats well, thinks the world of her new-born, and is so happy and sweet-tempered that I'm walking on the air.

The depression of years is passing away, and great happiness is in store. When Ida gets really well, as seems to be the case now, we shall enjoy so much that we shall be envied.

To merely say that all has been and is, transpired so splendidly, is to demonstrate the weakness of language. The happiness of all of us is inexpressible in words. . . .
Lovingly
Ed.

On September 7, my father died. He was thirty-eight years old. He died exactly nine years to the day after writing the note to my mother on that train from Chicago to Leavenworth.

9-12-27

Dear Florence:

We got letter to day from Ida. She states that Ed was not well since early part of July, he was home for 10 days and doctor prononsed it gall truble. so he drained the gall and found it full of puss. so I understand it was drained 4 times a week apart but got no better. so performed an operation on Aug. 31st removing gall bladder and appendix.

all went well till Sept. 2nd when he got a gase attack and was very ill
on 3rd & 4th, on the 5th he was better, but that evening incision got
busted, he passed over the 6th and died at 1:15 a.m. on the 7th.

We are O.K. and hope you are the same. You can let the girls know
by phone.

Dad

Amarillo, Texas
Sept. 12, 1927

Dear Florence,

You all have our sincerest sympathy in your loss. As friends and co-
workers we can appreciate your deep affection for your beloved
brother and son. I am so glad your Mother was so brave.

Mrs. Doree is bearing up far better than I expected. She is very
calm and collected. Friday morning after the funeral she wrote you
a long letter giving all the details.

Mr. Doree had not been feeling well for the past two months and
after consulting the doctors, found that he had pus in the gall bladder. For about six weeks he has been having it drained once a week.
He decided to have it removed at once against the advice of the doctors and was operated on Tuesday morning, August 30. They removed
the gall bladder and the appendix both of which were actually rotten.
The operation itself was a success and everything pointed to a rapid
recovery. However, he is of a very restless nature, and on the fourth
day he had severe gas pains and the bowels and kidneys refused to
function properly. For three days he suffered greatly and then the
bowels moved also the kidneys and he seemed fine. Monday night,
Sept. 5, during the night he tore off the bandages and tore loose the
stitches in his incision. I do not know how it happened. He had a day
and night nurse but somehow he got at the incision which previously
had been healing splendidly and tore it open.

He asked them not to tell Mrs. Doree. When we visited him, Mrs.
Doree & I, on Tuesday morning & afternoon, he appeared to be himself and greatly improved, and we, not knowing of the happenings of
the night before, supposed him to be doing fine.

The doctor called here for Mrs. Doree about 8:30 P.M. and we immediately went to the hospital and she was with him until he died at 1:30. I believe he knew he was going and he remained conscious until 15 minutes before he died.

Mrs. Doree's first thought was for cremation but the body would have had to be sent to Denver or Kansas City and would have cost around $500 or $600. She just could not afford it and the only other possible thing was to bury him here temporarily.

She is planning to leave here Thursday for Brooklyn, N.Y. to stay with her sister until she can adjust herself to the situation and can make some plans for the future.

If I can furnish you with greater details or can be of any service whatever, do not hesitate to call on me.

With deepest sympathy, I am

Your friend,

Mabel [Wilcox]

My mother was forty-three years old. She had lost and lost again. She saw my father buried in the Llano Cemetery in Amarillo, notified his family, disposed of her household, and boarded the train for New York with an infant in one arm and a small child holding her free hand. Feige and Walter were now in Brooklyn, and she would go there. Little Ivan's name would be changed to Edwin.

The Bedford-Stuyvesant section of Brooklyn, where Feige and Walter lived, was beginning its long decline from elegance. Some of the four-story brownstone houses were still occupied by single families: Congressman Emanuel Cellar, with his wife and wheelchair-bound daughter, lived in such a house. The Nefs's brownstone had been converted to "furnished rooms." They had done well and were ready to move on to a larger rental property on Marcy Avenue. My mother bought their brownstone on McDonough Street.

She struggled. She cleaned the halls and the common bathrooms and the vacated rooms. She fed the coal furnace and hauled heavy cans of ashes up the cellar steps. She sometimes sat at the window all night, watching who came and went, if she suspected that a tenant "nurse" was really a prostitute, or feared that a tenant would try to skip out owing several weeks' rent. It was the Great Depression and she could barely make ends meet, but we had a roof over our heads and food to eat.

My mother lived as much with death as with life. She sang "Oh my darling Nellie Gray, they have taken you away and I'll never see my darling any more." On the living room wall was a picture captioned "The Death of Mozart," with crying women kneeling before him. Her favorite poem was "Annabel Lee": "we loved with a love that was more than love— I and my Annabel Lee— . . . Yes! that was the reason (as all men know, in this kingdom by the sea) that the wind came out of the cloud, chilling and killing my Annabel Lee."

She smiled if I danced for her or Eddy put on a "clown act." But she was always sad, and vaguely absent, even when she was present. Eddy grew up and became the commercial artist his father had dreamed of being. In 1977, he gave me a page, printed in his artistic handwriting, titled "Third Person, Singular." It reads in part:

> He sat on his small ass on the top step of the stairs down from the parlor floor and thought how the dark down there was hell and how Jack Frost would come and take you away one day and maybe that's now.
>
> He held tightly to the rails on the staircase, in case it might be now. Except there was no noise down there and so probably there was no one there.
>
> He could hear the vacuum cleaner two flights up rattling against the stair rails, so mommy was alive so far, probably, if he didn't bother her. . . .
>
> I think he knew for the first time that his mother was dead, even though the vacuum cleaner rattled against the rails upstairs, and she would come down a few more times anyway, and if she lit a cigarette he might get a kiss and she would touch him and that somehow made things as clear as the black long shadows and the great bright sun pounding silently on the wall just above where he was sitting on that cold little ass.

In 1952 my mother met her first grandchild, and three months later she suffered a stroke that left her paralyzed and speechless. She died two years later. Of her seventy-one years, she was truly alive only during the thirteen years of her marriage. Her ashes and Bucky's were buried with my father's remains in Amarillo. They are all, as they should be, together.

This book is for them, for my late brother Edwin, for Ed and Chiky's five grandchildren, and for their seven great-grandchildren. I want them to know their progenitor was in prison and they should be proud of him.

NOTES

✥

INTRODUCTION

1. Peter Cole, review of *Harvest Wobblies: The Industrial Workers of the World and Agricultural Workers in the American West, 1905–1930, Labor History* 43 (Nov. 2002): 570.

2. Peter Carlson, *Roughneck: The Life and Times of Big Bill Haywood* (New York: Norton, 1983); Joseph R. Conlin, *Big Bill Haywood and the Radical Union Movement* (Syracuse: Syracuse University Press, 1969); Melvyn Dubofsky, *"Big Bill" Haywood* (New York: St. Martin's, 1987); *The Autobiography of William D. Haywood,* (New York: Masses and Mainsteam, 1929); Elizabeth Gurley Flynn, *I Speak My Own Piece: Autobiography of "The Rebel Girl"* (New York: Masses and Mainstream, 1955); Flynn, *The Rebel Girl: An Autobiography* (New York: International, 1973); Helen C. Camp, *Iron in Her Soul: Elizabeth Gurley Flynn and the American Left* (Pullman: Washington State University Press, 1995); Ralph Chaplin, *Wobbly: The Rough and Tumble Story of a Radical* (Chicago: University of Chicago Press, 1948); Covington Hall, *Labor Struggles in the Deep South and Other Writings,* ed. David Roediger (Chicago: Charles H. Kerr, 1999); and Ben H. Williams, "American Labor in the Jungle: Saga of the One Big Union" (Microfilm, Archives of Labor and Urban Affairs, Walter P. Reuther Library, Detroit, Michigan).

3. James Jones, *From Here to Eternity* (New York: Scribner, 1951), 640–42; Carleton Parker, "The I.W.W.," *Atlantic Monthly,* Nov. 1917, 651–62.

4. Aileen S. Kraditor, *The Radical Persuasion, 1890–1917* (Baton Rouge: Louisiana State University Press, 1981).

5. Paul F. Brissenden, *The I.W.W.: A Study of American Syndicalism* (New York: n.p., 1919) and Louis Levine, "The Development of Syndicalism in America," *Political Science Quarterly* 28 (Sept. 1913): 451–79. Cf. Melvyn Dubofsky, *We Shall Be All: A History of the Industrial Workers of the World* (New York: Quadrangle Press/New York Times, 1969).

6. Salvatore Salerno, *Red November, Black November: Culture and Community in the Industrial Workers of the World* (Albany: State University of New York Press, 1989), 144.

7. Donald E. Winters, Jr., *The Soul of the Wobblies: The I.W.W., Religion, and American Culture in the Progressive Era, 1905–1917* (Westport, CT: Greenwood Press, 1985), 131.

8. David R. Roediger, *The Wages of Whiteness: Race and the Making of the American Working Class* (New York: Verso, 1999); Roediger, *Towards the Abolition of Whiteness: Essays on Race, Politics, and Working Class History* (New York: Verso, 1994); Roediger, "Race and the Working-Class Past in the United States: Multiple Identities and the Future of Labor History," *International Review of Social History* 38 (1993, Supplement 1): 127–43. Also see James R. Barrett and David Roediger, "Inbetween Peoples: Race, Nationality, Class," *Journal of American Ethnic History* 16 (spring 1997): 3–44; Bruce Nelson, "Class, Race, and Democracy in the CIO: The 'New Labor History' Meets the 'Wages of Whiteness,'" *International Review of Social History* 41 (1996): 351–74; Stephen H. Norwood, *Strikebreaking and Intimidation: Mercenaries and Masculinity in Twentieth-Century America* (Chapel Hill: University of North Carolina Press, 2002); Joshua B. Freeman, "Hardhats: Construction Workers, Manliness, and the 1970 Pro-war Demonstrations," *Journal of Social History* 26 (summer 1993): 725–44; Steve Meyer, "Rough Manhood: The Aggressive and Confrontational Shop Culture of U.S. Auto Workers during World War II," *Journal of Social History* 36 (fall 2002): 125–48; Ava Baron, "Questions of Gender: Deskilling and Demasculinization in the U.S. Printing Industry, 1830–1915," *Gender and History* 1, no. 2 (1989): 178–99.

PROLOGUE

1. Valentine Huhta (T-Bone Slim), "The Popular Wobbly," in *Songs of the Workers: To Fan the Flames of Discontent*, 33rd ed. (Chicago: Industrial Workers of the World, 1970), 63.

CHAPTER 1

1. Florence Pettingill Howard, letter to the author, June 14, 1994.

2. Transcript of trial, *United States v. William D. Haywood, et al.*, May 2, 1918. Archives of Labor and Urban Affairs, University Archives, Wayne State University, Detroit, Michigan, p. 5905.

3. Ibid.

4. Len DeCaux, *The Living Spirit of the Wobblies* (New York: International, 1978), 11.

5. Wallace Stegner, *The Preacher and the Slave* (Garden City, NY: Doubleday, 1969), 106.

6. Transliteration of the original Yiddish:

Vu loyft es der vint
Azoy vi farsamt,

Vos aylt er, vos blozt er
Un fregt vu er shpahnt?
Meynt er miglekh der volkn tsu farnichten?
Meynt er miglekh der volkn tsu gedichten?
Oder geyt er on tsil
Azoy vi mir ale.

CHAPTER 2

1. *United States v. William D. Haywood, et al.*, 5905–15, passim.
2. Ibid., 5918–31, passim.
3. Florence Pettingill Howard, letter to the author, June 14, 1994.
4. Quoted in Dubofsky, *We Shall Be All*, 153.
5. Dubofsky, *We Shall Be All*, 321.
6. Ibid., 186.
7. Carlson, *Roughneck*, 248.
8. Patrick Renshaw, *The Wobblies* (New York: Doubleday, 1968), 162–63.
9. *United States v. William D. Haywood, et al.*, 5958–60.
10. Dubofsky, *We Shall Be All*, 286–87.
11. Joyce Kornbluh, *Rebel Voices* (Ann Arbor: University of Michigan Press, 1964), 230.
12. Ibid., 243–47.
13. Selig Perlman and Philip Taft, *History of Labor in the United States, 1896–1932*, vol. 4 (New York: Macmillan, 1935), 387.
14. Carlson, *Roughneck*, 231.
15. Ibid.
16. Kornbluh, *Rebel Voices*, 232.
17. Ibid.

CHAPTER 3

1. Carlson, *Roughneck*, 292.

CHAPTER 4

1. Quoted in Dubofsky, *We Shall Be All*, 424.
2. Dubofsky, *We Shall Be All*, 386.
3. Ibid., 390.
4. Carlson, *Roughneck*, 247.
5. Dubofsky, *We Shall Be All*, 98–101.
6. Ibid., 247.
7. Kornbluh, *Rebel Voices*, 317.
8. Dubofsky, *We Shall Be All*, 376.

9. Patrick Renshaw, *The Wobblies* (New York: Doubleday, 1968), 173.

10. Dubofsky, *We Shall Be All*, 360.

11. Stegner, *Preacher and the Slave*, 187f.

12. Dubofsky, *We Shall Be All*, 163.

13. Ibid., 399.

14. Ibid., 404.

15. Ibid., 396.

16. Fred Thompson, *The I.W.W.: Its First Fifty Years* (Chicago: Industrial Workers of the World, 1955), 112.

17. Carlson, *Roughneck*, 250.

18. Melvyn Dubofsky, *"Big Bill" Haywood* (New York: St. Martin's, 1987), 108.

19. Carlson, *Roughneck*, 255.

20. *United States v. William D. Haywood, et al.*, 12273–85, passim.

21. Carlson, *Roughneck*, 256.

22. William O. Douglas, quoted in Carlson, *Roughneck*, 257.

23. Ray Ginger, *The Bending Cross* (New Brunswick, NJ: Rutgers University Press, 1949), 152.

24. Carlson, *Roughneck*, 258

25. Ibid., 261–62; see also Chaplin, *Wobbly*, 233–34.

26. Renshaw, *Wobblies*, 179.

27. Dubofsky, *We Shall Be All*, 425.

28. Dubofsky, *"Big Bill" Haywood*, 116.

29. *United States v. William D. Haywood, et al.*, 5902–5, passim.

30. Ibid., 5935–40, passim.

31. Ibid., 5944–54, passim.

32. Ibid., 12295–307, passim.

CHAPTER 5

1. "Amnesty for Political Prisoners," Hearing before the Committee on the Judiciary, House of Representatives on H. J. Res. 60, March 16, 1922 (Washington: Government Printing Office, 1922), 14–15.

2. Testimony of Alexander S. Lanier in Hearing before the Committee on the Judiciary, 21ff.

3. Testimony of Dr. Frederick Edgerton in Hearing before the Committee on the Judiciary, 45.

4. Ibid., 54–55.

5. Ginger, *Bending Cross*, 428.

GLOSSARY

༶

Persons for whom no information is available are not listed in the glossary

FAMILY

Edwin Doree's family

Parents: Frederick and Maria Doree
Brothers: Frank and Alford
Sisters: Hilma, Florence, and Edna
Uncles: Axel Brandt and Gus Berquist
Aunt: Sophia Berquist
Cousins: Astrid and Florence Berquist

Chiky Doree's family

Parents: Lebel and Sarah Salinger
Brother: Yudel (also two brothers in England)
Sisters: Ruchel (married Philip Weber), Feige, and Belle (also one sister in Lithuania)

WOBBLIES

Ahlteen, Carl: editor and writer; Chicago trial, twenty years
Anderson, Olin B.: organizer; Chicago trial, five years
Anderson, C. W.: secretarial work; Wichita trial, nine years
Andreytchine, George: editor (Bulgarian), writer and speaker; Chicago trial, twenty years, jumped bail in 1921
Ashleigh, Charles: writer and publicist; Chicago trial, ten years
Avila, John: Chicago trial, five years
Baldazzi, John: speaker (Italian) and organizer; Chicago trial, ten years
Beyers, J. H.: Chicago trial, ten years
Boose, Arthur: secretarial work; Chicago trial, five years

Brazier, Richard: General Executive Board; Chicago trial, twenty years

Buckley, Dan: secretarial-executive work; Chicago trial, ten years

Chaplin, Ralph: editor, writer and cartoonist; Chicago trial, twenty years

Clark, Stanley J.: speaker; Chicago trial, ten years

Corder, Ray: Chicago trial, one year and one day

Doran, J. T. "Red": speaker; Chicago trial, five years

Eastman, Phineas: Wichita trial, seven and one-half years

Ebel, Godfrey: Sacramento trial, ten years

Edwards, Forrest: union head; Chicago trial, twenty years

Embree, A. S.: veteran of the "Bisbee Deportations"

Esmond, Fred: Sacramento trial, ten years

Ettor, Joe: case severed from Chicago Hundred; never stood trial

Fallino, C. H. (C. L. Filigno): organizer assisting the Brotherhood of Timber Workers in Louisiana in 1912. Arrested there with Doree on charges of jury tampering.

Fanning, Ray: no formal IWW role; Chicago trial, five years.

Feinberg, Harry: IWW Chicago headquarters

Fletcher, Benjamin: speaker-organizer; Chicago trial, ten years

Flynn, Elizabeth Gurley ("The Rebel Girl"): case severed from Chicago Hundred; never stood trial

Fraser, Ted: organizer; Chicago trial, five years; one of the "irreconcilables"

George, Harrison: Chicago trial, five years

Gergots, Louis J.: Textile Workers' Union, potential witness for Doree

Gordon, Joseph J.: Chicago trial, ten years

Graber, Joe: speaker (Polish); Chicago trial, five years

Hall, Covington: poet and writer

Hamilton, Ed: union head; Chicago trial, ten years

Haywood, William D. ("Big Bill"): IWW head; Chicago trial, twenty years, jumped bail in 1921, died in Russia

Hill (Hillstrom), Joe (The Wobbly Bard): songwriter, executed by Utah authorities

Hough, Clyde: Chicago trial, five years

Jaakkola, Fred: editor-writer; Chicago trial, ten years

Johannsen, Ragner: speaker; Chicago trial, ten years

Lambert, Charles L.: General Executive Board; Chicago trial, twenty years

Laukki, Leo: editor-writer; Chicago trial, twenty years

Law, Jack: organizer; Chicago trial, ten years

Lever, Jack (E. J.): potential witness for Doree, later executive secretary of the Pennsylvania Committee for Political Prisoners

Little, Frank: organizer, lynched by vigilantes in 1917

Lossieff, Vladimir: writer; Chicago trial, twenty years; jumped bail in 1921

MacDonald, J. A.: editor and writer; Chicago trial, ten years

McCosham (Herbert McCutcheon): no formal IWW role; Chicago trial, five years

Mahler, Herbert: publicist; Chicago trial, five years

Manning, James H.: Chicago trial; five years; one of the "irreconcilables"

McEvy, Pete: speaker: Chicago trial, five years

McKinnon (MacKinnon): Charles, organizer of Arizona copper miners

McWhirt, Charles: union secretary; Chicago trial, one year

Miller, Francis: General Executive Board; Chicago trial, ten years

Murphy, John L.: Sacramento trial, five years

Nef, Walter T.: organizer, union head; Chicago trial, twenty years

Nelson, Fred: no formal IWW role; Chicago trial, one year

Nigra (Pietro Nigri, also Peter Negro): speaker (Italian), Chicago trial, eighteen months

Pancner, John: organizer; Chicago trial, ten years

Parenti, Louis: speaker-writer (Italian); Chicago trial, five years

Perry, Grover H.: mine union secretary-treasurer; Chicago trial, ten years

Phillips, James: organizer; Chicago trial, five years

Plahn, Charles: organizer; Chicago trial, five years

Prashner, Albert: union head; Chicago trial, ten years

Quigley, Edward: Sacramento trial, ten years

Rey, Manuel: organizer; Chicago trial, twenty years

Rice, C. H.: Chicago trial, ten years

Rothfisher, Charles: editor-writer (Hungarian); Chicago trial, twenty years

St. John, Vincent ("The Saint"): secretarial-executive work; Chicago trial, ten years

Scarlett, Sam: speaker; Chicago trial, twenty years

Smith, Walker C.: editor of IWW paper, "Industrial Worker"

Speed, George: west coast organizer, sent with Doree to Louisiana in 1912, Chicago trial, one year

Stenberg, Sigfred: Chicago trial, ten years

Tanner, William: speaker (Finnish); Chicago trial, five years

Thompson, James P.: organizer, speaker; Chicago trial, ten years

Walsh, John: Chicago trial, ten years

Westerlund, Frank: writer, circulation editor; Chicago trial, five years

Wetter, Pierce C.: Chicago trial, five years

Weyh, William: Chicago trial, five years

GENERAL

Ashurst, Henry Fountain: U.S. senator from Arizona

Baldwin, Roger: head of Civil Liberties Board (later American Civil Liberties Union)

Beef Trust: indicted by the Federal Trade Commission in summer of 1919 for collusion to manipulate the meat market

Biddle, W. I.: Warden, Leavenworth

Biddle, J. S.: U.S. Deputy Marshal, brother to Warden Biddle

Borah, William: U.S. senator from Idaho

Burke, William Joseph: U.S. congressman from Pennsylvania

Burnham, E. Lewis: chairman, Philadelphia Civil Liberties Committee

Burns Detective Agency: company detectives

Christensen, Otto: lawyer for the IWW

Children's Crusade: delegation of children of political prisoners, petitioning President Harding for their parents' release from prison

Clabaugh, Hinton: head of Chicago Office, U.S. Justice Department

Clyne, Charles F.: federal attorney, Northern Illinois District

Cope, Mrs. Walter (first name unknown): widow of prestigious architect Walter Cope. Active in behalf of Philadelphia IWW prisoners.

Darrow, Clarence: lawyer, council to Debs, Haywood, later to Scopes

Daugherty, Harry: U.S. attorney general during Harding administration

Debs, Eugene V.: American Socialist Party

De Silver, Albert: American Civil Liberties Union

Douglas, William O.: fruit picker, later U.S. Supreme Court justice

Edgerton, Dr. Frederick: University of Pennsylvania, Pennsylvania Committee for Political prisoners

Emerson, A. L.: leader of the Brotherhood of Timber Workers in Louisiana

Evans, Edmund C.: architect, benefactor to the Dorees and activist for release of political prisoners

Evans, Edward W.: brother to Edmund C., benefactor to the Dorees, activist for release of political prisoners

Evans, Rebecca Winsor (Mrs. Edmund C.):, benefactor to the Dorees

Fels, Mrs. Samuel S. (first name unknown): wife of Philadelphia philanthropist

France, Joseph Irvin: U.S. senator from Maryland

Gaines, I.: organizer of black timber workers, Louisiana

G.D.C.: General Defense Committee of the IWW

Gregory, Thomas: U.S. attorney general during Wilson administration

Hendrie, Cathleen McGraw: posted bond for Doree

Hog Island expose, 1918: the Hog Island Ship Yard at Philadelphia was investigated by Congress because production lagged seriously while workers were poorly selected, trained, and managed.

Industrial Worker: IWW publication

Inglis, Agnes: advocate for labor and civil liberties

Johnson, Gustave: fellow inmate, not a Wobbly

Johnson, Jack: first black boxer to win the heavyweight championship of the world; sentenced to Leavenworth on trumped-up charges of violating the Mann Act. Appointed athletic director at the prison.

Jones, Mary Harris, ("Mother"): speaker and labor organizer

Kane, Francis Fisher: attorney for Eastern District of Pennsylvania and critic of the repression of radicals

Kaplan, Yetta (later Meranze): Chiky's friend, Philadelphia

Kiefer, Daniel: Philadelphia benefactor

Knox Resolution, 1921: a resolution to declare a state of peace between the United States and Germany, introduced by Philander Chase Knox, U.S. senator from Pennsylvania

Ladd, Edwin Freeman: U.S. senator from North Dakota

Landis, Kenesaw Mountain: U.S. District Judge, Northern District of Illinois

Lanier, Alexander S.: Captain, U.S. Army, testified at House Judiciary Committee hearings

Lenin, Vladimir Ilyich: founder, Russian Communist Party

Liebknecht, Karl: coleader of Spartacus League in Germany

Lind, John: ex-governor of Minnesota

Lloyd, William Bross: millionaire, ran as socialist candidate for the senate from Illinois in 1918; later organized the Communist Party of America.

London, Meyer: U.S. congressman from New York

Lowe, Caroline: attorney for the IWW

Mooney, Tom: labor leader, convicted of bombing, pardoned in 1939

Moore, Fred: attorney for the IWW

Moyer, Charles: mine union leader

MTW: Marine Transport Workers' Union

Nebeker, Frank K.: one of three special prosecutors in Chicago trial

O'Hare, Kate Richards: colleague of Eugene V. Debs and organizer, "The Children's Crusade"

Oleve, Dora: friend of the family, Philadelphia

Owens, Robert Nathan: U.S. senator from Oklahoma

Palmer, A. Mitchell: U.S. attorney general, 1919–21, led attack on radicals during "red scare" period

Pepper, George Wharton: U.S. senator from Pennsyslvania, facilitated Doree's leave to visit Bucky

Pouget, Emile: French anarchosyndicalist, author of "Sabotage"

Reed, Kenny: Sheriff, Merryville, Louisiana

"resolutionists" (also,"irreconcilables," "die-hards," "hard liners"), IWW prisoners opposed to individual release

Russell, Theresa (Mrs. Charles Edward): activist for pardons

Sacco, Nicola & Bartolemeo Vanzetti: American radicals, convicted of murder in 1921 and executed in 1927

Shatoff, Bill: friend, later chief of police in Petrograd

Trotsky, Leon: Russian Communist leader, later expelled by Stalin

Vanderveer, George F.: lead attorney for the IWW

Veblen, Thorstein: economist, author

von Bopp, Franz: at one time vice consul for the German Imperial Government at San Francisco. Part of a group of German secret agents engaged in sabotage against the United States in 1916. Paroled from Leavenworth in 1920.

Walsh, Thomas J.: U.S. congressman from Massachusetts

Weyh, Emily: wife of Bill Weyh, a Wobbly

White, William Allen: Pulitzer Prize–winning writer and journalist

Wilcox, Mabel: friend of the family, Amarillo

Winsor, Ellen: benefactor to the Dorees; Chairman, Pennsylvania Committee for Political Prisoners

Winsor, Mrs. James D.: mother of Ellen Winsor and Rebecca Winsor Evans

Index

www.ingramcontent.com/pod-product-compliance
Lightning Source LLC
Chambersburg PA
CBHW050646270326
41927CB00012B/2892